A Democratic Classroom

WITHDRAWN

Steven Wolk

HEINEMANN
Portsmouth, NH

Heinemann
A division of Reed Elsevier Inc.
361 Hanover Street
Portsmouth, NH 03801-3912
http://www.heinemann.com

Offices and agents throughout the world

The author and publisher thank those who generously gave permission to reprint borrowed material.

The excerpt from THE EDUCATION OF LITTLE TREE by Forrest Carter, published by The University of New Mexico Press, is reprinted by arrangement with Eleanor Friede Books, Inc. © 1976 by Forrest Carter. All Rights Reserved.

Library of Congress Cataloging-in-Publication Data
CIP is on file with the Library of Congress.
ISBN 0-325-00058-1

Editor: Leigh Peake
Production: Melissa L. Inglis
Cover design: Jenny Jensen Greenleaf
Cover photo: Steven Wolk
Manufacturing: Louise Richardson

Printed in the United States of America on acid-free paper
5 6 VP   05

for Laura, my best friend

My focal interest is in human freedom, in the capacity to surpass the given and look at things as if they could be otherwise.

—MAXINE GREENE
The Dialectic of Freedom

If you're going to repair a motorcycle, an adequate supply of gumption is the first and most important tool. If you haven't got that you might as well gather up all the other tools and put them away, because they won't do you any good.
Gumption is the psychic gasoline that keeps the whole thing going. If you haven't got it there's no way the motorcycle can possibly be fixed. But if you have got it and know how to keep it there's absolutely no way in this world that motorcycle can keep from getting fixed. It's bound to happen. Therefore the thing that must be monitored at all times and preserved before anything else is the gumption.

—ROBERT PIRSIG
Zen and the Art of Motorcycle Maintenance

Sometimes I've believed as many as six impossible things before breakfast.

—LEWIS CARROLL
Alice in Wonderland

Contents

Acknowledgments

This book may have only my name on the cover, but there are many people who helped to put it there. First and foremost are my students over the years. Not only have many of them allowed me to use their work and stories in these pages, but they have shown me firsthand that the ideas in this book can work and have humbled me along the way with how much I have yet to learn about making them work. It's funny how someone becomes a teacher yet ends up a student.

I had the pleasure to work with so many talented people at Heinemann. The greatest compliment I can pay them is that they allowed democracy to flourish in the publishing process. Even with me missing one deadline after another, they always welcomed my voice and input. They recognize the passion (and possessiveness) of the writer and I thank them for that. My heartfelt gratitude goes to Leigh Peake, Melissa Inglis, Victoria Merecki, and Melissa Dobson, all of whom helped make this a better book and me a better writer.

Teaching is a solitary job but being a teacher involves a network of supporters, colleagues, mentors, and friends. I've been fortunate through the years to have had just that, and their ideas and inspirations are spread throughout these chapters. These include Aleta Margolis, Lauren Keck, Barbara Versino, Richard Brogard, Erin Roche, Peter Fisher, Bill Pink, Ken Kantor, Chuck Cole, Sylvia Gibson, Kim Day, Diana Shulla, Brenda Kraber, and Jan Perney.

I owe so much to many past and present educational thinkers that have guided and nurtured my own practice. Their ideas and words have inspired me to be more than just a teacher, but an activist who works for educational and social change. My thanks to John Dewey, William Heard Kilpatrick, John Holt, Carl Rogers, Paulo Friere, Maxine Greene, Frank Smith, John Mayher, Nancie Atwell, Howard Gardner, Patrick Shannon, Carole Edelsky, Herb Kohl, Jim Beane, and all of the many others who have struggled over the past century and more to bring freedom, dignity, thoughtfulness, and democracy to our classrooms and to our communities.

Finally, if it were not for my immediate and extended family, none of this would be remotely possible. Without knowing it, they helped light the flames that gave birth to my teaching and the ideas in this book. My wife, Laura, gave up untold numbers of hours over many years for me to write (as she continues to do). When the words are flying she is always willing to graciously step back and let them fly, and when the words are stuck and frustrated, she knows just when to step forward with her own words of encouragement. *A Democratic Classroom* could not have been written without her. As this book was going to press, Laura and I had our first child, Max. How lucky we are for all of the years ahead to help our son think for himself, love learning, ask questions, create, become a compassionate and thoughtful person, and take an active role in making our world a better place.

Introduction: Classrooms as Spheres of Freedom

A straight-row, lesson-plan-in-place, learning-outcomes-on-the-chalkboard kind of teacher I ain't.

—SUSAN OHANIAN

The kind of school that I envision is one that offers a special place for philosophers, for people who ask "why" questions. Nothing is more important to building a culture of inquiry and a community of learners.

—ROLAND BARTH

In a way, teaching found me, I didn't find teaching. After studying design and photography as an undergraduate, and writing for six years, I wanted a change. I applied for a teacher's aide position in a local school district. I didn't want to be a teacher, I just needed a job. As fate would have it, I didn't get the aide position. But the school district asked me if I wanted to be a full-time substitute teacher. I didn't know it then, but my life was about to be turned upside down and inside out. I was assigned to sub at an elementary school and I went in every day, whether they needed me or not. The school was very traditional and I questioned none of it. Textbooks, workbooks, worksheets, tests, grading, book reports, spelling lists, neatly defined subjects, ability grouping. To me it was just school. It was exactly what I remembered from when I was a kid.

Two years later, as I was about to begin teaching in my own classroom, everything had changed for me. The summer before, I read Nancie Atwell's book, *In the Middle* (1987), and it was, without exaggeration, an epiphany for me. As I read about Atwell helping children discover the joys and powers of reading and writing through a whole language and "workshop" belief system, I was thrust into a new way of seeing the world. More than anything—more than any research could have shown me—what Atwell wrote *made perfect sense.* Suddenly, what I had been seeing (and doing) for the past two years as a substitute had profound new meaning. And my own schooling as a child and my own learning (or lack thereof) and my entire life suddenly had a new clarity. School and teaching and learning as I had once known them—a lifetime of insidious myths and assumptions—were toppled into a heap of dust.

From the first day in my own classroom I was determined to do things differently. I was determined to make my students' experiences in school purposeful and meaningful, because I realized how meaningless and purposeless—how *regressive*—my own had been. I don't remember exactly when the notion of *democracy* entered the picture, but from my very first day with my own students I consciously worked to give them freedom, to allow them voice, to give them ownership in their own learning process, to help and challenge them to see the world critically, to *trust* them. And what they have given me in return can never be seen on a standardized test. My students have shown me that schooling for freedom and democracy and dignity can work. They have created fabulous projects, written and read endless texts, engaged in important discourse, and become more caring and thoughtful human beings. This does not mean it has been easy or that I've created any miracle students or methods. Teaching is tough, no matter how you teach.

I strive to create classrooms that live and teach democracy, classrooms that nurture freedom, dignity, thoughtfulness, community, and a natural love and respect for learning and knowledge. Maxine Greene (1988) writes of classrooms that are "spheres of freedom," places where children and their teachers *are allowed to create themselves* (117). Schooling for democracy *requires* these spheres. We cannot advocate and nurture democratic habits of mind without building classrooms for the free exploration, creation, and sharing of ideas and knowledge; for Michael Apple's and James Beane's (1995) "open flow of ideas" (6). We cannot have classrooms and curriculums that silence children and their teachers, control and regulate their thinking and learning, rate them and label them, and then expect them to take part in what's supposed to be a democratic, pluralistic, and participatory nation. Schools that nurture apathy and passiveness in children help propagate apathy and passiveness in society.

As a classroom teacher I am after something more. In the hope of creating a better world, a more humane and caring and thoughtful world, I'm working to create classrooms that live those spheres of freedom, that allow my students and me to give conscious shape and meaning to our voices. But as other democratic educators have shown (Beyer 1996; Parker 1996), this is not easy. Schools are not only antiintellectual, they *control against* a free intellectualism, against an open flow of ideas, against democracy itself. This makes my job more difficult from the start. Schools were never designed to be changed from within and teachers were never supposed to be thinkers and creators and decision makers. But this can change. Teachers must realize that they are the primary agents of school change. Which means they must stop being followers and start being leaders and activists.

Democratic classrooms begin with teachers who have or strive toward certain attitudes and habits of mind. I consider these attitudes to be the foundation of my own practice. These teachers make critical reflection an important part of their work. They look deep into their own beliefs, beneath the facade of surface realities. They are, as Roland Barth (1990) said, "philosophers who ask 'why' questions": Why do students have to raise their hands? Why are children segregated by age and grade and so-called ability groups? Why are children not invested in school? Why is Julie struggling with her writing? Why do we need textbooks and worksheets? Why is there only one teacher for twenty-five children? Why don't schools have equitable financial resources? These are not fleeting questions we can answer in an afternoon. In fact, these are the kinds of questions that have no single correct answer. Henry Giroux (1988) writes of "teachers as intellectuals." I like that idea. To me, an intellectual is someone who thinks about important things and knows they're thinking about important things. What all of this means to me is that democratic teachers see themselves as *learners*.

Teachers who strive to create democratic classrooms want to make the world a better place. That may sound like a tall order, but I'm not being romantic here. Schooling has a profound impact on the lives of people and society. As a teacher, I believe that my actions in the classroom play a very real role in creating and changing and shaping the world, one child at a time. I need to ask myself what kind of neighbors I want, what kind of community I want, what kind of nation I want, what kind of world I want, and then I need to work to create a classroom that helps create that world. This involves far more then merely imparting certain knowledge to children. In contrast to that, I see my primary goal as being to create a classroom environment that allows everyone—my students and myself—the infinite opportunities to create and learn and question together as a community of critical learners.

Democratic teachers see themselves as political actors. Schooling is inherently political, which makes teaching inherently political. It is not possible to shape the minds of people, especially within a governmental institution like a school, and not play a role in developing and influencing their political selves. I know that my students (and I) are part of a political world, so I want to encourage them—and *teach* them—to consciously take part in the evolution of who they are and what they want their world to be. I also accept that knowledge is inherently ideological, so I take my choices of what to teach (and what not to teach) seriously. A curriculum may look simple and objective on paper, but knowledge can never be simple or objective; it shapes who we are and how we see the world.

These habits of mind are not just an important part of democratic teachers when they are in their classrooms, but are an inherent part of who they are as complex human beings. Maxine Greene (1988) wrote, "A teacher in search of his/her own freedom, may be the only kind of teacher who can arouse young persons to go in search of their own" (14). The ideals and hopes of democracy are not merely important to me in the context of schooling, but are critical parts of who I am, both in school and out.

This book is about my classroom experiences as a third- through eighth-grade teacher in several different school systems. The democratic classroom of the title is really an amalgam of classrooms in multiple and mostly mixed-grade contexts. The photographs included are of various locales. Some are of a university laboratory school attended primarily by upper-middle-class white children; others are of a Chicago public school classroom serving primarily Latino children of the working poor. Some of what I relate goes back to my first classroom, when I taught sixth grade at a Chicago suburban middle school. I consider this diversity of experience a strength of the book, because democratic schooling is not just for some kids in some schools, but for *all* children in *all* schools.

It is important to stress that I do not intend this book to be a recipe or a formula. We don't need any more "effective" teaching recipes. Recipes may work when you're baking a cake and formulas may work when you're mixing hydrogen and oxygen to get water, but teaching and schooling are suited to neither. Every school is different, every teacher is different, every child is different, every class is different, every day is different, and every classroom and school culture is different. Plug-in, learn-by-numbers, "teacher-proof" schooling will never solve anything, no matter how hard we try and no matter how much money we invest. Educating human beings is much more complex than any mandate could capture. Rather than looking at this book as an ending point, the reader should try and see it as a starting point, or just another point on the never-ending path of his or her professional (and personal) evolution. The very best that I can hope for this book is that it encourages teachers to talk, to look, to ask questions, to take risks, to be their own researchers. I am not offering this as a book of answers, but rather as a way to enrich the teaching and schooling conversation. That's what teachers need more than anything: time for good, honest, intellectual talk and debate.

Needless to say, the vision of teaching and learning in this book is not finished. My teaching is a continuous evolution along my own winding (and at times bumpy) path. And again, it's not neat and easy. Just because I may be a so-called progressive teacher does not mean that I'm always successful or that my job is problem free. But that's just fine. Democratic schooling believes that it's okay for teachers and children to fail, that failure is an important part of democracy and risk taking and *learning*. Teaching is messy, bureaucratic, unpredictable, idiosyncratic, confusing, unjust, and at times very frustrating. That's not the way it has to be, but that is the way it is for most teachers today, and that includes me. As a teacher, as an educational activist, I struggle on a daily basis to make my vision a reality. When it doesn't work, I pick myself up, dust myself off, salve my emotional wounds, and try again tomorrow. Good teachers know that we have never "figured it out"; we're always asking more questions, always seeking new ideas.

Challenging the norm—or as Marilyn Cochran-Smith (1991) writes, *teaching against the grain*—is not easy. It's lonely, highly political, very emotional, and professionally risky. But it's worth it. Not only do I feel better about myself, not only do I see myself offering my students a more purposeful and rich school experience, but I enjoy my job *infinitely* more. Being in our classroom is exciting, invigorating, and empowering. On most days I go home feeling that I played an important role in encouraging children to expand their minds, to be caring human beings, to think for themselves, to be creators and leaders, to develop a love for learning, to help make the world a better place. That's why I became a teacher.

One

Reinventing School, Reinventing Teaching

It is through and by means of education, many of us believe, that individuals can be provoked to reach beyond themselves in their intersubjective space. It is through and by means of education that they may become empowered to think about what they are doing, to be mindful, to share meanings, to conceptualize, to make varied sense of their lived worlds. It is through education that preferences may be released, languages learned, intelligences developed, perspectives opened, possibilities disclosed.

—MAXINE GREENE

Why are our schools not places of joy?

—JOHN GOODLAD

In his wonderful book, *Epitaph for a Peach*, fruit farmer David Mas Masumoto (1995) explains how and why he decided to change the way he works. For all of his life he was a typical farmer; he farmed like his father farmed the very same land, with pesticides, herbicides, and synthetic fertilizers, killing and removing all of the weeds growing around his crops. That's become the "norm" in farming. It is how the vast majority of farmers go about their daily business. It is what we could call the *dominant paradigm* of farming. Put simply, a paradigm is a model or a framework or a *belief system*. It is a common set of rules or assumptions that dictate our actions. Masumoto started thinking about his farming. He began to question his fundamental beliefs and assumptions about farming. He began to wonder if he could farm in a completely new way. He wanted to farm according to a new set of rules:

> I used to farm with a strategy of un-chaos. I was looking for regularity, less variability, ignoring the uniqueness of each farm year. But now my farm resembles the old pine at the Del Rey Hall; wildness is tolerated, even promoted. The farm becomes a test of the unconventional, a continuous experiment, a journey of adaptation and living

1

with change. I've even had to change my ways of counting. It's no longer important how *many* pests I have, what matters is the ratio between good bugs and bad bugs. I try to rely less and less on controlling nature. Instead I am learning to live with its chaos. (37)

The language we use is intricately tied to the rules of the paradigms we live by. Masumoto gave a new name to what he once called "weeds." Obviously, weeds are a common sight on farms. And to a farmer—a farmer, that is, operating from the dominant farming paradigm—they're the enemy. To Masumoto weeds became *indigenous growth*. There's a profound difference between seeing a "weed" growing on your farm and seeing an "indigenous plant" growing on your farm. Once he renamed them, once he gave them new meaning, once he *changed the rules*, he didn't have to get rid of them. He realized that they belonged there. In fact, he realized that they could *help* his farm.

What Masumoto did was have a *paradigm shift*. In a very real sense a paradigm is our reality. There's a saying: Fish are the last to discover water. The water is their paradigm; it's their reality, so they don't *see* it. People live in "water" too, most just don't see it, because it's their reality, the lens they see the world through. Masumoto was able to see his farming water. He learned that his earlier way of farming wasn't *the* way to farm, just *one* way to farm. He realized that farming could be seen through *multiple lenses*. Once he saw that, he could work toward meaningful change. Entirely new possibilities presented themselves, possibilities that he could not see through his previous lens. He worked hard to stop using chemicals; he let weeds grow; he planted wildflowers on his farm, creating a "cover crop"; he welcomed the animals and insects and amphibians that returned to his land. The place became alive again. Before, he and his neighbors labored endlessly to have "clean" fields, to remove any form of life other than their crops. They'd even compete for the cleanest field. We could say that that was a "rule" in the traditional farming paradigm: "A good crop field is a clean crop field."

But once he started to see through a different lens, he realized that such fields weren't "clean," they were *sterile*. How ironic! He tells of his neighbors coming by his farm, looking at its wildness, trying to figure it out. They didn't understand it. It didn't look like "farming." It didn't work according to their set of rules or assumptions. It is interesting that Masumoto uses the same word to describe his new farm that some have used to describe my classroom. He writes, "Chaos defines my farm" (34). To my critics, and to Masumoto, I quote Henry Adams: *Chaos often breeds life*.

This book is about a different kind of classroom. It advocates a radically different educational paradigm from what is found in most classrooms. It offers a different way to see and think about school. School should be so much more than it currently is. It should have so much more meaning and purpose and relevancy for everyone, children, teachers, society, our world. But we're stuck. We're stuck in old ways of thinking and seeing. And what makes it especially difficult to change our schools is that most people don't know we're stuck. Yes, we certainly know that we have problems, that our classrooms are not as successful as they could be, but most people do not see that we're stuck in an inappropriate paradigm, because most people don't see the paradigm in the first place. It doesn't have to be this way. We can significantly change the way we teach, even radically change the way we teach. But to do so will require us to at least temporarily wash away any preconceived notions of schooling and teaching and learning, and of what it means to be a student and a teacher. We must change our lenses.

Seeing the Water

The notion of *paradigm* is central to this thinking. We'll never really change our schools until we see the water, until we see and question our "school reality." Throughout this book I am going to refer to the *dominant paradigm* of schooling and teaching. Just like the farming "norm" that Masumoto left was the dominant paradigm of farming, there is what many refer to as the dominant paradigm of education. The word *paradigm* is a buzzword these days. It was made popular by Thomas Kuhn (1962) in his classic work on the history of science, *The Structure of Scientific Revolutions*. Since then, and especially in the last decade or so, the word has been used so much that it has lost much of its significance and some even snicker at its use. But I believe that it is referred to so much precisely because it has truly profound implications for change, and not just in education but anywhere, as David Mas Masumoto shows with his farm, or as the car company Saturn has shown by changing the car-buying paradigm, or how hospitals have so radically changed the rules for having a baby.

When my wife, Laura, and I were on our honeymoon four years ago, one of the places we visited was San Francisco. One day when we were walking through Chinatown, I wandered into a store. I knew I was in foreign territory right when I entered. The shop was rather small; long and narrow. There were maybe half a dozen people inside, and it was quiet. Three or four men of Chinese descent were working behind a long counter. Behind them was a wall of large wooden drawers. Above the drawers were shelves with glass bottles filled with what looked like dried roots and herbs. I stood watching for a while, wondering what was going on. One of the men glanced at a small piece of white paper, grabbed a handheld balance from behind him, and started to fill it with contents from the drawers. What were in the drawers? Well, it looked like more dried roots and crushed herbs. After he weighed an item, he would quickly spill it onto a small square of white paper on the counter and then weigh another. I watched quietly as he poured four or five different things onto the same piece of paper, folded it over, and taped it closed.

What was this place? It didn't take long for me to figure it out. I was in a *pharmacy*. The difference was that this pharmacy existed within the paradigm of Chinese herbal medicine, which operates from a profoundly different set of *rules* than the medical paradigm that I'm used to. When my doctor gives me a prescription, I go to my neighborhood pharmacy and get a bottle of pills or eyedrops or lotion. But there were no pills in this store, because pills aren't in this paradigm's set of rules just like dried roots aren't in mine. I'm not attempting a comparison here of Western and Chinese medicine. What's important is the idea that Western medicine isn't the only medicine, it's just *our* medicine, and maybe, just maybe, people could benefit from looking at other medical paradigms. The same is true for our schools. The schools we have, the paradigm that our schools operate from, isn't what school must be, it's just the school we made.

Paradigms are funny things, though. On the one hand they're all-encompassing. You can't get much more inclusive than talking about a person's reality. But on the other hand, changing paradigms, or having a paradigm shift, is not an all-or-nothing process. You don't need to change every aspect of the current schooling paradigm in order to begin teaching from a different belief system. You can have what could be called mini paradigm shifts (Covey 1989). Here's an example in an educational context. When I first started teaching I didn't use a regular teacher's desk, but a large table instead. I hate those bulky wood or metal desks. I wanted to use something cleaner, something neater. But my table was never clean or neat. It was constantly piled high with endless stuff. My students teased me about it.

The summer before my second year of teaching, I was determined to solve the problem. I thought about scheduling regular cleanings; I considered different filing and storage systems. For weeks I searched for the answer of how to keep my desk clean and organized. Finally it came to me: *get rid of the desk*. I realized that I never used it. Since our classroom was so active, I hardly ever sat at it, which is one reason I allowed it to pile up. Since I didn't need it, why not let the class use it as a work table? This was a paradigm shift. I solved a problem by completely reframing it, by considering a rule ("a teacher does not have to have a desk") that goes totally against a rule in the traditional school or teaching paradigm ("teachers have desks"). From that day I've never had a desk of any kind. If I have to sit down and do some work, I sit at one of our classroom tables, just like the students do. Of course, not having a desk does more than just solve a neatness problem. Desks can be power statements, especially since teachers have really big desks and students have really small desks. Not having a desk can also move the classroom supplies, like staplers and tape and paperclips, which are usually limited to the teacher's desk, to a common area for everyone to use. Getting rid of my desk helped make our classroom more democratic.

By saying that our schools have a dominant paradigm, I am saying that the vast majority, not every school but the vast majority of them, carry out their schooling within a common set of beliefs, assumptions, practices, or rules. Acknowledging that I am generalizing, which is something I normally don't like to do, I will say that most of these practices and beliefs are *pervasive* throughout American education; they comprise the *dominant* paradigm. There are certainly other educational paradigms—this book offers what I'll call a *democratic paradigm* of schooling—but the vast majority of schools exist within the same one. John Goodlad (1984) summed this up after studying over one thousand classrooms across the nation when he found an "extraordinary sameness" (246). Kenneth Sirotnik (1983), who worked on Goodlad's study, reached the same conclusion:

> What we have seen and what we continue to see in the American classroom—the process of teaching and learning—appears to be one of the most consistent and persistent phenomena known in the social and behavioral sciences. To put it succinctly, the "modus operandi" of the typical classroom is still didactics, practice, and little else. (16–17)

This does not mean that there are no public (or private) schools working against the dominant paradigm. There are. But, relatively speaking, very few. And I accept that the schools that do work within this paradigm differ in degree and school culture, but still, nearly all of them operate from within the same belief system. This can be seen rather simply by naming some of the paradigmatic rules that dictate how our schools and classrooms typically operate: homework, textbooks, tests, essays, book reports, grades, report cards, worksheets, grade levels, discrete subjects, the list is endless. These are some of the rules or assumptions that our schools operate from. If a school or a classroom doesn't function according to these rules, to most people they are not doing "Real School" (Metz 1989).

According to educational historian Larry Cuban (1993), this is one of the primary reasons our schools are resistant to substantial and meaningful reform. The beliefs of the dominant paradigm are so firmly entrenched in our schools and in our culture that it has become "school reality." Schooling in the United States has become reified. People see schooling and teaching the way they see gravity: as an absolute "God-given" thing, as a universal law of humankind. To most people—even most educators—there isn't a dominant paradigm of schooling because there is only one kind of schooling, the kind we have. If what I do in my classroom doesn't look like "school," the assumption is that I'm not doing "school," which leads to another assumption, that my students aren't learning. This is why it is so difficult for teachers to challenge the status quo. If my classroom looks different, if I want to teach from a different set of paradigmatic rules, to most people I am not really teaching and my students are not really learning. If there is anything I have learned as a teacher, it is that challenging culturally and institutionally accepted rules is not easy. It's swimming upstream. No matter how neat and easy things may appear on these pages, I assure you that in the reality of the classroom and the school they are not. Schooling and teaching are complex business.

But schooling and teaching are not like gravity, they are not natural phenomena. As Tyack and Cuban (1995) have written, "The grammar [or practices] of schooling is a product of history, not some primordial creation" (86). In this sense, school is a *human creation*, and all human creations are ideologically biased and all can be changed. Larry Cuban (1993) writes, "Cultural beliefs about the nature of knowledge, how teaching should occur, and how children should learn, are so widespread and deeply rooted that they steer the thinking of policymakers, practitioners, parents, and citizens toward certain forms of instruction" (14). What makes school "school" are our underlying cultural beliefs that began being formed with the early creation of schools, and the day-to-day practices that grew out of those beliefs, many of which are *myths* that our culture has labeled as "truth." So, if we want to change school—if we want to *reinvent* school—which is what this book advocates, we can. But to do so requires critically deconstructing our cultural beliefs. I don't believe our schools will ever meaningfully change until we crack open the myths and the assumptions of the dominant paradigm and reinvent what it means to be a teacher. Contrary to what a lot of people think, it is teachers, not principals or school boards or legislatures or education academics, but *teachers* who are the key to true school reform.

To be honest, when I walk into a school, there isn't a whole lot I find uplifting. Going to school is primarily a game of hoop-jumping. From the moment children enter their first classroom, they are taught the rules of the Game of School: Sit still, don't talk, listen to the teacher, bring your pencil, take tests, answer the question, read the textbook, write the essay, raise your hand, stand in line, pay attention, think. These are the rituals of daily life inside our classrooms. It's what Philip Jackson (1968/ 1990) called "the daily grind" in his classic study, *Life In Classrooms*. I'll repeat John Goodlad's (1984) question from the beginning of this chapter: *Why are our schools not places of joy?* School doesn't always have to be fun, but to me, going to school should be an experience of hope, an opportunity to open and expand the mind and the heart, to experience intellectual freedom. School should be a place that allows one to become empowered, a place that helps people become thoughtful human beings, a place that welcomes critical questions, a place where people—children and adults— work together as a community of learners to nurture our society, our nation, our world, and our selves. If there's a word that should describe our classrooms, it is *active*. Minds and bodies should be *engaged* there in purposeful, meaningful, and sometimes joyous acts. The daily grind of school, the dominant paradigm of education, fosters the opposite of this. It teaches children passivity. It teaches them that learning is not something *you do*, it's something that is done *to you*.

There are a lot of people who question that schools can be the type of active place that I envision. But they can. We just need to change them, in the words of Hilton Smith (1995), "one classroom, one school, one school district at a time" (68). Those who worry me more are the people who think our schools *shouldn't* change, who want to see school as a vapid experience of learning "the facts." I can't think of a more depressing, antidemocratic, antiintellectual, antisocial way to learn. It limits us. It hinders us. It fools us. It keeps us from what *could be*.

What Is the Purpose of School?

Here is a question: What is the purpose of going to school? Take a moment and think about that. Why do children go to school?

Admittedly there are many reasons why our society sends its children to school, and all of them are debatable depending on your opinions. But historically the primary purpose of going to school hasn't really been about learning, it's been about *eco-*

nomics. The main obligation of our schools throughout their history has been to propagate economic growth, or, to put it another way, going to school has mainly been about preparing children to grow up and get a job and fulfill certain economic roles. To see the frightening level to which our schools are pushed toward economic (and some may say military) ends, we can look at the document that helped start the "back-to-basics" frenzy in the early 1980s, *A Nation At Risk.* A product of the Reagan administration, this document begins:

> Our Nation is at risk. Our once unchallenged preeminence in commerce, industry, science, and technological innovation is being overtaken by competitors throughout the world. This report is concerned with only one of the many causes and dimensions of the problem, but it is the one that undergirds American prosperity, security, and civility. (National Commission on Excellence in Education 1983, 1)

Commerce? Industry? Science? Technology? These are the keys to "civility"? This is not the place for a critique of *A Nation at Risk* (see Arnstine 1995; Finkelstein 1984; Singer 1985; Wood 1984), but when I look at our country today, our world today, the problems that I see, the "risks" that I see, are far removed from mere commerce and industry: poverty, racism, sexism, impoverished schools and crumbling infrastructure, oppression, violence, a void of critical skepticism, fractured families, inadequate health care, corporate hegemonies, crime, environmental degradation, individualism and consumerism run amok, war, the growing chasm between rich and poor, famine, overpopulation, the inability of families and neighbors to talk and listen to one another. Why aren't any of these mentioned in *A Nation At Risk?* Some people like to say that these are "moral" issues, that they're about values and beliefs and character, so they belong in the home or in the college classroom. But how can we separate any of these issues from what it means to be an educated, informed, and literate human being? How can we say that we're preparing children to take a conscious and purposeful part in a nation and its daily life if we aren't addressing these issues in school and teaching students how to relate them to their everyday lives? And how can we call ourselves a democracy if our schools ignore the very issues that test our democracy, that can encourage us to be critical of our commitment to equality, to humanity, to empathy, to the common good? George Wood (1988) has offered some of the most potent words against our schools' intense focus on employment and economic ends:

> The consequence of schooling that seeks merely to respond to the demands of the workplace seems all too clear: Individuals patterned to take their place unthinkingly in a world that operates beyond their control with no respect for their needs. We become cultural and political isolates—with little sense of community or cooperative effort. And most essentially, we adopt a position of passivity, waiting to be "done to" rather than acting ourselves.
>
> The broadest, most public agenda for schooling is thus abandoned. The issue of preparing a public to live democratically, to share in collective decisionmaking, to participate broadly in public affairs, is lost to the simple memory tasks of mandated

minimum competencies. It is not simply an ignorance of the school's democratic mission that brings about these trends. Rather, it is a decidedly antidemocratic spirit that motivates reforms designed to keep the public ignorant and passive as opposed to enlightened and active. (174–175)

Issues of schooling and the economy become even more interesting when we consider that *A Nation at Risk* came out in 1983 with its dire reports of our schools' "rising tide of mediocrity" and a deeply threatened economy, and here we are in 1998 with our economy thriving. The high school class of 1983 has now been in the workforce for about ten to fifteen years, and clearly the report's warnings of American economic and technological doom and gloom have not proven true. And this report, along with an ignorant media and an unquestioning public, fueled so many of the so-called back-to-basics school "reforms." Such grim predictions are nothing new. Vociferous debates and complaints about low test scores and kids not learning the "basics" go back one hundred years and more. But after all of these years and all of these desperate educational/economic predictions, our economy is one of the strongest in history, with one of the lowest unemployment rates since 1970. And consider so many of the Asian economies—countries that are so often touted as the educational ideal with high test scores and long school years—and their economies are on the verge of catastrophe. Just maybe, as I'll argue in Chapter 3, most of the skills people need for their jobs are acquired not from school, but from life.

Considering that school is mostly about getting a job, should we be surprised that so few people come out of it with an ability to engage in meaningful dialogue? Should we be surprised that so few people vote? Should we be surprised that our backyard barbecues are filled with more talk about Disneyland and basketball and TV than about poverty and prejudice and violence and freedom? This is the case, at least in part, because of the superficial nature of schooling. In the words of John Taylor Gatto (1992), our schools are "dumbing us down" in an effort to create children who conform to the status quo rather than empowering them with the skills, the attitudes, the knowledge, and the voices to change it in whatever ways they feel it should be changed. This is why schools must stop placing so much emphasis on economic purposes. This way of thinking distracts us, it subverts our consciousness, it tacitly teaches children (and teachers) that the world we have is the world we have, like it or not, and encourages us to live our lives as if we were powerless, as if the decisions to be made and the actions to be taken should be accomplished by others, as if the only purpose of learning were employment. I certainly want to help prepare my students to get a job, but my teaching is not about creating complacent workers, but helping to shape thoughtful, active, caring, and critically aware human beings.

We will never reinvent our schools and our teaching until we break free from what Frank Smith (1986) calls the "tyranny of testing." Tests, and in particular standardized tests, fit perfectly into the assembly-line transmission methods and economic purposes of schooling. And these tests are built upon one of the longest held assumptions about schooling, learning, and human nature: that it is possible to quantifiably *measure* what a person knows or what a person can do. But this has *never* been proven because it is a personal *ideological belief*.

As John Mayher (1990) and Terry Meier (1995) point out, standardized tests only ask questions which have (supposedly) one *correct answer*, which eliminates the vast majority of knowledge that people can (and should) use to make sense of their lives. Contrary to popular belief, testing is also *subjective* since they expect specific answers and use selected knowledge from very limited disciplines and cultures, showing a clear bias to a white, middle-class experience. And testing drives the curriculum: because so many people are so concerned about test scores, schools and teachers teach to the tests. All of this works to perpetuate teaching in a fragmented, fact-by-fact, skill-by-skill, fill-in-the-blank process (Smith 1986).

In what is certainly one of our society's most undemocratic acts, the most popular standardized tests—the Iowa Test of Basic Skills, the California Achievement Test, the Stanford Achievement Test, the ACT, the SAT—are *norm-referenced*, which means *they are designed for children to fail*. Since one of their purposes is to compare and rank children, before anyone even takes a test the testing company expects half of the kids to score below the "norm" or the fiftieth percentile. This is a *dangerous* labeling of human beings that should not be a part of a democratic society. And this goes far beyond the tests since so many schools use the scores to track students in certain classes and to determine who goes to college, grossly limiting children's opportunities while creating a very real form of social control.

The Hope of Democracy

This brings us to the word *democratic*. I titled this book *A Democratic Classroom* for two reasons. First, in my practice I strive to make the classroom function according to democratic ideals such as equality, dignity, freedom, the common good, empathy, and caring. And second, I strive to make those ideals of democracy a critical part of the knowledge I hope my students will learn. A democratic classroom involves not only process, the methods by which we learn, but it is equally about *content*. I am not just advocating in this book that we change *how* we teach children, I am advocating that we change *what* we teach children.

So, what is the content of a democratic classroom? What, for example, does *democracy* mean to me? John Dewey believed that there are two forms of democracy. One is governmental democracy, which comprises the structure and functioning of our governmental systems. This is the democracy that our schools teach children. It's a very factual, sanitized, and mechanized vision of democracy. The three branches of government, voting, the electoral college. The second form of democracy, however, is what Dewey (and I) are most concerned about and have the most hope in. This is democracy *as a way of life*. Dewey wrote, "A democracy is more than a form of government; it is primarily a mode of associated living, of conjoint communicated experience" (1944/1966, 87). There aren't many "facts" here. Dewey believed that the democracy of our government was only as good as the democracy of our daily lives, our "associated living" and our "conjoint communicated experience." His hope was that our lives would be filled with talk, discourse, social interaction, of letting our infinite voices be heard about the important issues and questions of the day. This requires several things. It certainly requires having an informed and literate citizenry. But it especially requires involving ourselves in the lives, concerns, feelings, and conditions of others, in the functioning of our nation and our world as a whole, and in the forming of beliefs that are based in the common good. And perhaps more than anything it requires a certain *thoughtfulness* and *consciousness* in our daily lives. This may be the single greatest hope of democratic schooling. It can raise a person's consciousness to the world and to the people around them. Bellah et al. (1992), in the book, *The Good Society*, put it this way: *Democracy means paying attention.*

Dewey, who had a great concern for what would happen to democracy in a highly industrial society, saw this process of "paying attention" as our "search for the great community" (1927/1954, 143). The idea of *community* was central to his thinking, to his vision of what could be. He wrote, "The clear consciousness of a communal life, in all its implications, constitutes the idea of democracy" (149). School, on the other hand, makes children believe that the role of the general public in a democracy is voting every four years. Voting certainly has its place, but that's just the mechanical part of democracy. I agree with Benjamin Barber who considers voting to be "the least significant act of citizenship in a democracy" (Kohn 1993b, 20n). What democracy really requires—even *demands*—is the thoughtful dialogue and action that comes long before and long after and completely in between the voting. Democracy is not something we possess, like a house or a TV. It is something that each of us, working together, needs to strive for, needs to continuously question. It's never finished or complete, but rather like learning itself, it is an endless evolution.

So central to democracy as a way of life is the notion of community. But just as I'm advocating a very different conception of democracy, I'm advocating a different conception of community. We must stop seeing community as merely a physical thing, as a place *where* people live, but rather as *how* people live. Far too often when school teaches "community"—a subject usually, and shockingly, reserved for the primary grades—kids spend the vast majority of their time studying local streets and businesses and firehouses and parks. Rarely does school see community as people getting together as a regular part of their daily lives to enjoy one another's company, grow from one another, share perspectives and experiences, care for one another, and engage in important conversation. These are the requirements for a deep and thoughtful democracy. Americans like to talk about all of the individual rights we have, but perhaps instead of talking so much about our rights we need to start thinking more about our communal responsibilities (Etzioni 1993; Lasch 1995).

As social historian Christopher Lasch (1995) passionately argues, for this vision of community to thrive it must welcome economic, gender, ethnic, and racial diversity. As Lasch points out, one of the greatest failures of our current democracy is that the great conversation has been hijacked by the "elites" who do not invite the voice (or the power) of the "common" people. To Walt Whitman, one of the greatest champions of the hope of American democracy, it is the common person who is democracy's lifeblood. (It is no surprise to learn that Whitman—who was a country school teacher for five years—advocated a progressive, even radical, educational practice. In a notebook entry from 1855 he called for "an entirely new system, theory, and *practice* of education, viz: to do that which will *teach to think* everyone for himself" [Reynolds 1995].) It is not enough simply to nurture a democratic communal dialogue, we must constantly question what voices are being invited and allowed to participate in that conversation and what voices are being silenced. Throughout history, the voices of the less powerful, of the poor, of ethnic minorities, have been silenced and marginalized. And many people with important, though unconventional, perspectives to offer—often labeled iconoclasts, zealots, radicals, romantics, or idealists and including Noam Chomsky, bell hooks, Howard Zinn, Henry Giroux, and Wendell Berry—are rarely invited to take part in public debates by politicians and the mainstream media who reduce complex public issues to the two perspectives of Left and Right. What we end up with are "official" conversations and so-called debates whose parameters have been established before the debate even begins. Community and democracy can never exist in a society with a hierarchy of voices.

In a book as closely concerned with democracy as this one is, something must also be said of capitalism. For many Americans, capitalism has unfortunately become synonymous with democracy. But any form of critical study of capitalism is usually (and again, shockingly) reserved for the upper grades (if at all), when in fact so many of the most basic concepts of capitalism are passed on to children the moment they get their first piggy bank and unwittingly become members of Madison Avenue's youngest target market. Most curriculums preach the gospel of capitalism as merely the joys of consumerism and economic growth, the pursuit of profit, and the necessity of a corporate class system, rather than instill in children the freedom to question, change, and improve the economic status quo. Consider an alternative perspective. Tom Chappell is the cofounder and CEO of Tom's of Maine, a $20 million toothpaste company, which, among other things, gives 10 percent of its pretax profits to charity. Chappell has developed a radically different view of capitalism. He says, "The ultimate goal of business is *not* profit. Profit is merely a means toward the ultimate aim of affirming the health and dignity of human beings and their families, affirming aspirations of the community and affirming the health of the environment—the common good" (Barasch 1996, 27). In this view, capitalism is directed by social and environmental responsibilities; it serves the people and the planet, not the other way around. There is also the story of Aaron Feuerstein of Lawrence, Massachusetts, whose textile mill burned down. He and his wife could have cashed in the $300 million insurance policy and retired, but they didn't. They rebuilt the mill because they had a responsibility to their thirty-one hundred employees (Owens 1996). This is capitalism for the common good.

This vision of democracy is absent from the dominant paradigm of schooling. At best, it tries to make kids learn the names and dates and places of our nation's history (or at least one version of it). Even when it comes to teaching democracy in its simplest form, voting, it fails, considering the abysmally low voter turnout that exists.

Hilton Smith (1995) writes, "Schools in the United States have provided plenty of schooling *about* democracy, but very little *for* or *in* democracy" (63). School spends a lot of time on the virtues and heroics of our political past and present, but does little, if anything, about what it means to be an active participant in a democratic way of life, about the responsibilities, the complexities, and the messiness of democracy. It teaches children, both overtly and tacitly, that our nation is finished, that we have already reached the summit of democracy, rather than instilling in them the value of working toward the hopes and the ideals of democracy. It would be easy to dismiss this vision as romantic hokum. But the sad and insidious truth is that our common notion of citizenship has been perverted by an understanding of ourselves as spectators and consumers. This leaves us with the antithesis of an active, conscious, and compassionate citizenry—with the antithesis of a democratic society.

The Limits (and Hope) of Reinvention

As radical as what I'm advocating in this book is, it is not nearly as radical as it could be. There are schools that offer a much more extreme vision of what they call democratic schooling, such as Sudbury Valley School in Framingham, Massachusetts (Arnstine 1995; Ruenzel 1994), where children are pretty much allowed to do whatever they want. (And the school's been open for more than thirty years.)There is also Harmony School in Bloomington, Indiana, whose "democratic ethos" is largely about "liberating, enlightening, emancipating, and empowering" (J. Goodman 1992, 51–52). Many of the ideas, experiences, and theories that I include in these pages can actually be seen as quite traditional. In Chapter 6 I write about a project we did on the American Revolution, in Chapter 7 I talk about reading books and writing stories and essays and poems. All of these can be seen as traditional school fare. All of these ideas (except perhaps the reading of real books such as novels) continue many of the long-accepted rules and rituals of school. We can also look at the institution of school. I teach in a regular "school" building, we have a separate classroom, I have twenty-seven students, they have lockers and school supplies, I spend virtually all of my time alone with them, they leave the room for gym and art. So there are similarities between our classroom and most classrooms, at least in terms of basic structures.

There are two primary reasons for this. First, no matter how progressive I may want to be in my classroom, I must still function within an existing—and extremely traditional, and some would say conservative—system of schooling (Eisner 1992; Tyback and Cuban 1995). This returns us to that "against-the-grain" notion that I mentioned in the introduction. Teachers can bend and push and cut and shape our current schools and their traditional paradigms, but there's only so far that we can bend them before something or someone (usually us) breaks. This is one of the political realities of being a teacher-activist. We need to work to bring change to schools in ways that allow us to keep our jobs. As Marilyn Cochran-Smith (1991) wrote, "To teach against the grain, teachers have to understand and work both *within* and *around* the culture of teaching and the politics of schooling at their particular schools and within the larger school systems and communities" (284). So what I can and cannot do in my classroom is directly tied to the school I'm working in, as well as to the larger society. I would have much preferred to call this book "A Democratic *School*," but unfortunately I've never worked in a democratic school. So until schools and society become more open to serious, even radical, change, teachers are going to be somewhat limited in what they can do in their classrooms, at least in public education.

One suggestion I do have for a teacher who wants to question the status quo, change their practice, and work "against the grain," is to find a colleague who can be an ally and a partner. When I first started teaching I was very fortunate to have had another new (and excellent) teacher across the hall from me, Aleta Margolis, who shared many of my educational beliefs and teaching frustrations. Sometimes we actually joined our classes and taught together, like on our great kite-making project. Both in school and out, Aleta and I talked constantly, helping each other, supporting each other, commiserating with each other. We were both more successful—and more sane—teachers and activists because of it.

Another reason the pace of our (and my) reinvention is limited is because as a teacher I need to play a role in preparing children to take part in society. Even though I work to instill in each of my students the passion and the ability to transform our society and our world, the fact remains that they are going to be expected to—and they are going to *want* to—function and succeed in our society as it presently is, not necessarily as we might want it to be tomorrow or next year or in the next millennium. So no matter how much I might want to change how I teach, no matter how much I might want to implement a radical new idea I've come up with, I'm limited, sometimes *seriously* limited, in what I can do.

I've come to believe that this is my greatest challenge as a teacher: to be true to my self while being honest and practical to my students and at least somewhat agreeable to the powers that be. Grimmet and Neufeld (1994) have called this a teacher's "struggle for authenticity." Teachers who consciously work to transform the institution of schooling and the practice of teaching are steeped in this search to be authentic. These teachers are conscious of their missions, they ask hard questions, they work to uncover their tacit beliefs and assumptions about schooling and children and society, they have skeptical habits of mind, and they make critical reflection and personal and professional development an important part of their lives as teachers and human beings.

Reinventing schools and teaching is about much more than implementing new methods. When we reinvent our teaching we are really reinventing *ourselves*. David Mas Masumoto, the farmer I discussed at the beginning of this chapter, wrote something that struck a nerve in my teacher self. He wrote, "In the process of exploring the landscape, I discover a little bit more of who I am" (1995, 19). The same is true for myself when it comes to being an educator. It is a constant self-exploration. As much as I'm concerned with the growth of my students and the transformation of teaching and schooling, I am equally concerned with the growth and transformation of myself, and not solely as a professional educator but as a complete human being. More than being a teacher, I am a learner. I will always be a learner first. And in the process of teaching each day, I truly do discover more of who I am and who I wish to become.

Two

Respecting Children

I have spent my whole life learning how to paint like a child.
—PABLO PICASSO

The secret of education lies in respecting the pupil.
—RALPH WALDO EMERSON

When teachers stand before their classes each day, they have specific beliefs and assumptions about the nature of childhood. They may not volunteer these beliefs in a faculty meeting or at a staff party, but they have them. It's possible, even probable, that a teacher is operating on a daily basis from beliefs that they do not have conscious awareness of. This has been called "tacit" or "personal knowledge." Tacit knowledge is the silent or subconscious knowledge that directs our actions without our conscious awareness (Connelly and Clandinin 1988; Lincoln and Guba 1986; Polyani 1958). But whether the beliefs we have about children are tacit or conscious, we have them, and they determine how we act when we're with them. It's important, then, to make critical self-reflection a part of your teaching, to help you uncover your tacit beliefs and reconsider your conscious beliefs. This is one of the reasons Connelly and Clandinin write, "There is no better way to study curriculum than to study ourselves" (31). The more we study ourselves, the more questions we ask about what we believe and why, the more beliefs we can uncover, the more we will understand and be able to change and grow.

I can use myself as an example. Although I'm sure that I have knowledge or beliefs that I'm not consciously aware of, it's important for me to critically reflect on my teaching every day—to study myself—so that I have many *conscious* beliefs about children that I bring with me when I enter my classroom. The more that I know about myself and my beliefs about children, the better teacher I can be. Here are ten things that I believe about children:

1. Children have a natural love for learning.
2. Children grow and develop differently.

14

3. Children bring important prior knowledge and experiences with them to school.
4. Children are capable of learning without being taught.
5. Children are naturally good people.
6. Children learn from their models.
7. Children need guidance in making good decisions.
8. Children learn from their cultures.
9. Children like to talk.
10. Children can do a lot that society doesn't think they can do.

These beliefs are not facts. They're *beliefs*. They're my beliefs. And I have reasons to believe them. I have what could be called evidence that support my beliefs, such as research that I've read or conducted myself, and especially personal experiences, which are very powerful reasons for believing something. These experiences are not limited to my teaching, either. My experiences throughout my life have had a profound impact on my beliefs about children, especially experiences I had when I was a kid. And my beliefs are not set in stone; they're constantly evolving. I expect that some of them will change over time and some of them won't.

I remember when a preservice teacher was observing in my classroom when I was teaching in a suburban school. As you'll learn throughout this book, my classroom is a lot freer than most, with a lot of movement and noise. After school we sat down to talk. I wanted to know his thoughts about what he saw:

> PRESERVICE TEACHER: It's cool. I really like what you do. But it would never work where I've been observing in the city.
>
> ME: Why not?
>
> PRESERVICE TEACHER: Because it's Chicago. Those kids are *tough*. The teacher needs to do what she's doing.
>
> ME: What is she doing?
>
> PRESERVICE TEACHER: She has the kids sit in a circle and take turns reading from the textbook. What you do won't work with those kids.
>
> ME: How do you know that?

He didn't know that. He certainly believed it, but his belief was just an *assumption*. It wasn't based on actual experience. He hadn't seen those "cool" ideas fail when put into practice at the inner-city school he was referring to. During our conversation it was clear to me how his assumptions about teaching and his assumptions about those "tough" Chicago kids dictated his beliefs, which in turn, if they go unquestioned, will dictate his practice as a teacher. I'm not saying that he was wrong. I'm saying that he was confusing an assumption with a fact, and when it comes to teaching and learning and schooling, there aren't many facts.

I don't fault him for his thinking. He's coming from two of the most time-honored assumptions about children. The first is that if children aren't controlled, they will run amok, they'll be dancing on their desks and hanging from the lights. This is the monkeys-running-the-zoo assumption. The second assumption has to do with how most educators react to children who are not motivated or who misbehave or who happen to be difficult "city kids." The typical reaction is to get tougher on them, to implement more structure, to teach more "basics" through skill and drill and direct instruction. This is the school-as-bootcamp assumption. These assumptions are so widely accepted as fact that they're usually implemented without much evidence or support to justify their use. But seen from an anthropological perspective, every classroom, every teacher, every student is different, so what doesn't work in one class-room may work beautifully in the classroom right next door. Of course all of this depends on how you define *work*. A classroom that "works" for me, that accomplishes what I want it to accomplish, may not be working at all in the opinion of that preser-vice teacher.

So much of schooling and teaching today are directed by the assumptions of our culture. People assume that schools must use textbooks; that children must be divided by age and grade; that teachers should do most of the talking; that it's possi-ble to measure someone's "ability" or "knowledge" or "IQ" (that something called "IQ" even exists); that kids learn best in quiet classrooms; that kids learn how to spell from taking spelling tests; that any form of assessment is objective. The list is endless. Not a single one of these assumptions have ever been proven to be universally true and none of them will ever be proven to be universally true, because all of them depend on a long list of context-specific variables, personal assumptions about human nature, and a host of political purposes (such as, what is the purpose of school?). So what "works" wonderfully in one classroom or with one student may work terribly with the classroom next door or with another student in the same classroom. There are very few (if any) universal truths about schooling and teaching.

It is our unquestioned assumptions about what works and what constitutes school that dictate how most schools operate and how most teachers teach. Exposing these assumptions won't make a lot of people happy because it certainly isn't convenient and it certainly doesn't offer any final answers to how we should teach, and it most definitely eliminates any form of universal, standardized, cookie-cutter, factory-model vision of a classroom or curriculum. Americans have developed the habit of wanting definitive *answers*, and when they aren't available or they don't work, people get mad. But there are no easy or definitive answers when it comes to schooling. All educators need to be critical of what we do and what we believe and what we're told to do, and consistently work to shape and refine our practice.

If we fall back on our assumptions about children and teaching, we fail to con-sider alternative possibilities. Rather than looking at the situation from a new per-spective or trying the previously untried or the unimagined, far too often our automatic presuppositions kick in and we allow them to control what we do. In the context of schooling and teaching, this happens so often because it is difficult for most educators to see outside of the dominant paradigm, to see the water and reach beyond it. So rather than asking critical questions about his underlying assumptions about city kids and why they couldn't do what we were doing in my classroom, the preservice teacher reacts with the usual bootcamp scenario. He could have questioned, for example, what it is that the school wanted those inner-city kids to learn in the first place. If he's expecting those kids to be excited about reading the textbook and learning the names and dates of the ancient Assyrians, he might want to take some time and think about his own memories of memorizing names and dates. Mine are nightmarish. It's certainly possible that what I was doing in my classroom would not have "worked," in either his or my opinion, with the students he was observing in the city, but his beliefs, largely formed by his unquestioned tacit assumptions, eliminated the possibility of ever finding out.

In *To Teach: The Journey of a Teacher*, William Ayers (1993) asks, "When teachers look out over their classrooms, what do they see? Half-civilized barbarians? Savages? A collection of deficits, IQ's or averages? Do they see fellow creatures? We see students in our classrooms, of course, but who are they?" (28). Here is a question that can encourage educators to consider some of the strongest-held assumptions about children and teaching. How do we see children? Every educator must ask themselves what they see and what they believe when they look at children, and especially their students, and they need to dig deep for honesty. My image of children isn't all pristine and rosy and I don't expect anyone else's to be either. But I do believe that far too often, adults, and especially educators, look at children and see the enemy.

All of these ideas, for me, come down to the issue of respect. The dominant paradigm of education doesn't have much respect for children. This may seem incredibly ironic, and it is. (Education is fraught with ironies.) If schools had more respect for children, they would be more about meaningful learning, creating, and sharing knowledge and less about blind compliance; more about celebrating differences and less about advocating sameness; more about honoring what children bring with them into a classroom and less about trying to prove and remediate what they don't; more about raising children's critical consciousness and less about numbing their minds by making them memorize endless trivia; more about building community and less about fostering competition; and more about helping children to develop their voices and encouraging their use and less about making, as John Dewey argued against, silent schools a virtue. If schools had more respect for children, they would not only talk about democracy as part of their curricular content, they would be invigorating environments and communities that *live* democracy as an inherent part of their daily existence.

The people that have taught me the most about what it means to respect children aren't educational researchers or experts, but children themselves. By watching them, by listening to them, by asking questions about them and with them, by encouraging me to reflect on my own childhood and school experiences, my students never cease to remind me of what it means to respect another human being, whether they're thirty or thirteen.

I would now like to tell you a story of one of those children. I will call her Tracy. I had Tracy, a sixth grader, during my second year of teaching. Tracy helped me learn a great deal about what it means to respect children as learners, as teachers, as meaning makers, as complete and complex human beings. The story of Tracy, however, is not just the story of one student that I taught for one year. All across our nation, in schools in every state and every community, there are many, many Tracys. In fact, I believe there is a part of Tracy in every child.

Tracy Helps Me to See

Tracy was shy. She was the kind of student who disappeared in a classroom. She never raised her hand, she never misbehaved, and unless I specifically asked her something, I wouldn't hear her voice. If I didn't make a conscious effort to notice her each day, which some days I didn't do, she would very easily melt into the walls. Most teachers I know have had students like this, and when it comes time to grade them, without a whole lot of deliberation you give them a C. That's exactly what I did with Tracy. I'm fairly sure I gave her all C's for the first quarter of school. I saw her as an average, maybe even a below-average kid. She didn't seem to fit in with most of the class. Tracy's the kind of kid that other students would call "strange."

After three months of school I noticed that our classroom walls were pretty bare and needed some spicing up, so I created an art project. The class broke into small groups with the purpose of coming up with a theme and creating a large mural. I showed them several murals, like Picasso's *Guernica*, and we related the idea of a mural's theme to the themes of books, short stories, movies, and songs. Since a lot of thought had to be put into the project, I saw it taking at least two or three weeks. The kids had the option of working alone or in small groups. Not surprisingly, Tracy chose to work alone.

Whenever we worked on our murals, Tracy would go off across the hall to work on the stairway landing. It was a good space to work, large, carpeted, and private if you closed the stairway doors. I don't remember knowing much, if anything, about Tracy's project while she was working on it. I saw bits and pieces over the days and weeks, but I didn't have any overall sense of what she was doing. I suspect she was melting into the walls. And to be honest, I distinctly remember spending considerably more time during this project with the more verbal students.

Finally, the day came to present our murals. I don't remember what I was expecting, if anything, from Tracy, but when she showed her work to me, it absolutely took my breath away. She had taped together perhaps twenty pieces of white photocopy paper on which she had drawn. Her mural stretched more than *half the width* of our large classroom. Even more amazing was her theme: "The Evolution of Life." The mural began with the first microorganisms on earth, continued with the early primates, went on to the evolution of humans, and then followed some people through the course of life, from childhood to the teenage years (whizzing by in a convertible, hair flying about) to adulthood, and then finally to old age and death. Her drawings included the smallest details, like beams of light from the car's headlights, the knurled wooden cane of an elderly person, the engraving on headstones in a cemetery. But that was only the first half of her mural. On the other half were intricate drawings of the sky, some clouds, the planets, the sun, and some stars. I remember pointing to the scene with curious wonder, and asking about its meaning. I can still see Tracy standing next to me, answering my question. In her ever-so-quiet, matter-of-fact voice, she said, "It's how you get to Heaven." Heaven, I thought. It's how you get to heaven. I was in awe.

It was obvious that Tracy not only worked on her mural harder than anyone else in class, but that she did most of it at home, which hadn't been something I'd even suggested. This wasn't the work of a rainy day, this was the result of working every day for weeks with a passionate vision. I could not get over how much effort she'd put into the assignment. How important it was to her. The meaning it had for her. This assignment struck something in her heart and soul. Given the freedom to create the mural of her choice, Tracy had produced something I don't think I could have ever specifically assigned.

I was also amazed by what was included in her mural. Where did she *learn* about the evolution of life on earth? *In our own class.* We'd been studying it through our exploration of life science, which was part of the required curriculum. In writing workshop, we had read the poetry of William Carlos Williams, and Tracy had even included his name on one of the cemetery's headstones. Her mural was not only a testament to how much meaning what we were doing had for her, it was a perfect example of *authentic assessment*. No test, no workbook, no essay, not a single worksheet. And still I was able to see how Tracy assimilated the ideas we'd been exploring. I learned more about Tracy's learning—and more about Tracy—from her mural than I could ever learn from a test.

Imagine one's reality being changed in an instant. A snap of the finger. One moment I saw Tracy as an "average" kid, and the next moment I saw her as being one of the hardest working, most invested, and unique children I had ever met. How could it be? How can someone be average and spectacular at the same time? The answer lies in one of the things that Tracy taught me. *There is no such thing as an average child.* Seeing Tracy as an "average" kid reduces her to those C's that I put on her report card and destroys every ounce of character and vitality that makes her the unique person that she is. It takes away her humanity and her dignity, her sense of *self*. Schools and teachers need to celebrate everyone; they need to see that behind those test scores and grades and essays and worksheets and reports are very real, very unique, and very *complex* human beings. There may be a lot of kids in a classroom, but each and every one of them is special and deserves to be celebrated, and deserves the right and the freedom to celebrate themselves. A democratic classroom strives to make this happen.

But it's not easy. The very nature and structure of the dominant paradigm of school, with its assembly-line belief system, makes this celebration of uniqueness difficult if not impossible. The dominant paradigm is about *standardization*; it's about teaching (or covering) the same stuff to every child at the same time, and doing so in a predetermined, lockstep, unit-by-unit, lesson-by-lesson curriculum. How can anyone get to know the intricacies and complexity of a child this way? How can anyone encourage children (and teachers) to develop their selves, to share who they are and who they wish to become, and to think for themselves and create their own ideas if everything they're supposed to learn and everything they're supposed to do has been decided before they ever set foot inside the classroom? The dominant paradigm of schooling is built upon the *necessity* of having "average" children, an inherent part of a system that rates and ranks children. Democratic schooling is the antithesis of this. It strives to create classroom environments that allow every child to flourish in a caring classroom community where no one is average and everyone is unique.

Tracy got me thinking about notions of intelligence and academic success. What does it mean to be "smart"? What does it mean to succeed in school? What does an A or a B or a C or an F mean? And who gets to decide these answers? From the perspective of the existing paradigm of school, Tracy wasn't particularly strong in "school intelligence." She struggled with math, she didn't read the most difficult novels, she hardly spoke, and her writing had a certain naïveté. Historically, our schools have valued two forms of intelligence, analytical/logical and linguistic. Stated in simpler words, math, reading, and writing. This is what Michael Apple (1990) critically refers to as "technical knowledge," because it's the knowledge that our society sees as being key for our children to get a job and maintain economic growth, and it's the knowledge people assume can be *tested*. I'm not denying that some of these skills are important for our children's and our society's well-being, but Tracy helped me to seriously question our schools' devoting practically their entire existence to the transmission of technical knowledge and the subsequent devaluation (or complete neglect) of other forms of knowledge and intelligence, such as ability in the arts and the many forms of affective knowledge.

There are now greatly differing views of intelligence, such as Howard Gardner's (1983, 1991) theory of multiple intelligences. Gardner has identified at least eight forms of intelligence: linguistic, logical-mathematical, visual-spacial, bodily-kinesthetic, interpersonal, intrapersonal, musical, and naturalistic. These are eight very different ways of knowing; eight different ways of making sense of the world and interacting with others. We can add to Gardner's thinking Daniel Goleman's (1995) "emotional intelligence" and Robert Coles's (1996) "moral intelligence." Being human and "smart" is profoundly more complex and multidimensional than school makes it out to be. We all know the world through these different intelligences, but we differ in the extent to which we possess each intelligence. Unfortunately, our society, and hence our schools, has little respect for any form of intelligence beyond the first two. You would think the opposite is the case when we consider how revered Michael Jordan is, with his extraordinary bodily-kinesthetic and visual-spacial intelligence. How often do we hear about his SAT scores? But then again, who does our society identify as being "smarter," Mother Teresa, Picasso, or Einstein?

All of this points to how our schools force all children into the same educational mold, which is exactly what I was doing with Tracy. But children are people, and people, by nature, are *different*. Children have different experiences, different learning styles, different cultures, different genetics, different intelligences, different interests, different histories, different knowledge, different hopes and dreams. And yet there is basically one kind of school. Rather than creating classrooms that are able to shape themselves to all of the different children and all of the different possibilities, school forces children to squeeze themselves into one way of learning, one way of doing school. Those are the rules of school, and if you don't like to play by those rules, or if you don't know how to play by those rules, or if you can't play by those rules as well as others can, than you lose the Game of School. That's what school did to Tracy. That's what I'm sure school continues to do to Tracy as I write these words. That's what I did to Tracy until she helped me to see.

The difficulty I had with Tracy has its roots in the mind-set I began teaching with. This was a mindset of *comparison*. When I assessed my students, both formally and informally, I would compare one student to the next. This is another rule of the dominant paradigm of schooling. I would mentally rank my students, comparing Tracy to Joey and Joey to Mitchell and Mitchell to Latisha, and somewhere among all of those people there were lines of demarcation, lines that separated the academic elite from the academic average and the academic average from the academic failures, and somewhere in the middle of all that is what some people call the "norm." But Tracy helped to teach me that the only person I should be comparing Tracy to is *Tracy herself*. It should come as no surprise that our schools are based on competition, which is, after all, a foundation of our economic system. But assessment doesn't need to be— it *shouldn't* be—one against the other. Rather, it can be a recognition of one's growth and thinking and areas that must be focussed on for improvement. Once we remove the competitive factor, school becomes a much more humane and democratic place.

From the day that I saw Tracy's mural to the very last day of school, I never gave her another C. Tracy was Tracy and she was doing an amazing job of working hard on her own learning in her own way at her own rate. As far as I was concerned, in a snap, she became an A student. But with Tracy's help I realized that grading children at all is inhuman, medieval, undemocratic, and completely unnecessary. Grading is one of school's most disrespectful acts. It doesn't matter if you're giving a child an F, a C, or an A. By grading children, we're sorting and ranking them as if they were cattle at a county fair. Grading children may be convenient, but convenience should not guide how our schools function. Giving children grades is one of those entrenched rules of the dominant paradigm. People can't imagine how you can teach and do school without giving grades, but you can, you just need to see assessment through a democratic and noncompetitive lens.

Tracy taught me that every human being develops uniquely. I wish I had a nickel for every dirty look I get when I use the word *developmental*. A lot of people see the word as an excuse for bad teaching and lazy students. Many who see the developmental classroom as important for early childhood teachers think it amounts to bad touchy-feely teaching in anything above first or second grade. I like the way Zemelman, Daniels, and Hyde (1993) defined the idea: "Developmentalists recognize that kids grow in common patterns, but at different rates which usually cannot be speeded up by adult pressure or input" (13). Common patterns but different rates. If we accept this then we cannot blame children for who they are. We cannot blame Tracy for struggling with math or for being quiet or for wanting to experiment wildly with poetry. If I compare Tracy to her classmates, then I am claiming that I believe there is some scientific law as to what each and every sixth grader in the world should know at a specific time in their lives and how well they should know it. By doing so, I'm saying that I believe that norm exists; that I believe there is such a finite and defined thing as a "sixth grader" and that there are objective and measurable levels of "sixth graderness." Except for extreme cases, we would never expect this in a child's physical development. We don't expect all children to be a specific height and weight at age six. So why should we expect it in their intellectual development? Schools need to stop blaming and punishing children for being human.

I am reminded of Susan Ohanian's (1994) "learning-to-ride-a-bicycle" approach to teaching and learning. We would never expect every child to learn how to ride a bike at the same age. If an eight-year-old is still using training wheels, we don't ship him off to bike-riding remediation. We just figure that he needs a little more time, or perhaps that bike riding isn't one of his strengths. We make the learning-how-to-ride-a-bike fit the child, rather than forcing the child into a bike-riding "norm." If this is true with riding a bike, why isn't it true for adding and subtracting and reading and writing? Why is it so difficult for people to accept that requiring and expecting children the same age to learn or "master" the same material at the same time to the same degree goes against common sense?

I know that it is very fashionable to say, "All children can learn." I certainly believe that. All children *can* learn. But seeing learning through a developmental lens means that all children are not going to learn the same thing at the same time and at the same rate. It also means that all of us have a wide variety of strengths and abilities. Some of us are good at math and some of us are not. Some of us are great spellers and some of us (even avid readers and writers) are not. Some of us have great interpersonal skills and some of us do not. Some of us can weave a beautiful basket and some of us cannot. Some of us can pick up bike riding in a snap and some of us cannot. Some of these differences are caused by our home life and other cultural and personal experiences and relationships (nurture), but others are caused by our personal set of genes (nature). It makes no difference how hard I try, I will never be very good at basketball. Personally, I don't think I was born with what it takes. And during high school biology I specifically chose Alan to be my lab partner because he was a wiz at science and I wasn't. (Why was he a wiz? Well, for one, he loved science. Why wasn't I a wiz? Well, at the time I couldn't care less about science. It's only natural that many of the interests we have are so often intimately connected to our strengths.)

This doesn't mean we shouldn't encourage children to make sense out of the difficult and the confusing. In fact, that's exactly what we should be doing. When we look at an eight-year-old, we can't begin to assume what that child can and cannot do, either tomorrow or ten years from tomorrow. Herbert Kohl (1984) wrote, "One cannot look into children's souls and see the extent and limits of their potential. Potential is not located in any part of the brain or in any organ. We don't know what people (ourselves included) could become, and any limit on expectations will become a limit on learning" (58). Ask my sisters and they would probably tell you how shocked they are that I'm an avid reader and writer and that I became a teacher. Fifteen years ago I would have told you the same. Every child truly does have an unknown limitless potential. And that's why a democratic classroom is so important. Its intellectually rich and active environment, its freedoms, its thoughtfulness, its critical nature, its encouragement of talk and discussion, allows—actually encourages and teaches—children to go in search of themselves. Tracy, thankfully, helped me to see that.

Children's Knowledge

Children do not come to school with empty heads to be filled up. They bring powerful knowledge, history, experiences, interests, cultures, and theories with them to school. My students have knowledge that I need to respect. Just because they're children doesn't mean I can't learn from them. My students have had experiences that I have not had, read books that I have not read, met people that I have not met, belong to cultures that I do not belong to, and have interacted with the world in ways that I have not. When one of my students writes a poem, their poem is no less valuable or no less meaningful than a poem I wrote simply because they're ten and I'm thirty-seven.

I've had students that had *more* knowledge and ability than I. Kristi and Sarah were better writers, Adam knew more about science than I'll ever know, Caroline and Daniel were better at math, Andrew and many others were better at sports, Brian and a host of others were great at art, and Barrie had an amazing grasp of history and read more books by fourth grade than I read through college. In addition to this I could take any student (such as Tracy), and find their unique talents and abilities and knowledge. Nick, for example, knew a lot about computers; Adam knew a lot about the Navy Seals; Sojourner knew a lot about African American history; Abby knew a lot about horses; Neil knew a lot about skateboards; Franco and Becky could play the guitar (and Becky wrote her own songs). The list is endless. A classroom, any classroom, is truly a rich repository of knowledge and experience that I (and everyone) can grow from as human beings. I don't think kids have much conscious awareness that they know so much, or that their personal knowledge has value. Over the years school has taught them that they are the ones who do not know and that their teachers and other adults are the ones who do know. A democratic classroom wants everyone to know that everyone knows.

It's important to specifically note the *cultural* knowledge that children bring with them into the classroom. Imagine three different ten-year-old boys. An African American ten-year-old from Chicago's inner city, an upper-middle-class Jewish ten-year-old from a Chicago North Shore suburb (that's me), and a ten-year-old boy on a farm in rural Illinois. All boys, all ten, all in Illinois. But imagine the profoundly different cultural knowledge and cultural realities these three boys have. They do share some things in common. They're all kids, they have similar patterns of biological development, they may share a similar media and pop culture orientation, and they may have similar social realities in how they've been enculturated into the wide grasp of American consumerism. But their differences are profound, and respecting children means recognizing these differences, honoring them, allowing them to flourish in the classroom, and having the willingness to learn from them. Imagine for a moment how complex and amazing and rich the issue of culture becomes if we were to add a ten-year-old boy from Pakistan to the mix, or if we were to consider the different social and cultural knowledge and perspectives between boys and girls. Cultural knowledge is diverse. My students in Chicago, all African American, have taught me a lot about gangs because gangs are a very real part of their lives.

Children also bring meanings or *theories* about the world into their classrooms. This is an especially important point for teachers to consider, since a child's theory about something can often be in conflict with something the teacher wants to teach. Roger Osborne and Peter Freyberg (1985) offer a good example of this with their research into "children's science." They asked kids, "How far does light from a candle go?" Here are just three of their responses: "It goes out in rays and ricochets off objects"; "About one foot"; "Just stays there and lights up." Imagine if your job was to teach these children about light. You want them to learn certain knowledge about light, but they begin with knowledge of their own. In a sense, you're *competing* with their ideas. I see this all of the time. For example, I like to ask my students what *democracy* means to them. Here's five responses I've received from fifth graders:

1. Democracy means that we have a little power over the government. I also think it means that you are free to express your thoughts, feelings, opinions, and reactions.
2. Democracy is when everybody votes for people who they feel have the same ideas as they do.
3. I don't know what democracy means.
4. I think democracy is important because everybody gets their say and everybody listens to the people, besides the government's opinion. That is really important 'cause if you don't get to say what you think you feel helpless about your country's conditions.
5. Democracy means voting and freedom of actions.

Many theories that children have are wrong, but remember, to the child they *make sense* and they are *perfectly correct*. In the context of science, Osborne and Freyberg (1985) put it this way:

> Children naturally attempt to make sense of the world in which they live in terms of their experiences, their current knowledge and their use of language. Kelly (1969) suggests that we are all scientists of a sort from a young age. The child-as-scientist develops ideas albeit tacitly, about how and why things behave as they do, *which are sensible to that child*. (13, italics added)

This is just science. Imagine the complex theories children have about history, politics, geography, reading, math, art, even learning itself. (Go and ask ten kids— and adults—what it means to learn.) We must respect these theories, whether they're right or wrong; we must recognize that our students have them, and that they have a powerful influence on the meanings children construct. Of course, many theories are not right or wrong. That's why they're *theories*. Ask children "Why is there racism?" or "What causes poverty?" or "What is a good person?" and you will so often hear profound and thoughtful responses.

Respecting children also means respecting, honoring, and nurturing children's individual meaning making. This is a profoundly different vision of the learning process. No longer is school and learning simply a matter of transmission from teacher to student; it becomes a *transaction*. For me to respect my students I cannot corral their minds and thoughts by using a rigidly sequenced predetermined curriculum. Where is the place for a child to think, to make sense, to share their voice in a curriculum that decides they will begin to study the American Revolution on November 25, long before they ever step inside the classroom? Curriculums like these are recycled year after year after year, no matter what children walk through the classroom doors.

There is specific knowledge that I strive to help my students learn. Not only are there district, state, and cultural expectations about what I will teach, but I have much knowledge of my own that I want to share with my students. Doing this and respecting the knowledge my students bring with them are not mutually exclusive. In fact, they can compliment one another. Existing knowledge and new knowledge can share a symbiotic relationship, feeding off of one another. By learning and understanding who my students are and what knowledge they have, I can *situate* new knowledge within their lives and I can use their experiences, knowledge, and cultures to *create* curriculum. Ira Shor and Paulo Freire (1987) call this "situated pedagogy," and C. A. Bowers (1984) refers to this as basing schooling on a child's "phenomenological culture." As I will show in this book, situated pedagogy can be done with virtually any topic, and it not only helps children connect new knowledge to existing knowledge, it enables children to make better sense of new ideas by placing them within the context of their own lives.

Along with the dominant paradigm's model of schooling as a one-way process from teacher to student is the tacit belief that children are "incomplete." That's why, the belief system says, children come to school, so that they can get the knowledge they need to be complete. But children are already complete people, in the sense that all of us—adults included—are *never* finished, we're always under construction. Like me, my students have feelings, likes and dislikes, learning experiences, expertise, hopes and dreams, fears, struggles with friends and family, angst, laughter, and curiosities. We are all people living on the same planet. They are children and I am an adult. I have had many more experiences than they have had, and that does give me more knowledge and hopefully more insight. But we are all still learners and we are all still teachers and we all have knowledge and thoughts to share. That's what living in a democratic community means.

Children's Biology

Human beings are by nature social animals. That's why we live in families and communities and cities. That's why we like to go out to dinner and have parties. We spend a good amount of our lives seeking the company and companionship of others. There is a special truth to this for children, most of whom place tremendous importance on their social relationships. School, under the dominant paradigm, works against this. Until cooperative learning came along, talking with a classmate about math or social studies was considered cheating. But still, even with cooperative learning, which is implemented in relatively few classrooms and usually in a highly controlled manner, talking spontaneously and moving around freely is asking for trouble. In school, children's talk as a whole is the exception, not the rule (Goodlad 1984). Walk through the hallways of a school when classes are in session and the voices you hear belong to the teachers. If children are fulfilling their primary role in the school learning process under the dominant paradigm, they're sitting still and being quiet.

John Dewey ([1902/1915] 1990) wrote of an experience that speaks to this issue. He tells the story of going to buy desks for his famous turn-of-the-century school at the University of Chicago. It was very difficult for him to find desks that would work in a school that he saw as a child-centered "laboratory." The salesman finally remarked, "I'm afraid we don't have what you want. You want something at which children may work; these are all for listening" (31). Dewey goes on to comment:

> That tells the story of the traditional education. Just as the biologist can take a bone or two and reconstruct the whole animal, so, if we put before the mind's eye the ordinary classroom, with its rows of ugly desks placed in geometrical order, crowded together so that there shall be as little moving room as possible, desks almost all of the same size, with just enough space to hold books, pencils, and paper, and add a table, some chairs, the bare walls, and possibly a few pictures, we can reconstruct the only educational activity that can go on in such a place. It is all made "for listening"— because simply studying lessons out of the book is only another kind of listening; it marks the dependency of one mind upon another. The attitude of listening means, comparatively speaking, passivity, absorption; that there are certain ready-made materials which are there, which have been prepared by the school superintendent, the board, the teacher, and of which the child is to take in as much as possible in the least possible time. (31–32)

Dewey's description of "traditional education," offered nearly one hundred years ago, could have been written yesterday. To expect children to sit still and be silent and spend many hours a day passively yet attentively goes against all forms of biology, human nature, and post–World War II contemporary culture, with its cars and planes, televisions, telephones, video games, computers, movies, MTV, sports, and advertising. People—and especially kids—like to move and talk. For evidence I say visit a school faculty meeting or "inservice." Look who's whispering to their neighbors, scribbling notes back and forth, fidgeting in their chairs, even fighting at times to stay awake. It's hard enough for adults to remain quiet and still and focused during extended meetings and lectures, imagine what it must be like for a ten-year-old.

A quiet child is not necessarily a learning child, but our society equates silent children with learning children. This is one of those rules of the dominant paradigm: "Classrooms must be quiet so children can learn." But when the teacher is talking and the students are quiet, what's going on in the minds of those children? When I walk through the corridors of schools, I like to take passing glances through classroom windows and open doors. Usually the teacher is talking and the students are quiet, and some of them are looking at the teacher and at least appear to be paying attention. But others, most of them, in fact, are fiddling with pencils or staring out the window or doodling or passing a note to a friend or daydreaming or even sleeping. I know this because it's what I did in school. In a high school history class I perfected sleeping with my eyes open. This certainly isn't true for all children, but I don't believe the vast majority of children are paying even minimal attention to the talking teacher. That's why I strive to keep my talking to a minimum, and it's not easy, because as a teacher I have the urge to talk.

The goal of education shouldn't be to have quiet children, it should be to have children who are meaningfully learning and thinking and asking questions. Quiet times have their place, but most of what happens inside a classroom should be active and social. This means creating a classroom environment that builds off of a child's biology, that uses it, rather than fights against it. If you want to see what I mean, just take a peak inside a good kindergarten classroom. My friend Beth Kolhemanin's classroom is based on the belief that people are social beings, that learning is primarily a social act, that it involves much more doing than listening, and that it involves quite a bit of noise and movement. (The word *kindergarten* means "children's garden.") As I'll show in the following chapter, this is exactly how we learn in life. Five-year-olds may have their nap time, but most of their day together is spent being actively and socially involved, and this interaction *enhances* their learning by using their biology as a natural part of their learning process. Respecting children means recognizing that social involvement in the classroom should not be made to stop once a child becomes six years old.

Money

This book is not the place for a detailed discussion of school funding and resources; however, it is impossible to consider democracy and respecting children inside our schools without mentioning these issues. (See Jonathan Kozol's book, *Savage Inequalities* [1991], and the report *Rethinking Schools* [1995].) It is amazing to me that we can call our nation a democracy, that we can so easily flaunt our equality to the world, and yet have such blatantly unequal funding for schools. Democratic schooling demands equal educational opportunities for *all* children, in all of our cities and suburbs and rural communities. Our schools are primarily financed through state and local property taxes. In Illinois, the state that I teach in, this means that about half of a school's funding is based on a child's property value. How bad is it in dollars? Illinois has a per-pupil funding range from a high of around $12,000 to a low of around $2,400 (*Rethinking Schools* 1995). *This is democratic?* To me, this sounds more like schooling in medieval Europe, with the richest schooling automatically going to the aristocracy. Perhaps after five hundred years our society hasn't progressed nearly as much as so many think it has?

We can forget about the horrendous lack of resources inside most of our schools momentarily and look at the physical buildings themselves. A recent report by the U.S. General Accounting Office put the price of repairing our present schools (many of which are literally crumbling) at $112 *billion* (*Rethinking Schools* 1995). And this of course is only for our existing schools; it does not include the billions more desperately needed to build new schools to relieve the current massive overcrowding. Stories of schools, and especially urban schools, that conduct classes in hallways, bathrooms, and closets abound. There's a school in my neighborhood in Chicago that just put up its *eighth* temporary classroom on its playground. How do you tell children you respect them and want to give them the same educational opportunities that wealthier children receive when you are sending them to a school that looks like a trailer? You do not see these problems in middle- and upper-middle-class, primarily white schools. These schools have the system of funding on their side. This issue is about more than mere money and politics, it's a race and class issue.

All of this is not lost on our children. My students have joked about the peeling paint in our classroom, the holes in the walls, the lack of resources, the uneven heat in the winter. They know the score. They know exactly what society thinks of them. And it becomes insidiously ingrained in their psyches. Should we be surprised that the dropout rate in the Chicago public schools is nearly 45 percent? Should we be surprised that so many children in urban schools all across the country don't take their education seriously? If society doesn't take their learning seriously, if society doesn't want to give them the same opportunity and richness it gives to other children, if society does not show them the respect and dignity all people deserve, why should these kids care about it themselves? We can add to this what is surely one of the gravest insults to American children. Schools all across our nation that are strapped for cash are selling advertising on their hallway walls, their school buses, their sports fields. A student in a recent college class I taught showed me advertisements for Chefboy-ar-dee right on her son's worksheets. This, of course, is not just an issue of economics. Once an advertisement goes up in a school hallway or is shown on a school TV (through, for example, Channel One), it becomes part of a school's curriculum.

These problems are not to be left up to our legislators. Again, that is not my view of democracy. The concern of all children, whether they're African American or white, Native American or Latino, rich or poor, urban or suburban or rural, must be the concern of all people and all teachers. That's what is meant by the common good. That's what should be meant by democracy.

Trust

Respecting children to the degree that I am suggesting is not easy. It requires trust. The great psychologist Carl Rogers wrote in his classic book, *Freedom to Learn*:

> If I distrust the human being then I *must* cram him with information of my own choosing, lest he go his own mistaken way. But if I trust the capacity of the human

individual for developing his own potentiality, then I can provide him with many opportunities and permit him to choose his own way and his own direction in his learning. (1969, 114)

This is the idea behind the democratic classroom: to create an environment of trust that allows children and their teachers the freedom to explore, to ask questions, to inquire, to think. If we want children—and later, adults—who can and will think for themselves, then we must have classrooms that allow them to do exactly that. This cannot be done without trust.

Trusting and respecting children does not mean giving them free reign in school. That isn't respect, it's irresponsibility. John Dewey (1938/1963) was very clear that experience was not necessarily educative. Throwing kids in a room for them to "discover" their learning wasn't his idea, and it isn't my idea, of a stimulating classroom. According to Dewey it is the teacher's responsibility to very consciously create, or at least establish the framework to create, the classroom environment. But this environment must be built on a foundation of trust in children as natural learners, as people passionately interested and vested in their own learning, in being curious to understand their world, and in being more than capable of playing an integral role in directing their growth.

Teachers need to ask themselves to what degree they trust their students and why. We will never be able to break away from the dominant paradigm of schooling if we don't at least begin to have trust in children. Questions involving trust can be found in every aspect of curriculum and everyday school life: Do specific books need to be assigned for students to read, or can you let them choose their own books? What about allowing a student or a group of students to work in the hallway unsupervised? How about letting children create their own curriculum? Can children plan their school day? How about allowing kids free movement to go to the bathroom or get a drink of water when they need to? How about letting students write what they want to write? Or what about letting them choose their own collaborative groups to work in? All of these questions involve issues of trust and power and control. I'm not saying that we should blindly trust children to do what's right. Remember, one of my beliefs about children is that they need guidance to make good decisions. But I think it's very difficult to help children learn how to make good decisions if we don't give them opportunities to do so. That being said, schools must make it okay for children to fail. Schools need to start recognizing that making mistakes is a natural and important part of learning and taking risks.

We need to see children as naturalists see trees. There are millions of trees in the forest but not a single one the "same ol' tree," not a single one "average." Accordingly, naturalists believe that not a single tree—no matter how knurled or old or in decline—should be cut down, because they know that every tree breeds more life, every tree is an organic part of the whole, every tree has aesthetic and ecological value. Emerson wrote, "The creation of a thousand forests is in a single acorn." The same is true for children.

Three

Toward Meaningful Learning

I have never let my schooling interfere with my education.
—MARK TWAIN

I was determined to know beans.
—HENRY DAVID THOREAU

Several years ago when I taught fifth grade, I had a student whom I will call Nancy. Nancy was kindhearted and fun, with a great sense of gentle humor. She was capable of doing wonderful work when she wanted to, which wasn't as often as I would have hoped. I worked especially closely with her on her writing. Not only were her mechanics a mess, but she had, without a doubt, the worst handwriting I had ever seen. Every once in a while her penmanship would suddenly improve, so I knew that she could do better when she wanted to, and I showed her this, but it had little lasting effect.

At one point during the middle of the year, Nancy and another student started a class "advice column." They posted a large envelope on a classroom bulletin board, wrote a letter to the class explaining what they were doing, and distributed it to everyone's classroom mailbox. At first I went along with the girls' advice column. They were doing it as part of writing workshop (see Chapter 7) and I thought it showed great initiative. We talked about the aims of such columns and that the girls needed to take what they were doing very seriously. The only stipulation I put on their column was that they let me review their responses before they made them public. There were a few complex private issues being dealt with by some of the students, and I felt that it would be wise to take a look at what advice they were going to offer before they offered it. They agreed to my condition.

But after a week or so I nixed the advice column. The girls were not taking it seriously and it quickly became disruptive. This was not an easy decision on my part. I take pride in allowing my students to act on their ideas and be creative, so it was with reluctance that I put a stop to their efforts. Nancy was furious with me. She thought I was being unfair and told me so. She wasn't rude, just adamant and fighting

30

for her beliefs. I told her that she might be right, it might be unfair, but that I had made up my mind and my decision was final.

The next morning I came to school and found a sealed envelope with my name ("Mr. Steven Wolk") neatly printed on the front, sitting on a classroom table. I opened it. It was a letter from Nancy. A full page, handwritten. She was blowing off steam in a very determined, yet civil manner. And get this, her writing was *perfect*. Her handwriting was as neat as could be and her mechanics were flawless. It was the finest piece of writing she had done all year. And not just grammatically, but content-wise as well. She had stated her argument clearly and concisely.

I was amazed by this. Not only that Nancy would feel so strongly about the issue to take the time to write me a letter (a very democratic thing to do), but that she had put so much effort and care into writing it. Why did it look so good? Why, after months of struggling to get her to improve her writing, was her letter, in a flash, so beautiful? Because more than anything else she had done, the letter had tremendous personal *meaning* to Nancy. It was entirely an *internal* act. To use a word from Sylvia Ashton-Warner (1963), it was an entirely "organic" act. I didn't assign it, I didn't suggest it, I didn't expect it. It was one hundred percent Nancy. It came from within her, and she had a very real, very important, very personally meaningful purpose in writing it. That's what hit me about the letter more than anything. The meaningfulness it had to the author.

This was a rather humbling moment, standing in solitude in my classroom before school one morning, reading Nancy's letter. As a teacher I work hard to make my students' learning meaningful, personally important, and relevant to their present lives. But experiences like the one with Nancy serve as a reality check. They remind me just what it means for learning to be truly meaningful to an individual, how important it is, and how difficult and complex it is for me, the teacher, to help make this happen. Respecting children means not wasting their time in school, and if what's happening inside our classrooms is not about meaningful learning, then that is exactly what we're doing.

Learning and the History of Schooling

To most children, school has very little relevancy to their present lives. The content they are taught is so externally created and standardized, and delivered in such piece-meal fashion, that for something to truly connect to their lives, cultures, or selves, is rare indeed. As educators we must ask ourselves why learning in school is so meaning-less. This is obviously a complex question, but some of the answers can be found in a brief look at the history of schooling. One of the metaphors that's commonly used to describe schooling today is "school as factory." There are reasons for this metaphor. As Bowles and Gintis (1976), Edward Fiske (1991), and Herbert Kliebard (1987, 1992) explain, our modern system of schooling was largely modeled after our turn-of-the-century factories. The powers that be wanted schools that would create an "efficient" society, so they used a top-down system of management and assembly-line means of

31

production for inspiration. This is why the educational belief system that underlies the dominant paradigm is known as the "social efficiency movement." It was primarily concerned with creating and maintaining an efficient society, which in turn meant preparing a nation of complacent workers and separating people into predetermined social and economic roles.

Two of the easiest ways for us to see the school-as-factory mentality is in how it functions with specific, predetermined curriculums and lesson plans to supposedly increase efficiency, and in how it breaks knowledge down into discrete parts, teaching from part to whole, just like how an assembly-line operates, starting with a bunch of parts and ending up with a car or a toaster or a washing machine. Neither of these were made a standard part of school by accident. They were the results of years of advocacy of what came to be known as "scientific curriculum-making." Efficiency was the name of the game. Herbert Kliebard (1987, 1992) explains how our schools, in the early twentieth century, directly implemented the thinking of Franklin Bobbitt and W. W. Charters, two of the leading curriculum theorists of the time. For both of these men, schooling, learning, and teaching could be reduced to a "scientific technique" (Kliebard 1987, 116).

Our schools were not created in a vacuum; they did not just materialize one day in their present form. *People* created our schools, people with very specific beliefs and assumptions of childhood, learning, and human nature, and very biased and political notions about what school and society should be. Kliebard writes that few people have even read much of Bobbitt's and Charters' work, yet, "we pursue with somber dedication the techniques on which these works are based" (93). He adds:

> One of the most persistent and puzzling questions in this, the aftermath of the scientific curriculum-making movement, is why we retain, even revere, the techniques and assumptions we have inherited from Bobbitt and Charters, at the same time we reject, implicitly at least, the actual outcomes of their research. (93)

Scientific curriculum making did not stop with Bobbitt and Charters, but included the psychologist Edward Thorndike, who played a significant role in creating today's schools with his early work in the areas of intelligence—I.Q.—testing, and perhaps indirectly, ability grouping and tracking. Thorndike strongly advocated segregating children by their so-called abilities, native intelligence, and future potential. For example, he wrote, "The problem before the high school is to give the boys and girls from fourteen on *who most deserve* education beyond a common school course such a training as will make them contribute most to the true happiness of the world" (Kliebard 1987, 109; italics added). And since the scientific curriculum was based on the roles that someone determined children would (or should) assume in their later life, it strongly advocated, for example, one curriculum for boys and another for girls, thus assuring women the knowledge they would need to carry out their expected roles in society and the home. It is worth pointing out that research today continues to show that schools and their curriculums still favor boys (American Association of University Women 1991; Sadker and Sadker 1994).

But it didn't stop there either. Our schools also adopted the beliefs of the king of industrial efficiency, or what's known as "scientific management," Frederick Winslow Taylor. Taylor conducted intricate time-motion studies of assembly lines in order to first determine the most efficient means of production, and then to rigidly control them. (He had a big influence on Henry Ford.) In connecting Bobbitt, Charters, and Taylor to the dominant paradigm today, Kliebard (1987) wrote:

> One persistent legacy of the scientific curriculum-makers is the continued insistence upon stating precise and definite curricular objectives in advance of any educational activity. This is, of course, an argument by analogy from the world of manufacture where, at least according to Taylor, precise specifications and standards had to be established in advance in order to achieve the desired product with maximum efficiency. (121)

But standardized, mechanized, piecemeal teaching does not result in meaningful learning, it results in convenient, decontextualized, and strictly controlled schooling. Considering that it has been by far the single most dominant way of schooling and teaching since the days of the one-room schoolhouse, if it did result in meaningful learning, we would have a far more educated nation. I am puzzled why so many traditionalists place the onus on progressive educators such as myself to "prove" that the ideas we advocate can work. I look at our society and I look at our world, and it is clear to me that traditionalists have had nearly two centuries and I don't believe we've seen their ideas work.

What Does It Mean to Learn?

The word *learn* is the most abused in education. Consider how it's used: "In our school fifth graders learn fractions"; "On the field trip the students will learn about farming"; "During writing workshop students learn about the power of language and finding your voice"; "National standards will determine what all eighth graders will learn"; "In sixth grade kids learn the scientific process." To all of these comments and to the endless stream of others when it comes to the word *learn,* my reaction is the same: How does anyone know what a class or what any student will learn during fifth grade, or on a field trip, or during writing workshop, or from national standards?

"Fifth graders will learn fractions" is not a statement of fact. At best, it's a *hope.* We can say that we *work toward* fifth graders learning fractions. Or we can say that fifth graders are *presented* with fractions. Or we can say that fifth graders *experience* fractions. But whether they "learn" fractions or not, or to what degree they learn fractions, depends on each *individual* fifth grader. Learning does not happen inside a classroom, it happens inside each child's head, so there is no way of knowing beforehand what about fractions any of those fifth graders will or won't learn. In fact, when I'm teaching my class something about fractions, just about the only thing I know for certain is that it's highly probable my students' learning will cover a wide spectrum. I'm not saying that some kids can't learn, I'm saying that all kids learn differently.

Schools, teachers, parents, legislators, and textbook publishers bounce the word *learn* around as if the learning part of school is a foregone conclusion. As if *covering* fractions is the same as *learning* fractions. It isn't. There is a grand confusion—perhaps *myth* would be a better word—whereby people assume that what is taught in school is learned, and that for someone to learn something it must be taught. These two assumptions have seriously blinded educators (and the public) to the complexity (and, I will explain, the ease) of the human learning process. Frank Smith (1986), in his book *Insult to Intelligence*, wrote:

> In school, teaching and learning are generally regarded as the same thing, or at least complimentary. Although teachers may be heard complaining that they have taught something four times but some students still have not learned it, there is a general assumption that teaching should result in learning and that learning is the consequence of teaching. . . . The truth is that a good deal of teaching goes on without children learning anything that they are intended or supposed to learn, and enormous amounts of learning occur without conscious teaching or formal instruction. Most learning takes place without anyone even suspecting that it is occurring. (80–81)

In support of this position I point to virtually any school's official curriculum for a single school year. Anyone who believes that children can meaningfully learn so much stuff in such a short period of time (or perhaps ever) is seriously confusing teaching with learning. Simply because it's "in the curriculum," simply because the kids read the textbook chapter or "do the unit" or "cover" geometry, the assumption is that the content not only should be learned, but that it *will* be learned, maybe not "mastered" (whatever that means), but certainly learned, at least to some degree. If our children's learning was not assumed from the beginning, how can our schools have such *predetermined* curriculums? If school did not confuse teaching with learning, curriculums would not be set in stone and teachers would not be under so much pressure to get through the book by June. But rather, curriculums would be fluid and alive and largely determined and created along the way, depending on what's happening in each unique context.

But this isn't the case at all. Teachers know that after they finish teaching ancient Greece, it's on to ancient Rome, and the question of the students actually learning ancient Greece is a moot point because they need to move on to the next chapter in the textbook or the next topic in the curriculum. So in the end, school is not really about learning, it's about covering what's expected to be covered, it's about going through the motions of "Real School" (Metz 1989). This is why Ted Sizer (1984) and George Wood (1992) advocate the "less is more" philosophy. They want children to meaningfully learn, and they know that won't happen until we slash curriculums to a fraction of their size, having students spend much more time on far less content.

If we want to point a finger at why so many children are not meaningfully learning in school, two primary reasons are that *we think they are* and that *we think they should be*. When I was in school virtually everything I did I did because I was told to do it. Learning wasn't on my mind, getting it *done* was. That was my primary goal, *fin-*

ishing what I was told to do. It may have looked like I made a connection in answering a question correctly about ancient Greece on a test, but the end result was not usually me learning in a meaningful and purposeful context, but merely me *jumping through a hoop*. I did a pretty good job of going through the motions of school. I jumped through enough hoops that they let me graduate.

So here's a question: Think about your own schooling. Think about all of those years and all of that stuff you were made to study and read about and write about and take tests on. Now ask yourself this: How much of all of that content is an important part of who you are today? Let's make the question even easier: How much of all of that stuff, the lectures and textbooks and worksheets and essays full of the history, the science, the math, the reading and writing, do you *know* right now?

Learning and Meaning

In *Freedom to Learn*, Carl Rogers (1969) communicated a rather simple, yet profound idea about learning, and it has become a guiding light for me as a teacher. Here it is: *Significant learning takes place when the subject matter is perceived by the student as having relevance to his own purposes* (158). Now I am going to simplify this sentence even further (and perhaps change it a tad). Here's mine: *People learn best what is most meaningful to them.* This is true whether it's the learning of a nine-year-old or the learning of a thirty-nine-year-old. This is true whether you're learning the ABC's or you're learning how to do a kidney transplant. What this means is this: The more we can *situate* our students' learning within each of them, the more meaningful their learning will be. I don't believe I'm exaggerating when I say that when it comes to learning, *meaning is everything*.

When I write of a person's *meaning making* I am referring to the knowledge that each of us constructs as we take in information from the world around us and the significance that new knowledge or information has for us as unique individuals. It is the making sense of and learning from our lived realities. This is the basis of constructivist learning theory, which argues that people are not passive vessels to experience, they interact with it, they *construct* it. People make meaning all of the time. You are making meaning right now as you read these words. Having children make meaning is not an option. It's not something that teachers and schools can decide to have their students do or not do. They do it whether we want them to or not. It's a natural part of human consciousness. We can, however, enhance their meaning making by creating constructivist classrooms that nurture and celebrate it.

I don't think the idea of people constructing their own meaning will come as a big surprise to most teachers. I would say that when asked, most people would agree with it. The idea seems rather obvious. But our schools continue to function as if this weren't the case. As if when an entire class reads a book, the individual members of that class create—and *should* create—identical meaning, as if when they hear a lecture they make sense of it in the same way, as if even the more "factual" information like math and science must have the same meaning for everyone. Human meaning making, and I would think common sense, says this is not the case.

Meaning may be most important to learning, but meaning is dependent on *perception*. Carl Rogers's statement included the phrase "perceived by the student." Imagine what this means. As the teacher I can do a lot to help my students learn. I can especially play the primary role in first establishing the environment that allows them to learn. But the actual act of each student's learning is a product of their own individual perception and their meaning that results from it. This takes the emphasis in the learning process off of the teacher and puts it where it rightfully belongs, on the learner. *Learning is up to the learner.* I have a huge role in furthering my students' thinking, but no matter what I do, no matter how well-intentioned I may be, it's the learner who perceives experience and then constructs meaning. It is impossible for me to put "unconstructed," sterile, neutral knowledge into a child. Teaching is not just about opening up a kid's head and dumping something in. That's assembly-line teaching, and it does not result in very much learning.

Our learning, our meaning making, is not an isolated activity. Although it may ultimately happen inside each of us, making meaning is also a social activity. In their classic work *The Construction of Social Reality*, Berger and Luckman (1966) explain that human sense-making, is a *social construction*. Think about it this way: If you ask ten people who were at the same birthday party to tell you about the party, you're going to get some similarities, but you're also going to get some startling differences. Ten people at the same birthday party, ten different birthday party realities, but *all of them are interdependent on each other.* Everyone at the party influenced each other's construction of their "party reality." Why is this important for teachers to consider when they're responsible for teaching kids about sentence structure, multiplication, and George Washington? Why should I give my students' perceptions a second thought? Imagine how impossible it would be for you to throw that birthday party with the *intention* of everyone afterward sharing the same party reality. It can't be done, and if it can't be done at a birthday party, then it can't be done in the classroom. But yet, that very assumption forms one of the rules of school under the dominant paradigm: that everyone will learn the same thing at the same time and in the same way.

Suddenly the very "simple" act of teaching takes on a whole new, and rather mind-boggling, complexity. If our goal is for our students to construct meaningful learning in our classrooms, then we better take their meaning making very seriously, and we better be asking ourselves what we as educators can do to help bridge what it is we want them to learn, the prior knowledge they bring with them into the classroom, and what it is they're going to construct from the process of schooling. One of the key answers to that question is to *start with the child*. Starting with the child not only recognizes the child's critical role in their education, but actually uses the child's life and existing knowledge to help them learn.

Situating Knowledge

What exactly does it mean to start with the child? It means, in part, that we try to *situate* new knowledge within each student. I do this in a number of ways. First, as I will explain in Chapter 6, I give my students time each day to work on a project of their own choice. This does *not* mean that a student with an interest in rockets goes off and studies rockets for six months at his own leisure. Here's a more *purposeful* process: say a student wants to know more about dolphins. Their learning *begins* with them; they decided to study dolphins, they *wanted* to study dolphins, so there is a much greater chance that they will assimilate this new knowledge, as well as the supplementary or collateral knowledge, such as research skills, collaboration skills, and reading and writing skills.

But it doesn't stop there. In the process of their study of dolphins, I can situate new ideas about dolphins or new ways of thinking about dolphins within their project. Put more directly, I can help them expand their learning, and not just specifically about dolphins. For example, I could suggest that they add a geographical component, having them look at where dolphins live and why. Or I could suggest a physiological perspective, encouraging them to look at the anatomy of dolphins. I could also suggest adding a *critical* and *moral* component that would have them look into the politics and the economics surrounding this species, such as the ethical controversies over the netting practices of the tuna industry or whether dolphins should be held in captivity and "trained." I could also suggest they add a mathematical component by looking at various dolphin populations over the years, or possibly creating a survey about dolphins. Even though the subject of study may be their choice, as the teacher I play a crucial role in facilitating the process, suggesting new directions and perspectives, challenging and guiding students in relating knowledge, and helping them understand new and complex information.

As I'll explain in Chapter 7, through our writing and reading I can also help students situate their growth in their own lives. In writing workshop I allow students to select what to write, so that their writing has direct relevance and meaning to them. I do the same for reading, allowing students to choose their own books and giving them a wide variety of mediums for responding to the text. Projects that originate from me or a school's official curriculum can also be situated in a child's life by building student choice and ownership into the project. For example, instead of making everyone in the class study "religion" by reading from the same textbook, children can choose one religion that they want to know more about and use the world to explore it. I did this my first few years of teaching when "religion" was in our ancient history curriculum, and I was fascinated by what religion each student chose to study. Sophia studied Judaism because she knew very little about it, but had a lot of Jewish friends. The questions she formed about Judaism didn't come from me or a textbook, they came from *her*. In addition to reading books about Judaism, she visited a synagogue and interviewed a rabbi and one of her Jewish friends. By starting with something from a required curriculum I was able to change it, shape it, open it up, and allow my students to make it their own.

There are many projects and activities that we can do as a class that can help me learn more about my students' lives, as well as allow them to situate their learning within themselves. One example is a project that I call our "personal maps." The idea is for each student to create a "map" of a part of their lives. Matt made an "injury map," which was a lifesize outline of his body, showing eleven years of cuts and bruises and broken bones; Sylvia, who was from Ecuador, produced a map of her native country showing all of the places she visited; Esmeralda created a map of her neighborhood, showing her home, our school, and all of the places she likes to hang out; Franco devised a topographical map of the desk in his bedroom, which showed the varying heights of his books, pencils, and papers; Crystal made a "map of my heart," showing all of the things she loved; Roger created an "emotional map," which showed where in his house he experienced certain emotions over the years; Jerry came up with a map of the enormous mess under his bed (reminding me of my own childhood!); Nick created a topographical map of the neighborhood path where he rides his bike; and David made a map of his refrigerator (Figure 3-1).

Not only did I use this project to learn more about the lives and interests of my students, I used it to help them learn map skills such as symbols, keys, grid coordinates, and the concept of scale. There's no question that the primary reason the project is successful (and enjoyable), is because it directly involves the lives of each of my students. I recently found a wonderful picture book on the same idea, My Map Book, by Sara Fanelli (1995).

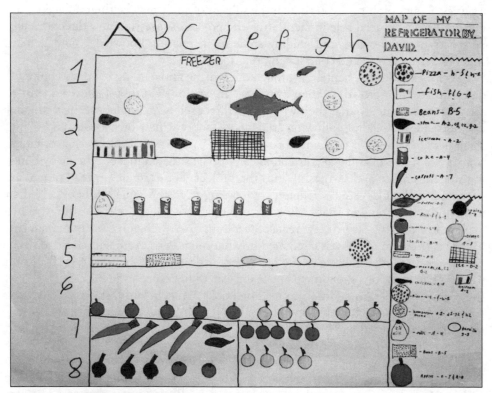

FIGURE 3-1 David's personal map of his refrigerator

As I will explain in Chapter 8, I can also encourage our learning to emanate from our own lives through formal and informal talk and discussion. Just by asking children what's going on in their lives or what news they have heard, I can encourage dialogue that's situated within each of them. Just the other day, when I asked the class what they wanted to talk about at our class meeting, Jamar, a fourth grader who is African American, asked, "Why are black people killing other black people?" Children rarely get to talk about their own lives and concerns in school. According to the rules of the dominant paradigm, that's not what matters. What matters isn't what children bring with them into their classroom, but what they *don't* bring with them, what teachers are supposed to "give" to them. Encouraging talk and discourse about our lives changes all of this. In a very real way it makes our own lives, questions, and ideas a central part of our curriculum.

But the reality of schooling is that as a teacher I'm given explicit curriculums that I'm expected to teach. So I make a very conscious effort to situate this "external" knowledge within the lives of my students. For example, earlier this year our class was looking at the Renaissance as part of our required curriculum. Since kids love stories and since history has an endless supply, I began our exploration by sharing with them the story of Galileo, who, to me, stands as a symbol of the Renaissance. To summarize, Galileo lived in the late sixteenth and early seventeenth centuries and built some of the first good telescopes. Using his telescopes he was able to prove that the sun did not revolve around the earth (geocentrism), as the Church and the Bible taught, but that the earth revolved around the sun (heliocentrism). (This actually wasn't new knowledge; Galileo further proved what the Polish astronomer, Nikolas Copernicus, knew a century before, which is why our modern system of astronomy is known as the Copernican system.) But Galileo got into serious trouble. When he did not heed the Church's warnings (and the warnings of university professors) to not teach and write about his ideas, which were considered heretical, they brought him to trial at the Inquisition, where he was made to recant his beliefs and sentenced to live his final eight years of life in a monastery. (Just six years ago, in 1992, the Vatican officially apologized to Galileo! He would have been 429 years old.)

After the story I gave the class a journal writing assignment. They had to write about a time that *they* clashed with authority or a time that they were prevented from expressing their ideas or feelings:

> There was a time when I couldn't express my feelings. It all began when I walked in the door. My aunt started yelling at me. I didn't know why she was yelling at me. I asked what was happening. My mom said, "One of our neighbors called the house saying that you and your cousin were yelling and wouldn't stop."
>
> I told my mom that it wasn't true. My aunt didn't believe it. My mom had always told me to tell people how I feel, so I did. I told my aunt that she never heard my side of the story and asked why couldn't she wait instead of just yelling at me. At that very moment was when I knew that I will never end up leaving the kitchen without getting in trouble. My mom told me to go to my room. I asked her, "Why?"
>
> "Because you talked back."

I told her, "You said that I should tell people how I feel and not keep it inside."

That was when everything got quiet. After that my aunt went to her house and my mom went back to what she was doing.

That night I went to sleep feeling proud because that was the first time I let my feelings out instead of having them in. And I felt really good. That was a time that I couldn't express my feelings. I think kids and adults have a right to express their feelings whenever and to whoever they want to. That's my personal opinion.
Elizabeth

It was quiet reading time and I was sitting next to Pedro, John, and Nick on the rug. We were looking at *National Geographic* and reading our books, when Mr. Wolk came up to us and said [that] he heard me talking. But I wasn't. He made me go to my desk and read. That made me real mad because he didn't listen to me when I tried to tell him that I wasn't talking. He just walked away and told me to sit down at my desk and read.
Danny

Learning and Purpose

Let's say a teacher wants their students to read Roald Dahl's book, *James and the Giant Peach*. He probably has specific purposes for having them do that. But the teacher's purposes have little to do with the *students'* purposes. Within the dominant model of teaching and learning, most kids would be reading the book because the teacher wants them to. They don't have any innate purpose for reading the book. The only reason they're reading the book is because their teacher told them that they had to. This doesn't mean they won't enjoy it. And it doesn't mean they won't get anything out of it. It just means that the reason for reading it, the reason for giving it a second thought, the very purpose for holding it in their hands, is the teacher's.

Now imagine a different scenario, and this is partly what the philosophy of whole language is based on. A teacher gives the class the freedom to choose their own books. A child goes to a library shelf and scans for a book. She comes across *James and the Giant Peach*, looks at the picture on the cover, reads the back, maybe remembers a friend telling her that it's a fun book and that Roald Dahl is a great author. So she takes it and reads it, or at least starts to read it. Different purpose entirely. If a person does something for their own purposes, because it is *relevant* to their own life and their own being, they will learn and grow significantly more than if they are doing something for someone else's purpose. The former comes from within the learner, the latter is driven from some external source. The former is an *authentic* experience, the latter is a falsely manufactured one. William Heard Kilpatrick, a contemporary of John Dewey's and a strong advocate of learner-centered schooling, succinctly put it this way: "The stronger the purpose the stronger the learning that takes place" (1925, 202).

Once again, Carl Rogers (1969) beautifully summed up the power of purpose and relevance in learning when he wrote, "We need only to recall what a brief length of time it takes for an adolescent to learn to drive a car" (158). Why don't schools ability-group driver's education? Why don't we have classrooms for driving remediation? Because we don't have to! Every adolescent that I know, including myself when I was fifteen, desperately wanted to learn how to drive and get their license. More than being just symbolic of freedom, being able to drive *was* freedom. Why, all of a sudden, do all of those so-called barriers to learning science and math and history and reading and writing in school, disappear when we're teaching driving? Because when it comes to learning how to drive, we can actually see the power of a child's internal purpose. I admit that there aren't many other things that so many children, almost universally, are driven (to use a pun) to learn, and that's exactly one of the problems with the dominant paradigm. It basically says, We don't care, you're going to learn it anyway. The trouble is, they don't.

Ask a child why they're studying fractions or why they're studying geography or why they're studying the human circulatory system or why they're reading Hemingway, and I'd be surprised if you get any form of coherent, meaningful answer. Most would probably say that they're studying it because they "have to" or because they "need to know it to graduate" or to "get into college" or to "get a job." The passion for learning for the sake of learning, or the idea of being an informed, caring, critical, thoughtful, responsible, and participating member of a democratic society is totally absent. Learning in school, from the perspective of most children, isn't seen as an important human endeavor or even an enjoyable endeavor. That's not the purpose from their eyes. To them it's seen as a necessary evil. As what their parents had to do. As a graduation requirement. I believe this is true for the vast majority of children, but I know this is true for at least some kids for two reasons. First, they've told me so, and second, when I was in school, that's exactly how I felt.

Learning as a Natural Act

If one were to base their beliefs of learning on "school learning" it would be hard to come to any other conclusion than to say that learning is a very difficult thing to do. After all, most kids in school don't get A's and B's, most get C's, with a significant percentage getting grades below that. This leads one to draw the reasonable conclusion that learning—at least the learning that's supposed to take place in school—is a difficult thing. If it wasn't, then everybody, including me in high school, would get much better grades.

But learning as a human process can actually be easy. Human beings are learning all of the time. In fact, it would be difficult—actually impossible—for people *not* to learn. The human brain's primary purpose is to learn and make meaning from our environments and experiences (Caine and Caine 1991; Smith 1986). One of the best ways to see this is to look at ourselves. Earlier I asked you to think about how much of all of that stuff you were expected to learn in school was a significant part of who you are today. I'm going to answer this question for myself. I know a lot. I've learned a lot.

How much of what I know right now as I sit at my computer typing these words did I learn in school? Maybe one percent, and that's being generous. Granted, as I type these words I am a thirty-seven-year-old upper-middle-class white male, but the same idea applies equally to my students, who are African American and largely children of the working poor. As I watch them and interact with them each day, it is very clear to me that the vast majority of what they know they did not learn in school. Of course, the idea is anything but new. The late John Holt (1964, 1989), for example, wrote passionately about the ease and the pleasure of learning as a natural part of life outside of school, and contrasted this with the stultifying difficulties of school learning.

Sometimes when I'm with adults, including preservice teachers, I'll ask, "If I gave you a piece of paper, could you somewhat accurately list the major historical events from the past five thousand years?" I'm not looking for trivial names and dates, but approximations for the big events, like ancient Egypt or the fall of Rome or the signing of the Magna Carta or the Russian Revolution. Not surprisingly, I hardly get a taker. And many of those adults went to "good" suburban schools and got "good" grades and did very nicely on their standardized tests. And yet, the question usually results in a slightly humorous and embarrassed silence. (My assumption is that most of them believe that they *should* know these things.) From there I go on to ask about major scientific events and concepts, about habits of reading and writing, about math. Once again, a lot of silence. Most know enough math to balance their checkbook, are scared of science, use writing for grocery lists and work, and rarely pick up a book. Most of the people that I ask this of had *seventeen years* of this stuff drilled into them and what do most of them have to show for it? Not a whole lot.

The same is true for me. When I graduated from high school I was a functional illiterate, and I attended schools that are considered by many to be among the best in the country. (All of my schools have won "Academic Excellence" awards from the U.S. Department of Education.) I had very good grades until high school, when I became the model C+ student. When I graduated as an undergraduate I wasn't much better. I distinctly remember being in my early twenties and unsure which side was which in the American Civil War. (I'm not kidding.) A few years later, in my mid-twenties, an urge to learn about the world overcame me, and that's when I started reading and having an *internal purpose* and insatiable thirst for learning.

Still, five years later during my first year of teaching I had to teach my students "ancient Egypt." Our textbooks were our curriculum, so I followed the topics, but I hardly used the books themselves. I remember sitting in my dining room, thumbing through the textbook chapter on ancient Egypt, preparing what my class was going to do. The truth is, and an honest teacher will admit this, I had to read about ancient Egypt in the textbook in order for me to learn it so I could then teach it to my students! The same was true for other subjects. The summer before my first year of teaching, I spent a good deal of time in the public library learning all about life science, because that was our sixth grade science curriculum and I couldn't have even told you what *life* meant. This is a reality of teaching you rarely hear because it points directly to the utter failure of our schools to help children meaningfully learn. When it comes time for teachers to start teaching certain knowledge, they don't know much of it themselves. (And what they do know well is usually what they like teaching best, because that's where their personal interests are.) So, while I was sitting in my dining room, reading about ancient Egypt, a thought suddenly entered my mind: What do *I* know about ancient Egypt? I made a list:

> The ancient Egyptians made pyramids and sphinxes.
> The pyramids were the tombs for the pharaohs, who were buried with treasures.
> They wrote with hieroglyphics.
> It was near the Nile River and the desert.
> In the movie *The Ten Commandments*, they were the bad guys.
> King Tut was an Egyptian pharaoh.

I'm not sure if you consider this a lot or a little knowledge of ancient Egypt, but sitting in my dining room I asked myself why I should bother teaching my students a textbook full of mundane trivia about ancient Egypt that I didn't know myself as an adult. Chances are I studied all of that stuff in school, was bored silly by it because it had little relevance to me, and forgot 99 percent of it, so why would I do the same to my own students? Surely, I thought, there must be better ways to spend our time together.

The simple truth is that most adults don't know so much of what we continue to teach kids. It amazes me that we worry about what our kids know and don't know and hardly offer a question to what *adults* know or don't know. In the much-referenced study by Diane Ravitch and Chester Finn (1987), *What Do Our Seventeen-Year-Olds Know?* the conclusion, and I'll take license to paraphrase, was "not much." This study sent off alarm bells from the halls of our schools to the halls of our legislatures, and it was Ravitch and Finn's further justification for sending our schools back-to-the-basics. But the question that rarely gets asked is one that Benjamin Barber (1992) offered: "What Do Our *Forty-Seven-*Year-Olds Know?" (italics added). If we want to gain some understanding of how our schools are doing, of how much meaningful learning is going on in them, then we have to set our sights on what it means to learn much higher than simply asking what last year's high school graduates know or don't know. By limiting our inquiry to kids, we're seeing school as simply a means to graduation. If children are meaningfully learning, their knowledge will not suddenly disappear as they're handed their diplomas. It will, at best, be the seeds for a lifetime of learning.

It might be worth a look at how American adults answer the kinds of questions that we worry so much that our children can't answer. Not too long ago the *New York Times* (Cronin 1995) published exactly this. For example, they asked adults what "D-Day" referred to. Only 27 percent knew that D-Day was the Allied Normandy invasion during World War II. Twenty-nine percent, almost a third, didn't even offer an answer. Only 60 percent knew that Germany was an enemy of the U.S., and even fewer, 53 percent, knew that Japan was our enemy. They also asked what side Russia was on during the War. Forty-nine percent knew that Russia was on our side. Thirteen percent thought that Russia, who lost *twenty million* people in the war, didn't even take part in World War II. I'm not surprised that these adults don't know this information, but outraged that we point so many fingers at kids for not knowing it, when just as many—if not more—adults don't know it. My point here is not one strictly of history. The *Chicago Tribune* published the results of an adult survey on "basic" science. Less than half of the two thousand surveyed adults knew that the Earth orbits the sun each year, and only 9 percent could say what a molecule is.

All of this is further evidence that our current school and learning crisis is not a contemporary crisis. Our schools have not taken a terrible tumble since their glory days of the past because they had no glory days of the past. As Vito Perrone (1991) and Deborah Meier (1995) have pointed out, the so-called golden age of education is a *myth*. When my parents and grandparents went to school, many people, primarily minorities and the poor, weren't welcomed into school, especially high school, or were the victims of horrendous education and social stereotypes. And it wasn't until 1950 that we finally graduated a majority—only 51 percent—of students from high school. So most people, including those that had high test scores and high grades, didn't really learn all of these facts. They simply memorized the stuff for the test, just like students today do. My mother, to her credit, admits this. But not many adults want to admit that we didn't learn all of that stuff we were taught in school. Why? Probably because all these years later, we're still blaming ourselves; school was supposed to work, we think, but we didn't allow it to, we didn't take our learning seriously enough, we didn't apply ourselves, it was our fault. The notion that school isn't designed for meaningful learning in the first place hardly enters our minds.

If we don't learn most of what we know in school, where did we learn it? How did I learn what I know? Most of my learning came from the greatest teacher there is: *life itself*. Imagine for a moment how much you know right now as you read these words. I'm not talking about just "school" type knowledge, like how to read and write and add and subtract, or even having the ability to recognize a fraction or knowing whose side Russia was on in World War II. I'm talking about any knowledge or information, including attitudes, that you possess and draw on in your everyday life. The list would be endless, even for a young child. Here's ten things that I know:

1. how to load a dishwasher
2. how to floss
3. that adolescence is a tough period
4. how to use this computer that I'm typing on right now
5. my sisters' birthdays
6. what my father looks like
7. how to develop film
8. where I live
9. that it's important to be a kind person
10. that I respect Martin Luther King Jr.

And on and on and on. The list truly is endless. And every item on the list above is important to me. None of it is trivial. Sure, I could have written "how to read" or "how to write" or "how to add," and perhaps we could make a value judgment and say that those are more important than knowing how to load a dishwasher or how to floss or perhaps even respecting Dr. King. But still, so much of what I know now—that I clearly did not learn in school—is important to my day-to-day existence.

And so much of what I know now that I didn't learn in school I know *really well*. This is my point about learning being easy and school learning being difficult. I not only know how to load a dishwasher, I'm quite good at it. I can fit a lot of dishes into a single load and increase our dishwashing efficiency. I'm also very good at organizing closet space and programming our VCR and shopping for groceries. How did I get good at these things? Why did I learn them so well? Because they had *meaning* to me and because I did them for a *real purpose*. I didn't do them just to learn how to do them, I did them to fulfill a real need. I didn't sit down and learn how to use my computer for the sake of learning how to use a computer. I did it because I knew that knowing how to use the computer would help me with my writing, my learning, and our household finances. This is Frank Smith's (1986), "Can I have another donut" system of learning. Smith writes, "Every child learns to say, 'Can I have another donut?' not in order to *say* 'Can I have another donut,' but in order to *get* another donut. The language learning is incidental, a by-product of the child's attempt to achieve some other end" (27).

There is a tremendous difference between the ease with which most people learn from life and the difficulty that most kids have learning in school—even, once again, the kids who get the good grades. This is the case because learning within the dominant paradigm of school is a "false" learning. Caine and Caine (1991) call it "surface knowledge, which is basically content devoid of significance to the learner" (93). David Perkins (1992) refers to it as "fragile knowledge," which "students do not remember, understand, or use actively" (20). Rather than design school around the natural ease with which most humans learn and assimilate new information in personally relevant contexts, school breaks up knowledge into bits and pieces, "subjects," and teaches it from external textbooks, falsifying the learning process. When children make organic connections to knowledge, a learning of "deep meaning" has a much greater chance of happening (Caine and Caine, 97). Consider the chilling comment one boy made to researcher Michelle Fine (1987): "I never got math when I was in school. Then I started sellin' dope and runnin' numbers and I picked it up right away" (164).

This is not to say that all meaningful and purposeful learning is easy. A lot of meaningful learning can be very difficult for a variety of reasons. Perhaps someone doesn't have a natural propensity, or as Howard Gardner (1983) might say, "intelligence," for a particular type of knowledge. For example, learning music for me would be (and has been) difficult, considering my rather limited musical intelligence. On the other hand, music is a snap for my wife, who was born to sing. This doesn't mean that I shouldn't take up a musical instrument or that my schools and my parents shouldn't have tried to musically enrich my life. It just means that assimilating that knowledge might take more effort and time on my part, and it's probable that I won't assimilate it as well as someone like my wife would. However, if I were to take piano lessons because I *want to learn how to play the piano*, even lacking any innate musical ability, my learning will be infinitely easier and more meaningful to me than it was when my mother forced me to take piano lessons when I was ten. I lasted a year and I can't play a note today.

If we want to see how easy it is for people to learn, all we need to do is look at five-year-olds. Some of them are reading before they enter kindergarten. Others know that reading is done left to right, or top to bottom, or recognize the correct way to hold a book. Take some time and watch a five-year-old child before they start kindergarten. They already have *enormous* amounts of knowledge. How to walk, how to talk, how to pick up a ball, how to ask for something, how to use a tool to accomplish a task, how to turn on the television, what a doll looks like, what a gun looks like, the meaning of a box covered with wrapping paper and a bow. I've watched my niece, Melanie, grow up now for five years, and I am continuously amazed by what she knows, by what she can do, by the conversations we have, by the fact that she can *read*. And she hasn't had a day in "school," at least not the formal kind. Her school has been life. This is the learning that John Mayher (1990) referred to as *osmotic learning*. It's how I learned most of what I know and how you learned most of what you know. Mayher wrote, "The commonsense [or traditional] views of learning have tended to ignore or minimize the significance of such osmotic learning, and yet it is clear that most of the competencies we need to function in life are learned just that way" (90).

I am reminded of the scene in Harper Lee's *To Kill a Mockingbird* (1960) when Scout's new first grade teacher discovers that she can read, a fact that distinguishes Scout from every other student in her class. Her teacher, Miss Caroline, is outraged. Why? *Because she wasn't the one to teach Scout how to read.* In her own defense, Scout tells Miss Caroline that nobody taught her how to read. In fact, she has no idea how she learned to read. Was it in church, while holding the printed hymnal? Or was it sitting in her father's lap each night while he read the newspaper or his legal papers or a book, and followed the words along with his finger? Whatever it was, Scout was sure about one thing: nobody taught her how to read. Miss Caroline, however, has a different opinion:

> "Now you tell your father not to teach you anymore. It's best to begin reading with a fresh mind. You tell him I'll take over from here and try to undo the damage—"
> "Ma'am?"
> "Your father does not know how to teach. You can have a seat now."

After being ordered by Miss Caroline to stop reading with her father, Scout goes on to make a beautiful analogy: "Until I feared I would lose it, I never loved to read. One does not love breathing." Most of the learning we do in the daily course of our lives we do without even knowing that we're doing it. We learn most of our knowledge without being conscious that we're learning. That's how easy it can be to learn. It's like breathing. Learning like this results in what Caine and Caine (1991) call *natural knowledge*.

But of course, all learning doesn't just happen. I highly doubt that Scout's father, Atticus, followed the words with his finger for his own sake. He did that for Scout, as she sat on his lap. She's not there only because Atticus wants her near him, she's there because he knows that the chances are excellent that she's going to learn by watching him read. This is an example of Frank Smith's "literacy club" (1988). By creating and living in literate environments, and by inviting (usually tacitly) children to be members in the club, children will become literate human beings. Atticus wasn't just loving Scout each night, he was inviting her into the literacy club, and she happily became a member without even knowing it.

Learning and Culture

People learn from the culture they grow up in. That's why there are such profound differences between the reality of those three ten-year-old boys I wrote about in Chapter 2. One in the inner city, one on a farm, and one in an upper-middle-class, largely Jewish suburb, and all enculturated into a unique way of life that they learned through the osmosis of daily participation in their particular culture. Cognitive psychologist Barbara Rogoff (1990) calls this social and cultural—or sociocultural—learning an "apprenticeship." Rogoff explains that children's cognitive growth is a result of their being naturally "apprenticed" through their social relationships within their cultural community. Sociocultural learning theory is based on two major beliefs: first, that our learning is inherently a *social act*, based on an infinite number of interactions with other people in our cultural communities; and second, that knowledge is communicated or "taught" to us through these social relationships. And Rogoff's word *apprentice* is an important one because it comes from one of the most time-honored, successful, and authentic processes for learning: apprenticeship, which has been formally used for thousands of years to teach so many crafts and skills—all done without the rules and rituals of school as we know it.

In his wonderful book *The Education of Little Tree*, Forrest Carter (1976) writes of his childhood in the mountains of Tennessee, raised by his Cherokee grandparents during the Depression.[*] Carter's story is full of examples of a boy being apprenticed and learning osmotically in a social and cultural context. Consider, for example, the learning that young Little Tree might have experienced while plowing their small field with his "Granpa":

> Sack by sack, we got the field covered with leaves and pine straw. And after a light rain, when the leaves clung to the ground just enough, Granpa would hitch up ol' Sam, the mule, to plow; and we turned the leaves under the ground.

---

[*]   I've recently learned that Carter's book may not be the autobiography that he claimed it to be. According to Arthur Applebee (1996) and Henry Louis Gates (1991), Carter's book is fiction and Forrest Carter was really the late Asa Earl Carter, a Ku Klux Klan member. The idea that *The Education of Little Tree*, a wonderfully warm and humorous book with an antiracist theme, might have been written by an avowed racist is hard to believe. Nevertheless, this posed an interesting question: If Applebee and Gates are right, does that invalidate Carter's book? I don't think it does, and decided to keep this illustration in my book.

I say "we," because Granpa would let me plow some. I had to reach up over my head to hold the handles of the plow stock, and spent most of my time pulling all my weight down on the handles to keep the plow point from going too deep into the ground. Sometimes the point would come out of the ground, and the plow would skitter along, not plowing. Ol' Sam was patient with me. He would stop while I pulled and strained at getting the plow upright, and then would move ahead when I said, "Giddup!"

I had to push the handles to make the plow point go into the ground; and so, between the pulling down and the pushing up, I learned to keep my chin away from the crossbar between the handles, for I was getting continual licks that jolted me up pretty bad.

Granpa followed along behind us, but he would let me do it. If you wanted ol' Sam to move left, you said, "Haw!" and if you wanted him to move to the right, you said, "Gee!" Ol' Sam would meander off a little to the left and I would holler, "Gee!"; but he was hard of hearing and would keep meandering. Granpa would take it up, "Gee! Gee! GEE! DAMMITOHELL! GEE!" and ol' Sam would come back to the right.

Trouble was, ol' Sam heard this so much, that he begun to connect up the total geeing and cussing, and would not go right until he heard all of it; figuring natural, that to go right, it took the whole amount. This led to considerable cussing, which I had to take up in order to plow. This was all right until Granma heard me and spoke hard to Granpa about it. This cut down on my plowing considerable when Granma was around. (48–49)

This scene shows what the Russian psychologist Lev Vygotsky (1978) called the "zone of proximal development." This "zone" is the separation between what a person can do on their own and what a person can do with help. Little Tree couldn't plow the field by himself yet. He could operate the plow stock more or less, but his Granpa "followed along behind" because he needed his guidance. The more his Granpa helps him, the more Little Tree will be able to do on his own. As Barbara Rogoff (1990) explains, that's how people learn within a sociocultural context. The "experts" apprentice the "novices," both formally and informally. In Rogoff's words, it is "guided participation" (189). If you think of your own life, going back to the day you were born, you'll realize that's how you learned a lot of what you know.

That is not, however, how school functions within the dominant paradigm. First, learning in a sociocultural context is a highly *active* process, on the part of both expert and novice. School usually controls against action on the part of the novice. Second, learning socially and culturally is not a one-way process. It's quite possible that as Little Tree plows the field he can teach something to his Granpa. This is especially true as Little Tree gets older. He might get new ideas about plowing, or he might come up with a better way to farm. (As we saw in Chapter 1, with fruit farmer David Mas Masumoto.) Which leads us to a third characteristic of learning in a sociocultural context: the roles of expert and novice *change*. I'm sure that as I was growing up there were many things that I helped my parents to learn. Suddenly, I was the expert and they were the novices. How many children all across our country do you think are currently using guided participation to help their parents learn how to use a computer? How often do our schools nurture this changing of roles by allowing children to be the teachers, the experts, the ones who know?

Little Tree's childhood was a constant stream of tacit or osmotic learning experiences within the zone of proximal development, like his plowing the field with his Granpa. They picked berries, ran a whiskey still, cured snakebite, and "walked like a Cherokee" in order that they could get close to the creatures of the wild. At one point a theory of learning is disclosed: "Granpa said there was so many things to handle in your head that I was not to worry about picking it all up at oncet; that it would come and be nature to me after a while. Which it did" (70).

Sociocultural learning can consciously be extended into the community of the classroom. This, however, requires the classroom to be a *social* environment. With learning in a social context, *talk is the key*, and I am not referring to the talk of the teacher, which dominates most classrooms, but to the talk of everyone, and especially the students. Without that naturalistic verbal give-and-take, a classroom cannot function as a social community. But with it, framed within a purposeful structure that I will discuss in the following chapter, meaningful learning can flourish. That's why Wells and Chang-Wells (1992), who have done extensive research into social learning and meaning making within a classroom context, wrote, "In a very important sense, education *is* dialogue" (32).

Learning by Doing

Throughout my life photography has been a passion of mine. When I was ten years old I started to roam the alleys and streets of my suburban Chicago neighborhood, camera in hand. The images from those early days remain etched in my mind. Close-ups of rusty nails in wooden fence posts, reflections of telephone poles in puddles, building facades, garbage cans against chain-link fences. When I was around fifteen I started to look at the pictures of famous photographers, like the great Harry Callahan, whose work was, and continues to be, inspirational to me. I also started to read about photography. I had books on both the technical aspects and the aesthetics of taking pictures. I built a darkroom in my basement and printed my pictures until all hours of the night. Before I became a teacher I studied photography in college. This led me to look at the work of noted photographers such as Robert Frank, Barbara Crane, Ray Metzker, Diane Arbus, Bill Brandt, Walker Evans, Edward Weston, and Garry Winogrand. The beauty and intensity of their images literally sent, and still sends, chills down my spine. In college we would have class "critiques" and display our pictures for open discussion. Later, in graduate school, I studied photography from philosophical and political perspectives, reading and discussing, among others, Freud, Marx, Engels, and the French philosopher and writer Roland Barthes.

Of all of those experiences, the early readings on technique and the later readings on philosophy, looking at pictures taken by my college classmates and by famous photographers, and participating in class critiques, none were as meaningful and significant to me as my own practice as a photographer, picking up a camera and *taking pictures*. They were all important experiences, they all contributed to making me who I am today both as an artist and as a human being, but what really counted, what helped me to learn the most about photography and make the most sense of my world aesthetically, was *doing photography*. The same is true when it comes to school learning. In the dominant paradigm, learning is done *to* students rather than *by* students. What should be clear from this chapter (and from your own life) is that the best way to learn something is by actually doing it. That's why we learn so well from life: nobody teaches us life, we *do* life.

Carol Porter and Janell Cleland, both terrific high school teachers, told me a great way to think about learning and school. They do this with educators who attend their workshops. Follow along with me. Suppose I offered to financially support you for an entire year, with one stipulation: you had to spend that year learning something that you've always wanted to learn. The question is this: How would you go about your learning? I've asked this of many adults. It's fascinating to learn what adults would love to learn. Everyone has something: the Spanish language, how to paint, how to fly an airplane, a foreign culture. So think about this for a minute. What would you love to spend a year learning and how would you go about it?

Not a single adult that I've asked this of would ever do their learning from a *textbook* or a *worksheet* or a *lecture*. To learn Spanish they would go to a Spanish-speaking country; to learn to paint they would buy canvases, brushes, and paints, and start painting; to learn to fly they would find an instructor, get into a plane, and take off; to learn about another culture they would pack their bags and go live in that culture. It's as simple as one could get. If you want to learn how to play tennis, you might read a book or two on tennis and you may even take a lesson, but you're never going to get very good at the sport if you don't spend time—a lot of time—on a tennis court whacking tennis balls around.

Most schools rarely emphasize actual experience. Much more often they offer children desk-based pseudoexperiences. They're supposed to become better writers, not by writing real and meaningful texts, but by doing discrete writing tasks and exercises one at a time and by filling in worksheets and workbooks. They're supposed to become better readers, not by reading real books that hold interest to them, but by answering out-of-context comprehension questions and doing "reading exercises." They're supposed to better understand science and math, not by doing authentic science and math that has relevance to their lives, but by reading textbooks and solving lists of problems. They're supposed to gain an understanding of history and the social sciences, not by seeing these subjects as intimately connected to their present lives, but by memorizing facts and answering fill-in-the-blank questions and writing reports.

Once again, this thinking is not followed in good kindergarten classrooms. Five- and six-year-olds don't read (at least the ones who can read) textbooks on "blocks," they *do blocks*. They don't fill in worksheets on "dress up" or complete workbooks on "finger painting," but rather they *play* dress up and they *do* finger painting. Kindergarten is all about *learning by doing*. This is why osmotic or natural learning is so powerful. We don't spend our daily lives reading about and listening to someone tell us about the things we do and the things we experience, we're actually doing them and we really experience them. If our own lives can teach us one thing about learning and schooling, it is that experience is the best teacher.

Four

Classroom as Community

*The clear consciousness of a communal life, in all its implications, consti-
tutes the idea of democracy.*

—JOHN DEWEY

*There is not just one teacher and all the rest are the learners. Instead, we
are all teachers and we are all learners.*

—STEVEN, THIRD GRADER
(in Short and Burke, *Creating Curriculum* [1991])

In his essay "The Lives of a Cell," the late Lewis Thomas, a doctor, found his perfect metaphor for our planet earth: a single cell. Earth, according to Thomas (1974), is complex and has "many working parts lacking visible connections," just like a single, living cell (5). The same, I would say, is true for a classroom. On the surface, classrooms may not look like much. Walk down a school hallway and glance into the rooms and what do you usually see? Desks, kids, a teacher, a chalkboard, textbooks, maybe a plant or two, a globe. It seems like a very simple room made up of very common elements. That's at least what it looks like on the surface. But in fact, the classroom—any classroom and every classroom—is an extremely complex and unique environment with "many working parts lacking visible connections."

To show the complexity and uniqueness of the classroom environment, I return to my first year of teaching. My school at the time had five sixth-grade classrooms, which were all down the same hallway. Those five classrooms were all in the same school district, the same school, at the same grade level, and had the same official curriculum, yet each of them had unique educational experiences. What was *taught* in each of those classrooms was a different version of the same official curriculum. On paper we were teaching the same content, but in reality there were differences—many of which were *profound* differences—in what was being taught in those five classrooms. This means that those classrooms really weren't teaching the same content or the same curriculum.

For example, I used the textbooks minimally, while three teachers used them extensively, and the last teacher used them moderately. Three of the other teachers gave regular tests, something that I and the other teacher rarely did. Most of them had their students do some form of spelling or vocabulary and gave specific assignments for most, if not all, of their writing, while my class had writing and reading workshop each day and worked on spelling and vocabulary in the context of the workshop. The rules and rituals of the classrooms also differed dramatically. I'm not making a value statement here and saying that what I was doing was any better than what anyone else was doing. My intention here is for the reader to imagine how *different* each of these classroom experiences—or the *experienced curriculum*—must have been for the students in them, even though they were identical on paper. That's the power of the classroom environment. Schooling truly is context-specific. It takes on a life, a classroom culture, of its own.

Classroom as Ecosystem

What I am envisioning is the classroom as a *living thing*, a breathing, interconnected, ever evolving entity. Imagine a glistening pond on a beautiful summer day. I've seen ponds like this, in Wisconsin, in Maine, in my own state of Illinois. Imagine your pond. What do you see? Look at the big picture, the sky, the water, the vegetation, but also look at the details. Maybe there are cattails rustling in the breeze, a bumblebee at a flower, a frog on a lily pad, worms and centipedes along the ground, and maybe evidence of pollution in the water, in the air, or on the ground.

This is how I see a classroom. As an *ecosystem*. Edward O. Wilson (1992) defined an ecosystem as "the organisms living in a particular environment . . . and the physical part of the environment that impinges on them" (396). A *community* is the first part of the definition, the organisms themselves, but the ecosystem is holistic, and also includes the physical environment. It is the totality of the classroom space. Looking at the complexity of the pond might help us see the complexity of the classroom. Let's take a look at some of the *variables* that make up the ecosystem of our imaginary pond:

water	plants	animals
air	sun	pollution
climate	soil	

A seemingly simple pond is actually an extremely complex system of interconnected variables. How complex? Well, let's break down some of those pond variables into subvariables. For example, animals:

amphibians	insects	birds
fish	mammals	one-celled organisms

Any of these can be broken down into sub-subvariables. For example, the insects:

butterflies	bees	grasshoppers
dragonflies	beetles	mosquitoes

And these can be broken down further into different species. Of course, the actual list would depend on the particular pond.

Now remember, in the pond's ecosystem everything is interconnected. That's the idea behind a *system*, whether it's an ecosystem, a circulatory system, an exhaust system, or a family system. If you change one thing, no matter how small—even the plankton floating in the water—you affect the entire system, because all of its parts are "interrelated and interdependent" (Capra 1982). The same is true of classrooms. It makes no difference if a teacher is consciously aware of the power and complexity of the system in their classroom or not, it still exists. You don't have to know about the subatomic particles in atoms, but they still exist, and your existence is seriously affected by (and dependent on) their existence. To look at a classroom this way is to see it systemically. There is a field of study called *systems theory* that sees and studies biological, ecological, social, cultural, and even commercial environments in just this way (Capra 1982; Senge 1990). One of the most important beliefs of systems theory is that the "whole" is much more than merely the sum of its parts. In other words, the whole pond is something *different* from the collection of all of its variables.

Now let's extend the systemic idea to the classroom and consider some of its variables:

teacher	students	physical space
curriculum	budget	administrative policies
legislative policies	relationships	parents
classroom rules (specific and implied)		race/culture (teacher and students)

Once again, just as in the pond, we can take any of these variables and break them down into subvariables. The variable of students can be further broken down as follows:

age	interests	gender
race/culture	family life	prior knowledge
behavior	individual development	attitudes
socioeconomic status	social/emotional	

Subvariables of the classroom's physical space include:

size/shape	temperature	physical condition
windows	lighting	desks and furniture

Seeing a classroom as a living ecosystem with a seemingly infinite number of variables can help us appreciate and respect its complexity and uniqueness. It can shed some light on why list after list of so-called generalized effective practices don't work, and why much-touted rigid "standards"—even national standards—won't work either. *Every classroom is a unique environment with a unique set of variables.* That means that every classroom using the same "effective" teaching recipe or the same official curriculum or the same set of "standards" bakes a different cake, and sometimes a very different cake. This is an anthropological way of seeing a classroom, and offers a paradigm that is totally different from the one embraced by Bobbitt, Charters, Thorndike, and Frederick Winslow Taylor who advocated the antithesis of this with their "scientific curriculum-making." Educational researchers who hold an anthropological belief system do not conduct empirically-based quantitative (or positivist) research in order to determine a generalized "truth." They work in the radically different *qualitative* (or interpretive and ethnographic) paradigm which recognizes the uniqueness of people and environments and attempts to convey an *understanding* of them, which *might* benefit others in their own unique schooling contexts. Just in the last ten to fifteen years the long-in-coming credibility of qualitative research has truly launched a revolution in how we can see and improve teaching and learning. Finally a researcher can tell the story of just a few (or even just one) teachers or students or schools (or a teacher can tell his or her own story), which is (in my opinion) more useful to school and teacher change than an empirical research study with hundreds of "sample" participants. (For more on interpretive research, see Denzin and Lincoln 1994; Geertz 1973; Goetz and LeCompte 1984; and Lincoln and Guba 1986.)

The Classroom Ethos

There is yet another way of seeing a classroom. It can be understood as being part of the classroom's ecosystem, but it has a life of its own. This is a classroom's *ethos.* Simply put, the ethos of a classroom is its climate or atmosphere. It includes a classroom's *values,* and in some ways involves its *spirit.* A classroom's ethos is like the wind. You can't see it, but you can feel it and you can observe its effects.

The classroom ethos is the overall climate of the environment (Rutter et al. 1979). It's important to see the entire ecosystem, the classroom-as-pond, but it's also important to see the ethos, the wind that's blowing through the space. It's the ethos that's going to tell the students what their classroom is about; what's valued and what isn't; whether the classroom is about making your voice heard or about remaining silent; about being a conscious creator of knowledge or a repository of someone else's knowledge; about empathy and caring and consideration of the common good or about competition and individualism; about developing empowering critical habits of mind or about going through life indifferent and ignorant. A classroom's ethos sets the tone of the experience.

What Is Community?

Here are some ideas and images that come to my mind when I think of community:

together	values	common	talk
sharing	movement	active	responsibility
respect	bond	helping	trust

caring	differences	empathy	inviting
thoughtfulness	celebrate	safety	discourse
acceptance	friendship	purpose	democracy

These are the ideas that come to my mind; yours may differ, but I don't think that they would differ that much. It would be very difficult for me to envision community taking place without most of the characteristics above being valued and at least worked toward on a regular basis.

I have heard the word *community* used a lot in an educational context over the past few years, but to be honest, I have rarely seen a school or a classroom that truly functions as a community. The reason community is so rare in schools is precisely because of the list above. The dominant paradigm of schooling offers us the antithesis of community. School today, with its top-down structure, competitive belief system, rating, ranking, labeling, and segregating of children, is not about promoting or practicing community, and in many ways it advocates the exact opposite, fostering qualities that tear people apart rather than bring them together. It's easy to call a school or a classroom a community, but if we were to hold those environments to a realistic vision of the idea, it would be extremely difficult to locate community anywhere inside a traditional school, except perhaps in the lunchroom or on the playground.

If my students and I share something communally (or strive to share something) beyond just being in the same room together, what exactly is it that we share? My answer to that question is a *value system*. My hope is that we can collaboratively work toward creating what David Hansen (1992) calls a *shared morality*. The goal is for everyone, including me, to think about and accept a common set of values regarding our purposes, our conduct, and our responsibilities inside the classroom, and to use our classroom experiences as opportunities to question and develop these ideas. A classroom's shared morality is not a finite thing; it's never finished. As Hansen writes, it is both "emerging," in the sense that it is continually evolving, and it is "fragile," in that a classroom's shared morality is constantly being influenced by changes both inside and outside the classroom.

The word *morality*, used in an educational context, scares many teachers, parents, and legislators, but it shouldn't. *Teaching is a moral act* and *all classrooms have a moral dimension*. Morality is basically about *goodness*, about right and wrong, about our individual and collective decision making, actions, and responsibilities. It would be difficult to deny that these issues are central to every classroom, especially since students' behavior is so important to teachers. Gary Fenstermacher (1990) writes that the most powerful moral dimension of a classroom is the teacher, who serves, whether he wants to or not, as a moral model:

> Here the teacher acts justly while assisting and expecting just conduct from the students; the teacher shows compassion and caring, seeking these traits from his or her students; the teacher models tolerance while showing students how to be tolerant. Nearly everything that a teacher does while in contact with students carries moral weight. Every response to a question, every assignment handed out, every discussion on issues, every resolution of a dispute, every grade given to a student carries with it

the moral character of the teacher. . . . Teaching is a moral activity not simply because teachers exercise authority and control over those in their care. Perhaps more important, it is a moral activity because teachers have a specific responsibility for the proper and appropriate moral development of their students. (134–135)

Being a moral model doesn't mean that I dictate moral stances to children, but rather that I work to make certain that values such as respect, caring, empathy, thoughtfulness, trust, responsibility, the common good, and a shared sense of purpose are important in our classroom and serve as topics for discussion and reflection. These are the traits that I would like my neighbors to have, and these are the traits that I believe are central to democracy. What meaning these ideas or values have for each of my students is ultimately up to them; they need to live their own lives and to think for themselves. Of course, creating community is a *collaboration*. Just as I bring values and beliefs into our classroom, so do each of my students; our shared morality is actually a social construction. My students help me question and shape my own value system, as I help to question and shape theirs.

A Thoughtful Life

Two excellent teachers I know, Kim Day and Diana Shulla, work to teach exactly these qualities to their students. The primary way they do this is through teaching what they call "The Disciplined Life." I've recently adapted their idea into what I call "A Thoughtful Life." I put a placard with the phrase A THOUGHTFUL LIFE up on our classroom wall (as Kim and Diana do with The Disciplined Life), and all around it I placed cards inscribed with qualities or habits of mind that I believe are important to living a thoughtful life in a democratic society. Some of these qualities I've taken directly from Kim and Diana, others I came up with myself. (The list is by no means finished.) Here are the qualities I've initially displayed:

Be Helpful	Be Responsible	Create Art
Ask Questions	Have Dreams	Seek Wisdom
Be Critical	Think for Yourself	Promote Peace
Make a New Friend	Improve Yourself	Thank Someone
Practice Empathy	Be Open-minded	Engage in Dialogue
Love Yourself	Write Something	Celebrate Differences
Think Before You Act	Be a Giver	Be Kind
Take Time to Listen	Do the Right Thing	Appreciate Nature
Read a Book		

Throughout our days together, our class discusses these qualities and how they contribute to a life lived thoughtfully. Instances of us having and not having these habits of mind occur every day in our classroom, offering valuable, real-life learning opportunities. The other day at our class meeting, we were discussing whether or not it is racist for sports teams to use Native American names, symbols, and mascots. One student, I'll call him Louis, said that it wasn't racist because no one took sports teams seriously. But Somer, whose great-great-grandmother was part Native American, passionately spoke up, saying she took them seriously and was offended by their depiction of Native Americans. Louis became louder, waving off Somer's objections as if they were a joke. It was a perfect opportunity for me to point out an idea from A Thoughtful Life (the cards hang right above where we have our meetings). I told Louis I respected his right to hold an opinion, but that he needed to be open-minded enough to at least have respect for Somer's perspective rather than belittling her and her beliefs.

Once I started A Thoughtful Life in our classroom, it did not take long for its precepts to pervade our classroom ethos. It is not unusual now for students to point out when someone is being empathetic (or needs to be empathetic), when someone is being a giver, when someone needs to think for themself rather than being directed or manipulated by others, when someone thought before they acted. These ideas and this language have become an important part of our classroom community. They can also play a role in other parts of our curriculum. I decided to read the book *Shiloh* (Naylor 1991) to my class because of a lengthy discussion we had on empathy. The story is about a boy who steals a dog because he hates how it's being abused by its owner. The word *empathy* has become much used in our classroom now.

Since creating, maintaining, and evolving a classroom that functions as a community of learners is a communal effort, it demands that teachers and students take on roles that are different from what they are used to. *Roles must change.* You can't have a real community while maintaining the common notions of what it means to be a teacher and a student. Classrooms that are communities have *teachers who are learners* and *students who are teachers.* No longer is learning strictly a teacher-to-student transmission; it is an ongoing *communal collaboration.* This does not mean that I as a teacher relinquish my authority. But being the final authority doesn't exclude me from being an eager learner or my students from being genuine teachers. A classroom that functions as a community of learners is about sharing an appreciation of learning, asking questions about the world, seeking solutions, and doing so in a classroom culture of caring and thoughtfulness.

A classroom community does not come easily. I've struggled—and continue to struggle—to make my own classrooms work as communities. Most kids not only lack the social skills that are necessary for community, they lack the knowledge and experience for defining community. The idea of working together and putting the good of the group in front of the good of ourselves is a foreign idea to most people today, adults included. Our consumer culture sends a very powerful message that those with the most toys win. This means that living as a community is not enough. It's the first step and the most important step, but the ideas of community, the ideas in the list above, ideas such as equality and dignity, need to be made an important part of a classroom's curriculum. We need to set aside at times our mounds of math, science, history, reading, and writing, and *teach community.* If we don't, if through omission we make these ideas part of the "null" curriculum (Eisner 1994), then what we're doing is tacitly teaching children that they aren't important, that they don't count in life as much as addition and subtraction do.

Being a community does not mean having a conflict-free classroom. Just because you're a community doesn't mean that everybody gets along. Communities may strive for a sharing of values or purposes, but they're equally about *differences*, because whenever you bring people together, no matter how much they may share, they are different people with different experiences and ideas and values; it's inevitable that they're going to disagree. This should, of course, be looked upon as a good thing, as allowing diversity to flourish, as adding richness to the discourse. Somewhat ironically, living in democracy means anticipating conflict. I'm not talking about violent conflict here, but *healthy* conflict. This is the Deweyan vision of democracy's life-blood. It's exactly how larger democracies and communities shape and reshape themselves—by people with different thoughts and values and experiences lending their voices and minds to discourse and debate. Classrooms that are communities should not only expect and welcome conflict, they should have inherent structures in place to work through conflict as a natural part of the classroom life.

The notion of the *common good* is central to creating a classroom community just as it is central to democracy itself. The idea revolves around thinking of others. Its hope is twofold; first, to have students who are consciously aware that their actions and words move outward, affecting other people and the world around them, including that which is not a part of their immediate community. This is largely what Jesse Goodman (1992) means when he advocates his compassionate and democratic "connectionist perspective" for our schools' curriculums. This is, according to Goodman, "a perspective that places one's connection to the lives of all human beings on our planet at the center of the educational process" (28). For me, central to this is teaching and modeling *empathy* and *caring*. Nel Noddings (1992) has offered an argument for our schools to be based on the idea of caring, such as caring for the self, caring for friends and family, caring for strangers, caring for the planet and living things, and caring for ideas. Imagine the possibilities if our schools devoted as much time and energy to caring as they do to reading and writing and math and history. We just might have a more humane society.

The second hope is to have children who will consider the good of the group before the good of themselves. If children can begin to understand and appreciate selflessness, they can become the central underlying force of a healthy classroom community. This isn't easy for children to do, and not just because it's difficult for them to step out of their egocentric selves and into the shoes of another person, but because our culture often works against this idea. However, by making the common good a value in our classroom through discussion, journal writing, projects, reading, writing, poetry, historical examples, and the sharing of experiences from our everyday lives, children are more than capable of understanding and practicing what it means to be thoughtful human beings.

What Community Looks Like

Once again, the classrooms that come to my mind as exemplifying community are kindergarten classrooms. These are the only classrooms that consistently have regular social interaction built into their systemic structure and curriculum. Even the most ardent educational traditionalist would agree that a kindergarten without social play and talk is not a kindergarten. More than anything, the first requirement of community is the promotion of *social interaction*. Without a social context in which children and teachers are encouraged to interact as a regular part of daily life, community simply cannot take place. Community is about being active and alive and communicative.

The social interaction in a good kindergarten classroom amounts to much more than simply talk and play, however. When five-year-olds fool around in the sandbox, play house and dress up, draw, write, count, build, construct, there is *spontaneity* to their action. There is a great degree of *freedom* in what they do and say. Because social learning is an inherent part of the philosophy of kindergarten, the children's actions are natural extensions of their phenomenological (or conscious) selves. Since there's so much less external control in good kindergarten classrooms, children are free to act instinctively, and their instincts are seen as being an important part of their learning. If this weren't the case, then playtime in kindergarten would be like filling in a worksheet. But it's not. It's more like freewriting, the act of spontaneously writing whatever comes into your mind (Elbow 1973). Play or discovery, which makes up so much of a good kindergarten experience, truly comes from the mind of the child, rather than being dictated from an external source such as a teacher, a worksheet, or a textbook.

These ideas work well in kindergarten not because they work well with five-year-olds, but because they work well with *human beings*. For a classroom to be a community, there must be *spontaneous social interaction*. Students must be free to interact and communicate, not all of the time but as a regular and important part of the classroom life. For this to be possible there must be a lot less of what many would call "structure" than there is in traditional classrooms. This is one of the most controversial points when it comes to progressive and democratic schooling. The following chapter deals more specifically with classroom structure, but for now let me say that rather than being a set of "rules" based on silence and stillness, *the structure of a classroom should emerge from the daily functioning of the classroom as a community*. In other words, it is the community itself and its underlying values that maintains a classroom's structure. John Dewey (1902/1915/1990) wrote, "If the end in view is the development of a spirit of social co-operation and community life, discipline must grow out of and be relative to such an aim" (16).

Along with less overt structure in classrooms that are communities, there is less overt *planning*. Now, if there was ever an idea that is in conflict with the dominant paradigm, this would be it. It does not mean, however, that as the teacher I don't plan our day. I do. But my planning is not in the traditional sense of devising a "lesson" or preparing specific "learning objectives." Because I believe my students learn much more through our self-directed spontaneous interaction, I can't possibly plan what will happen beforehand—it is, after all, *spontaneous*. I *can* plan, for example, when we'll work on certain projects or when we'll have writing workshop or what the topic of a minilesson or journal reflection will be, but what actually happens during the time that we're engaged in these activities, I not only can't plan, but *I wouldn't want to plan*. That would defeat the purpose. Most of our classroom learning is osmotic, just like it is in life; it happens as a natural part of our social interaction.

If community demands social interaction, then social interaction demands *noise* and *movement*. Classrooms that are communities can't seek quiet as their ultimate goal or value. Sure, some quiet time to read or think or rest or watch a movie is important for everyone, but to be a community demands noise, and sometimes a lot of noise. It's simply not possible for children and teachers to interact meaningfully for the purpose of learning in silence and stillness. The idea of noise and movement scares a lot of teachers. This is understandable, especially considering that the teaching that most people experienced during their childhood and the teaching that attracted most people to the profession in the first place did not involve considerable noise and movement. In an article I wrote on project-based learning (1994a), I described what our classroom looks like while we're working on projects (I'll explain this more fully in Chapter 6):

> Walk into our classroom during project time, and you might see children sprawled on the rug taking notes from books on the habitats of beavers or on medieval life, or two students across the room watching a videotape on Jane Goodall, or others conducting tests on the aerodynamics of paper airplanes. Go to the library down the hall (past the students rehearsing a play they have written), and you might find members of the other half of the class conducting research on virtual reality or the history of Halloween. If you then go to the computer lab, you'll see, for example, one student inputting survey data while another learns to write a new computer language. In short, you never know what you might experience next, or, most important, what the students might experience next. . . .When the work is really flowing, there is a certain ethos in the air; students are into their work so intently, so genuinely, and they are constantly interacting and collaborating with one another. One student conducts a science experiment creating a vacuum with a candle, a jar, and some water; and three other children come to watch. Two students research the history of shoes, and classmates wander over to listen to an interesting anecdote. Another student builds a model set for his animated film, and someone offers suggestions. There is something infectious about this spontaneous give-and-take. (43–44)

This environment may seem rather chaotic and perhaps it is, but it worked for us at this particular school. Each situation is different. In my current school in Chicago, movement from room to room is impossible (partly because we don't have a library or computer lab to go to, and partly because my students aren't yet ready for this much freedom). But our classroom and our hallway still experience a great deal of spontaneous activity. Some days our community works better than others, and on days that it's not working, we stop what we're doing and have a class meeting to talk about it, to process it, to *learn* from it. That's exactly what we would want our children to do when something is not working in life, isn't it? Stop what they're doing, define the problem, talk it out, offer solutions, and try again.

Cooperative Learning

Some educators might equate my idea of community to "cooperative learning." I have some problems with this label, so I think it's important to draw a distinction. (If anything, I prefer "*collaborative* learning.") On its surface, cooperative learning looks like a radical departure from the dominant paradigm of schooling. Teachers certainly appear to be relinquishing control and power in allowing their students to work in pairs or groups. However, how much does this really deviate from traditional schooling? And does cooperative learning as it is traditionally implemented qualify as community?

Having children sit in groups and do math problems together does not necessarily create community and does not necessarily engender learning in a social context. Talk in cooperative-learning groups (at least the officially sanctioned talk) is rarely spontaneous. In the dominant model of cooperative learning, the *content* of what is to be learned is rarely changed, it's just the *process* that's been changed, and the process is usually highly controlled by the teacher. If everything students do in cooperative groups has been predetermined, if they have assigned "roles," if their thinking has been narrowly defined, if the content to be learned is externally dictated and remains embedded in technical knowledge, then the notion of spontaneous social interaction is being hindered and any sense of community is a false one.

Mara Sapon-Shevin has written on cooperative learning, not strictly as a teaching method but more from a political and social perspective. She argues that the implementation of cooperative learning over the past ten years hasn't amounted to much of a change from the status quo of schooling. It may *look* different, but the overall purpose remains the same: having kids learn the same facts and skills and names and dates and get higher scores on tests. In other words, we're having kids work together not to redefine the purpose of schooling or to have children examine their value system or issues of power or to promote community and democracy, but because it is a more child-friendly way to transmit knowledge from a textbook or a teacher or a worksheet to the students. In the end, not much has really changed.

In contrast to understanding it via commonly held assumptions, Sapon-Shevin advocates seeing cooperative learning through a *critical* lens, with social and political implications and learning opportunities. "Critical" ideas, which stem from *critical pedagogy* (totally different from "critical thinking"), will be explained in more detail in the following chapters; however, it would be beneficial to briefly look at them in the context of cooperative learning and community. In looking at cooperative learning critically, Sapon-Shevin writes:

> Cooperative learning can provide a framework for thinking about how power is allocated, how decisions are made, how multiple perspectives can be heard and validated. Cooperative learning can allow us to create participatory communities, classroom models of democracy, spaces for discourse and the critical examination of the ways in which certain voices are silenced by . . . our current models of schooling and government. (1991, 12)

Seen this way, having kids work together takes on a whole new meaning. No longer is working together "cooperatively" simply a way *of* teaching, but something *to be taught* and something *to be examined in itself.* To Sapon-Shevin, cooperative learning offers the opportunity for "liberatory praxis," a way of thinking about, teaching, and understanding freedom and power, the responsibilities that go with them, and their social and cultural consequences and implications. *Praxis* is an important word in both democratic schooling and reflective teaching. It is the combination of theory, reflection, and action, and truly can liberate students, teachers, and knowledge itself.

This is not an idea that should be reserved for middle school or high school kids. Children living together cooperatively in the classroom has implications for power structures and relationships from our playgrounds to our families to our corporations to our legislatures. Kindergarten teacher Vivian Gussin Paley (1992) shows us this in her book *You Can't Say You Can't Play.* In writing about children rejecting and excluding other children, she writes:

> By kindergarten . . . a structure begins to be revealed and will soon be carved in stone. Certain children will have the right to limit the social experiences of their classmates. Henceforth, a *ruling class* will notify others of their acceptability, and the outsiders learn to anticipate the sting of rejection. Long after the hitting and name-calling have been outlawed by the teachers, a more damaging phenomenon is allowed to take root, spreading like a weed from grade to grade. (3, italics added)

What Paley writes could have been written about our *society,* with its "ruling classes" that have power over others. Paley sees that what's happening with her five-year-old students has enormous implications far outside the classroom. She believes that by helping children, even five-year-olds, consider the social structures and relationships in their classrooms, their playgrounds, and their friendships, we can have a positive effect in building community both inside and outside our schools. Again, this isn't necessarily easy. It's a slow process that happens inside the mind of one child at a time.

Removing the Teacher Mask

I don't see myself as a teacher so much as a guide, a facilitator, and a coach. Most importantly, I see myself as a *learner.* That's the role I enter my classroom in each day because it is the role that I want my students to develop themselves. I want them to go through life as learners.

Being a learner for me is not limited to being a learner of education. That's important. Reading education books and journals; visiting other classrooms and attending conferences; and engaging in professional dialogue and critical reflection are important elements in my day-to-day teaching and of my professional self. But more than being a professional learner, I am simply a learner. This means that I live a curious life, that I'm a reader, that I ask questions about the world and seek answers, that I am metacognitive (or conscious of my thinking), that I make a point of being informed of local and world events, that I go out of my way to meet people and learn from their experiences, that I love learning for the sake of learning, and that I share my learning with others. I don't so much want to present myself each day as a learning teacher but as a *learning person*. That's what communities are made up of, and that should apply to teachers as much as it applies to children.

Last year my class got into a discussion about what each of us can do to make the world a better place. Somewhere along the way, the issue of the relationship between adults and kids entered the dialogue. Later in the day, three boys, Nick, Jaime, and Pedro, "challenged" me with a question: "How can kids change the world if the world won't take kids seriously?" I told them that I thought their question was an excellent one, and that I would give them my response the next day. I saw this as a great opportunity to model myself for the class as a learner, a thinker, and a writer. I also saw it as an opportunity to further our dialogue. That night I went home and wrote a letter to my class. The next day during our class meeting I passed out copies to everyone, read it aloud, and began another discussion on the topic. This was the letter that I wrote:

> Dear Class,
>
> Yesterday, Nick, Jaime, and Pedro brought a question to me. Here it is: How can kids change the world if the world won't take kids seriously? This is an outstanding question and one that demands serious thought, so I decided to put my response in writing.
>
> My first reaction is to define what I meant by "change the world." There are many different kinds of change. Every person makes an impact on the world; every person interacts with the world in some way; everyone, we can say, leaves their mark on the world. This means that how a person acts—including how a *child* acts—will have a certain impact or influence on the world. If this is true, then just by acting in a certain way, just by living your life a certain way, you can help to create a certain type of world, and I think a better world.
>
> For example, if a child decides to not involve themselves in violence (including verbal and emotional violence), then they are helping to create a less violent world. The same is true for all forms of prejudice. People have to decide how to live their lives, what kind of human being they want to be. By choosing to live without prejudice, to celebrate differences and respect others (and possibly even to help others do so) you are helping to change our world and make it a more humane place. You should not wait until you "grow up," as so many adults are fond of saying, to make a difference. It makes no difference whether you are twelve or thirty or eighty, you still interact with other people, you're still "leaving your mark" on the world. All of us must ask ourselves what marks we want to leave.
>
> But there is another way of looking at "changing the world." This idea goes beyond a person's day-to-day living. This idea is about consciously deciding to change something specific and be willing to work toward that change. For example, there are many things about how schools operate today that I would like to change, so I devote a large part of my life studying schools and teaching and learning, and writing about and discussing my ideas with others in the hope that I can help create

change. This kind of change happens slowly—*very slowly*. I'm an adult, and in many ways the world doesn't take *my* ideas seriously! Why? Because change is difficult for most people. It's a lot easier staying the same. (And it's worth noting that the more I learn about the world, the more knowledge and ideas I have to help me change it.)

But changing the world is very possible. Hard, but possible. Once again I point your attention to people like Martin Luther King Jr., who worked to end prejudice, and Mahatma Gandhi, who peacefully worked for the freedom of India, and Jane Addams, who devoted her life to helping children and the poor in Chicago. Are there still poor people in Chicago? Absolutely. But because of Jane Addams I believe there were far fewer people in physical and emotional pain, and I also believe that her work and what she believed in encouraged others to change the world as well. People can inspire each other. Like tossing a pebble into the middle of a pond, the ripples extend outward. A very famous writer, Ralph Waldo Emerson, once wrote, "In every acorn there are a thousand forests." Imagine that! Each one of us can be an acorn, living our lives and planting seeds to create change.

Now what about being a "kid"? Well, Nick, Jaime, and Pedro make a good point. I agree with them. Most adults—in fact, society itself—do not have much respect for children, do not take children seriously. But by *doing something*, by the way they live their lives, even by talking about this very issue to adults, kids can have a positive influence on the world. Maybe instead of writing two or three letters to the newspaper to get one published, you'll have to write five or six or maybe even seven. But that's okay. If you want a better world, if you want to change something you disagree with, then you need to be willing to work for that change. Some of it is hard work, but some of it isn't. Many of my past students have written poems and stories in our classes against racism and about the importance of *empathy*, which is being able (and willing) to put ourselves in another person's shoes so we can feel what others are feeling. Writing a poem may not seem like a lot, but it is. Other people can read it, talk about it. It can encourage them to think about these ideas. Maybe work for change themselves.

Change doesn't happen overnight. It usually happens a tiny bit each day. But those tiny bits add up. And remember, in a rather short number of years *you* will be adults yourselves. If you remember these feelings and these beliefs that you have now, then when you're an adult, when the world will take you a little more seriously, you can have an even bigger impact. But it's wrong to wait until then. Our world isn't a world just for adults. It's everyone's world. Kids' too.

Keep Thinkin',

Mr. Wolk

This letter helps me be a real person to my students. Carl Rogers (1969) wrote, "It is quite customary for teachers rather consciously to put on the mask, the role, the facade, of being a teacher, and to wear this facade all day removing it only when they have left the school at night" (107). I make a very conscious effort not to wear a teacher mask. When I walk into my classroom each morning, I want to bring all of me. Just like my students, I have likes and dislikes, emotions and feelings, hobbies, parents, pet peeves, worries, dreams, frustrations, failures, and victories. And just as my students bring their whole selves with them to school each day, I bring my whole self. If I've had a difficult and frustrating day (especially because of them), then I will let them know that in an honest way. If I have had a tragedy or a triumph in my life, I may share that as well. Consistently, the best teachers that I have met are not afraid to show their true emotional selves to their students. This isn't easy for many teachers to do, but what better way is there to get your students to treat you like a human being than to act like one?

Physical Space

The classroom space is important to me. As long as going to school means spending most of your day within four walls, how the space within those walls is used is going to be crucial not only to developing a sense of community but to learning. The physical space of a classroom can either help or hinder the creating of community. For example, in his history of teaching, Larry Cuban (1993) points out that one of the hindrances to early progressive educators was that their classroom desks were bolted to the floor. They wanted the freedom to physically structure their rooms differently for teaching, but their classroom furniture prevented it. Once classrooms started to have movable furniture, teachers had more options available to them as to how they taught.

I have always set up our classrooms to have a large open space for kids to move, build, draw, construct, act, read, discuss and interact. I've always liked sitting on the floor in a circle with my students. It removes artificial barriers, brings the class together as a unified whole, and is a wonderful way to encourage discussion and debate. If a classroom doesn't have carpeting, then getting a large rug is my first priority. Figure 4-1 (on the next page) is a diagram of my classroom. In many ways the open space off to the side is the centerpiece of our classroom. Interestingly, it's probably the one physical feature of my classroom that, year in and year out, visitors have commented on the most. It's large, it stands out, and it makes our classroom the antithesis of the one offered by the dominant paradigm.

The open space lends itself to many purposes. First, it's used for our daily morning meetings, class meetings, and discussions. It's also used for student presentations, video watching, collaborative games or activities, play production, and as a place where students can sit or lie down to read, write, or work on a project. The carpet or rug is usually scattered with a lot of large pillows, so kids can get comfortable while they read or write. I might also have some beanbag chairs, and at my last school I had a couch, which was a favorite place for kids to kick back and read a book.

This space is the result of a very conscious effort on my part to "de-school" our classroom. Considering that we learn a lot more at home and outside of school than we do inside of school, it makes sense to make our classroom more like home. A lot of people see this kind of classroom setup as not conducive to "rigorous" learning. This is another one of those assumptions about school. There is no scientific law that says

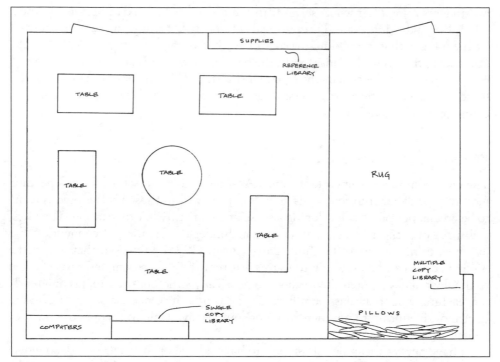

FIGURE 4-1 *Floor plan of our classroom*

that learning happens only when kids are sitting straight up at a proper desk. I know a lot of college students, including myself, who did a substantial amount of serious studying either lying down on a library bench, planted in a comfortable chair or couch in their living rooms, or even in bed. The important thing about a classroom isn't that it looks like a classroom, but that the space nurtures growth.

I like tables. A good table brings people together, and that's what community and democracy are all about. If I have to have desks at the school I'm at, we'll put the desks together in groups and have at least four good-sized tables for kids to work at. I've always allowed my students to choose where to sit at the start of the year. Choosing where to sit is an issue of power, and that makes it a democratic issue. I explain to them, however, that this choice is a privilege, and if they abuse it, by, for example, allowing their seating to interfere with thoughtful and respectful schoolwork and class community, then they lose it, and that means having me assign their seating. This is an opportunity for me to emphasize (or teach) the idea that *with freedom comes responsibility*. Most kids do great but some kids don't, which means I must assign seating for those students who need it. If an entire class can't handle the freedom, then I have no problem assigning seating for the entire class. But my goal is always to give them back this freedom as soon as possible. Assigning seats is not an end, it's a beginning.

Seating can also be an opportunity for thinking about community and critical social issues. This year, when I gave two classes, one with third and fourth graders and the other with fourth and fifth graders, the freedom to choose their seats, both classes sat completely segregated by gender. There were two all-girl tables and three all-boy tables. On the second day of school this became our first journal-writing topic of the year. I asked the classes to write about why the boys don't want to sit with girls and why the girls don't want to sit with boys. Not surprisingly, at first they didn't get what I was after. Not only is this an abstract idea, but rarely are kids asked to write about topics such as these in school. After they did their journal writing, we had a class meeting where volunteers read what they wrote. Many of the kids had difficulty coming up with much more than "girls are ugly" or "boys are dumb." But some of them were able to articulate some meaningful ideas about gender:

> The reason why girls don't like sitting with boys is because they can't relate to stuff girls can or like talk about boys. They always be talking about Pamela Anderson. The reason I don't like sitting with boys [is] because they are annoying and they do not understand girls.
> *Christina*

> Girls don't like to sit with boys because we don't like them. The reason why we don't like to sit with the boys [is] because they talk about ladies that [are] walking down the street. The reason we don't like to sit by the boys is because they talk about the ladies butts and look at them and want to marry them and they tell their friends.
> *Rachel*

> Why don't I sit with girls. [It's] because they're always talking about boys and they be talking about that I like a girl in this classroom. And girls are always hitting me and they be asking the boys for their phone numbers. And girls like trying to play ball with the boys. [And] girls be talking about their birthday and their makeup and they're always smashing the boys.
> *Samuel*

Once we finished reading, the class had a discussion about what "community" means. The kids had a lot of wonderful things to say about community, some of them being in my list at the beginning of this chapter. I pointed out that nowhere in their ideas about community is the notion of "just boys" or "just girls," but rather the overwhelming idea of everyone coming together. I told them that I did not think we could be a true community as long as we were separated by gender, and that I wanted them to change their seats, creating mixed-gender tables. There wasn't a single complaint. In fact, some of the kids verbally agreed with me. Everyone got up and five minutes later—totally on their own—they were sitting at integrated tables.

This seating arrangement did not magically change these children. The next day, during our class meeting, I watched to see where they sat down on the rug, and sure enough, they were completely separated by gender. By continuing our reflection and discussion of gender issues throughout the year, however, I'm hoping that the situation will change. And in fact, later that very day while I was reading a novel aloud, with the class sitting before me on the rug, Gregory pointed out that the boys and girls were once again separated. I highly doubt he would have made this observation if I hadn't made gender an important issue in our classroom.

All of the areas in our classroom are considered community space. For example, we have a classroom library filled with high-quality fiction, nonfiction, and reference books. We also have a classroom supply area, with various papers, pencils and pens, paperclips, index cards, erasers, staplers, glue, tape, and so on. These are not my supplies, they are the classroom's supplies, and early in the year we have a class meeting or two to discuss what it means to respect these materials. (This also offers the opportunity to talk about respecting natural resources in the interests of the common good.) We also have a computer area where we put together our class publications. Finally, as I mentioned above, there are a lot of big pillows lying around, which helps create a comfortable learning environment. The pillows have never failed to create conflict at the beginning of the year; there are never enough for everyone, so they become the object of fights and arguments. But this means that they also become the topic for further discussion about the notions of sharing, community, and solving conflict peacefully. When I first started to teach I never imagined that our pillows would be an important part of the curriculum, but that's exactly what they've become.

Fun and Games

Playing games is one of the best ways to develop a healthy and trusting classroom community. When we play a game, we create a special bond, a shared purpose of having fun. I start playing class games on the first day of school and continue them regularly throughout the year. Games are a great way of breaking down barriers, building a healthy classroom ethos, and bringing levity to the sometimes serious business of learning. I want to emphasize that the games are not just for fun. They are valuable learning opportunities. In order to play a game you have to follow the rules, and in order for the game to work, *everyone* has to follow the rules. Games can serve as a powerful analogy for the underlying values of community. Here are a few games my classes have liked to play:

Electricity

I like to play this game on our first day together. It requires everyone to hold hands, so right from the start we're breaking down barriers, bringing the class together. There's nothing quite like seeing two students who normally wouldn't talk to each other (a boy and a girl, a "popular" and an "unpopular" student, a fourth grader and a fifth grader) more than happy to hold hands for a game. To play, you have the kids (including yourself) form two single-file lines facing each other. Both lines need to have the same number of people. Everyone holds the hands of the people next to them. Put a chair at one end of the two lines, and on top of the chair put either a Nerf ball or a piece of paper crumpled into a ball. Setting the ball on top of a roll of masking tape helps it to stay put. On the other end of the two lines is the "starter," who, facing the chair, holds the hands of both people on his end. The starter squeezes both hands at once. Once your hand is squeezed you squeeze the person next to you. This action continues down the lines like a pulse until it reaches the last two people. The first one to grab the ball wins. The two students at the end of the line then go to the start of the line and the game repeats.

Group Sit

This is not only a lot of fun, but it requires everyone to work together. Everyone stands, forming a tight single-file circle. Each person puts their hands on the shoulders of the person in front of them. At a slow count of three, everyone sits down. If it works, if everyone is trusting, each person will sit on the lap of the person behind them. Once you're sitting, the goal is to hold the position for as long as you can. A fun way to do this is by choosing a song like "Rudolph the Red-Nosed Reindeer" or "Row, Row, Row Your Boat" that the whole class has to sing before the circle breaks apart. A photo of one of my classes demonstrating a "group sit" can be seen on the back cover of this book.

Ball Toss

Everybody sits in a circle on the floor. A ball, such as a volleyball, is tossed out into the circle. As in "hot potato," as soon as someone catches the ball, they have to quickly toss it to someone else. The goal is to keep the ball going without it touching the floor. This means tossing the ball softly, and not invading the space of the person sitting next to you when you catch it, and paying careful attention. Once the class does well with one ball, throw in a second ball to be tossed around simultaneously. If this works well (it's tough!), add a third ball. I suggest using different sized balls.

Trust Fall

This game requires small groups of around six. The groups stand in a very tight circle with their hand palm-out in front of their chests. A volunteer stands in the center of each circle, with their eyes closed and their arms at their sides. This person slowly falls toward the circle of people around them, and is gently passed from palm to palm around the circle.

The Number Game

My friend Aleta taught me this simple, less active, game. Someone starts by saying, "Ready . . . one." A different person then says "two," and then someone offers "three" and then "four," and so on. The goal is for only one person to say each number. If more than one person says the number, you have to start over. (There can't be any planning. That's cheating!) This is a great game for helping kids see the value in listening, in being patient, and in setting goals. One year I had a class that got up to seventy-five.

Follow the Leader

This is a rather well-known game. The whole class sits in a circle on the floor. One student leaves the room and a circle leader is chosen. The circle leader begins by, for example, patting their hands on their knees, and everyone in the circle follows along. The person who left the room comes back and stands in the center of the circle. As the leader changes what they do (from patting their knees to tapping their ears to clapping their hands to snapping their fingers and so on), the person in the middle has three guesses to find the circle leader.

Block Building

Playing this game is one of the few vivid memories I have of elementary school, no doubt because it's so "un-school" like. It's great for building listening skills. Only two kids participate at a time; the rest of the class sits in a large circle around them, watching and analyzing silently. The two students sit back to back, preferably on the floor. Both of them have an identical set of about twenty wooden blocks (if you don't have some, borrow them from a kindergarten classroom). When I did this as a kid we used sugar cubes, but the blocks are much better, since they are of different shapes and sizes and possibly color. One student, the "builder," builds a structure. As the student builds, block by block, he or she describes each block they're using and how they're using it in the structure. The other student's goal, the "listener," attempts to build the identical structure by following the builder's instructions. The listener is allowed to ask questions for clarification. After about ten minutes, the two students compare structures and the entire class talks about what worked and what didn't, and then two other students try. My students love doing this, and it's really hard to keep their excitment down if the listener's structure begins to take a life of its own.

We also have board games, decks of cards, puzzles, and CD-ROMs for the class to play during free time. I like free time. At the very least, free time gives kids ownership over their school day; ideally, it helps create community. Just like during the rest of the school day, at free time everyone needs to be respectful, share, and work together.

The fact that we're "playing" does not mean that we're not learning. It's rather amazing how much thinking can go on when kids are playing Monopoly or checkers or just sitting and drawing. You can also learn about kids by watching them during free time, both by how they relate to others and in what they choose to do. I was amazed earlier this year when one of my most demanding students, a boy who has had behavioral problems and has put forth minimal effort on his schoolwork, took a chess board out during our very first free time and sat down to play. Chess, it turned out, is a passion of his. I had no idea. Here is a child who has great difficulty focusing on his work and putting forth quality, and yet, there he was, sitting with another student, putting serious thought and time into a chess game. Just when you think you know a child, they go and surprise you.

Games also offer a wonderful opportunity to sit down and talk with students, either just to get to know them better as people or to discuss a problem they may be having. Over a game of checkers the labels of "teacher" and "student" can fall to the wayside and suddenly we're just two people playing a game. It's amazing the problems that can be solved, or at least begin to be solved, over a quiet game of checkers or Connect Four. Free time gives me the opportunity to do this. It also allows us to have a little fun, to enjoy each other's company, and to celebrate our living as a community of learners.

Five

Freedom Versus Control

Except for rare instances throughout history, schools have been bastions of autocracy.
—WILLIAM SCHUBERT

Make the work interesting and the discipline will take care of itself.
—E. B. WHITE

When it comes to democratic classrooms, and perhaps education itself, I don't think there is a more controversial issue than the debate between freedom and control. This debate is certainly not new. Jean-Jacques Rousseau advocated a child-centered education in his eighteenth-century classic *Emile*. Friedrich Froebel and Johann Pestalozzi continued these ideas into the nineteenth century (with Froebel inventing kindergarten), and later John Dewey and William Heard Kilpatrick, among others, brought them into the fierce curriculum debates of the first half of the twentieth century (engaging, for example, Bobbitt, Charters, and Thorndike). Half a century before Dewey, Leo Tolstoy (1967), the great Russian author of *War and Peace*, offered his vision of a Rousseauist, child-centered education by creating a school for peasant children on his estate and then building seventy progressive schools in nineteenth-century Russia (Schon 1983).

Drawing from these thinkers and their ideas, the "open classroom," learner-centered movement of the 1960s and early 1970s was supported by a long list of educators including Sylvia Ashton-Warner, George Dennison, Ronald and Beatrice Gross, John Holt, Herbert Kohl, Jonathan Kozol, Carl Rogers, and Charles Silberman. The movement was shot down by the very political push for "basics" in the late 1970s and early 1980s. In the midst of the conservative education crusade of the 1980s and 1990s led by people such as William Bennett, Allan Bloom, Chester Finn, E. D. Hirsch Jr., and Diane Ravitch, child-centered, constructivist, and democratic classroom practices began to bloom once again, fostered by whole language activists such as Nancie Atwell, Lucy McCormick Calkins, Ken and Yetta Goodman, Donald Graves, and Frank Smith, among many others.

To some this looks like a healthy (and democratic) tug-of-war over the years. The important thing to remember from this history, however, is that after all of these debates and contradictory theories and endless reforms and initiatives, *our schools have never really implemented child-centered schooling.* As Larry Cuban (1993), Herbert Kliebard (1987), and Tyack and Cuban (1995) have explained, schooling practices that are child-centered, holistic, and democratic have been put into effect throughout the last century, but in very limited geographic areas and usually for very limited times. Throughout the history of American schooling, going back to the one-room schoolhouse, the basic model, process, and paradigm of education as a one-way transmission has not changed.

Since I first began teaching, I've frequently heard the comment from teachers and parents that "schools tried all of those progressive ideas twenty years ago and they didn't work then either." A more accurate reading of educational history is that schools *didn't* try these ideas twenty years or even fifty years ago. Kliebard (1987) specifically points out that although John Dewey is perhaps the most honored American educational philosopher, when it comes to actual classroom practice, he's also the most ignored. When I write of child-centered, democratic, holistic education, I am not writing about a form of education that has been widely practiced throughout the history of American schooling, because the history of American schooling is not one of freedom, it is one of control.

When teachers move away from highly controlled classrooms and give their students more freedom, they are accused of being soft, liberal, touchy-feely, unstructured, and inattentive to "basics" and "skills." I've been accused of all of these and worse. Within the dominant model of schooling, "serious" learning takes place only in structured, disciplined, orderly, and extremely quiet schools and classrooms. Anything less, as the popular belief goes, isn't "real school." We must remember that there are many private progressive schools in this country that have flourished for many years and that continue to flourish outside of the dominant paradigm. I highly doubt these schools would remain open if they were graduating illiterate children who could not get into college or get a job.

I find it incredibly ironic that in a nation that considers itself one of the freest on earth, if not *the* freest, we raise our children in schools that are, as William Schubert (1986) wrote, "bastions of autocracy." Isn't there a contradiction here? How can we advocate and flaunt our freedom while raising children in schools that are so rarely about personal freedom? Should we be surprised that so few Americans take part in the many freedoms that we do have? The most powerful symbol for learning in our society, our schools, are not about practicing freedom in body, mind, spirit, and voice, they are about blind compliance, learning through competition, maintaining the status quo, silencing voices, and ignoring critical habits of mind. Everything students are supposed to learn in school is given to them from someone else, and usually someone they can't see and don't even know. The direct deliverer of knowledge may be the teacher, but it is legislators, textbook publishing companies, corporate executives, university academics, and school board members that have the most influence on what they are officially taught.

None of these people have ever stepped foot inside my classroom and asked me what I think or asked my students what they think. Recently, Louis Gerstner, the CEO of IBM, headed the second "Education Summit" in New York. There were forty-one governors, thirty corporate CEOs, and a smattering of education "experts." President Clinton even stopped by. How many *teachers* were invited to the summit? *None*. Evidently, our job isn't about thinking, making decisions, and having a voice, it's about doing what we're told to do by legislators and corporate executives, most of whom cannot even begin to understand the realities and complexities of teaching and classroom life, and measure the success of a school in extremely narrow economic and political terms. I wonder how our country's CEOs would feel if all of our teachers got together for a corporate summit and didn't invite any of them?

Seen in this light, the two people most directly involved in my students' learning, me and each of my students, have the least amount of control in the schooling process. We're supposed to just go along with the so-called experts. Follow the leader. Listen and obey politely. There is a reason women have historically been our teachers and men have historically been our school administrators and legislators. Women were supposed to be as compliant in the classroom as they were in the kitchen. To break that pattern, teachers must see themselves as educational *activists*, as critical questioners, as professionals who make issues of freedom and control, regarding both themselves and their students, central to their daily work.

Theory X and Theory Y

In a now classic study, Douglas McGregor (1960) differentiated between two philosophies of management, what he called Theory X and Theory Y. Although McGregor was writing in the context of business and industrial management, his ideas offer profound insight into education and teaching. (I am not, let me emphasize, equating schools with corporations.) McGregor's theories ask us to question our beliefs and assumptions about *human nature* in the context of management. When I speak of management here, I am not referring to "classroom management," but rather the management of *human beings*.

Just as teachers have conscious and tacit beliefs that dictate what they do in their classrooms, managers, according to McGregor, have beliefs that guide their actions. He wrote, and I'll emphasize it because it has important implications for teaching, "*Behind every managerial decision or action are assumptions about human nature and human behavior*" (1960, 87). What this means in the context of a classroom is that when teachers make managerial decisions, decisions that are about the freedom and control of their students, they have conscious and subconscious beliefs and assumptions about *human nature* and *childhood* that dictate the decisions they make. So here

74

is a question that every teacher must ask themselves: When it comes to the freedom and the control of my students, what do I believe about human nature and childhood, and why do I believe it?

McGregor's Theory X, what he called the "traditional view of direction and control," has three underlying managerial assumptions:

1. Most people have a natural dislike of work and if they can, they will avoid it.
2. Most people need to be forced and threatened with punishment to get them to put forth appropriate effort.
3. Most people prefer to be directed by others, do not want responsibility, have little motivation, and more than anything, want security.

In stark contrast is Theory Y, which McGregor called "the integration of individual and organizational goals." Theory Y has six underlying assumptions, but for my purposes here I need include only three of them:

1. "Work is as natural as play or rest."
2. Force and punishment are not the only methods for motivating people to put forth effort. A person will have "self-direction and self-control in the service of objectives to which he is committed."
3. "Avoidance of responsibility, lack of ambition, and emphasis on security are generally consequences of experience, not inherent human traits." (1960, 47–48)

While I would not want to reduce the complexity of teaching to the black and white of an X or a Y, I believe it is fair to say that schooling within the dominant paradigm is clearly built around Theory X. If this was not the case, then rigid curriculums and coercive practices such as testing and grading would not be such high priorities of our schools. School tells children what they should learn, when they should learn, and how they should learn. It assumes from the start that if it does not do this, children will not learn. It exhibits, at its very heart, a failure of trust in children and their desire to know and understand. If we trusted children, we would happily invite them in on the creation, the process, and the responsibility of their own education. (Giving people control over their learning is not only giving them freedom, it is also giving them—actually teaching them—responsibility.) Frank Smith wrote, "There is one reason only for the insistent control of programmatic instruction and tests in classrooms. That reason is *lack of trust*" (1986, 149).

The irony of Theory X is that even though school tries to control every aspect of the learning process to the most minute detail, its efforts result in little meaningful learning. Controlling a child's body so he or she sits still at a desk and a child's mouth so he or she remains silent and a child's fingers so he or she clutches a pencil to fill out worksheets does not amount to controlling their minds. In the end we *think* we're in control, it *looks* like we're in control, but we're not. The usual end result of Theory X schooling is that students do not learn what we think they learn.

They learn things—such as passivity by means of the hidden curriculum—that never even occur to us.

The children who play the Game of School according to the rules of Theory X get good grades, gold stars, and high check marks on their report cards. As Alfie Kohn (1993a) aptly points out, these external reinforcements are just a way to pay children to perform and the net result is actually damaging. The children who do not perform, or the children who do not want to play the Game of School, get poor grades, no stars, low check marks, calls home, and the wrath of angry teachers and principals. As Philip Jackson (1968/1990) and others have written, children begin to learn the culture of school from the first day they enter it. They know the Theory X rules, the regulations, the values, the tacit expectations of school, from the start. Most children learn immediately upon entering their schooling career that they have very little control over and very little say about what happens inside their classrooms. Some even argue that one of the primary purposes of kindergarten is to indoctrinate children into the rules and rituals of school (Apple 1990).

Why does school teach using Theory X beliefs? Because getting most kids to take school seriously is a struggle. Disinterest is something I have seen in children from the entire range of economic classes, not simply poor urban kids. Kids don't really care about school, because school is meaningless to their present lives. Yes, most kids complete their assignments, study for their tests and quizzes, do their homework, and come to school (more or less) smiling, but how many of them are truly *invested* in what they're doing? To use a word put forward by Chris Stevenson (1993), how many children have their hearts and minds truly *engaged* in what they are studying? Stevenson says that "by *engagement* I refer to a *personal intellectual investment in learning*" (76). It has been my experience, both as a teacher and as a student myself, that not many children possess this vision of learning at all. School is seen as a boring requirement. After studying many classrooms, John Goodlad (1984) wrote:

> How would I react as an adult to these ways of the classroom? I would become restless. I would groan audibly over still another seatwork assignment. My mind would wander off soon after the beginning of a lecture. It would be necessary for me to put my mind in some sort of "hold" position. This is what students do. . . . Students may not simply get up and leave. For many, there is no visible perceived alternative anyway. School is where their friends are. To resist or rebel would be to shake up the controlled ambiance and go against the grain of the trade-offs necessary for peaceful coexistence in a small space. One learns passivity. Students in schools are socialized into it virtually from the beginning. (233)

But for a child to learn does not require, as the behaviorist B. F. Skinner wanted us to believe, force, external motivation, or controlled environments. Force *is* required to get kids to work on things that they don't care about, on things that have little relevance to their lives. That's what fuels the struggle of school, the struggle that goes on beneath the facade of "school learning." I don't think that many people like to admit that this struggle exists. People don't talk about it, certainly not in faculty meetings and teachers' lounges. That's because children's resistance is accepted as being a given. When kids complain to adults about the mundane and purposeless work they have to do, most simply smile understandingly and tell them that that's the way things are. They had to do it, so their children have to do it. That's what school is. Teachers think the same way. The fact that so little of the work done in school results in meaningful lifelong learning, positive attitudes and self-esteem, and participation in a democratic society, makes little difference. School is school, like it or not.

Linda McNeil (1988) has written about our schools' "contradictions of control." She writes, "When the school's organization becomes centered on managing and controlling, teachers and students take school less seriously. They fall into a ritual of teaching and learning that tends toward minimal standards and effort" (xviii). Her point is that the primary goal of school is *not* meaningful teaching and learning, but the *controlling of children*. If control is a teacher's primary concern, then intellectual pursuits and the growth of the mind and the heart become a distant and superficial secondary purpose. Freeing a mind to think for itself, especially a child's mind, can be a dangerous thing when one's purpose is to maintain a quiet and orderly classroom.

We can take our schools' Theory X beliefs beyond their influence on children and see their influence on the control of teachers. As I have already noted, teachers are almost as highly controlled by school boards, textbook publishing companies, testing, and cultural and professional expectations as their students are controlled by them. Education and society have very little trust in teachers as thinkers and creators and nurturers of imaginations and ideas. This is why we are given "teacher-proof" curriculums and materials. In forcing so much predetermined curriculum, with its rigidly produced texts and materials, on teachers, the expectation is that they will not deviate from what is expected and cannot fail in teaching their students the required knowledge. This is schooling by numbers.

A Theory Y Classroom

What would a classroom look like if it were built around Theory Y? Here again is Douglas McGregor's first assumption of Theory Y: *Work is as natural as play or rest.* This accepts from the start that children want to learn, that they have an innate curiosity about the world and about life, and that they are more than willing to explore it and question it. It makes coercion and controls in the form of grades, sitting in rows, silence, textbooks, handraising, and "busy work" unnecessary and ill-advised. It gives us a dramatically different way of seeing children and learning. We enter our classrooms with an inherent trust in children and in their capacity and desire to make sense of the world.

Alfie Kohn (1993a), a harsh critic of Theory X schooling, makes a profound point when he questions the myriad of teachers who ask how they can motivate their students. I used to ask this all the time myself. But the question indicates a lack of trust in children. It assumes that unless they are externally provoked, children will remain disinterested in schooling. If students aren't interested in learning, it's usually not because they don't want to learn, it's because they don't want to learn what they're being told to learn and in the highly dull and passive and rote way they're being told to learn it. In echoing John Dewey, Kohn writes, "The job of educators is neither to make students motivated nor to sit passively; it is to set up the conditions that make learning possible" (199). What I try to do now is create a classroom that acknowledges and respects children's intrinsic motivation.

The second important idea underlying a Theory Y classroom is that it is inclusive of multiple objectives and purposes. Rather than learning being dictated by the school board, publishing company, standardized test, or teacher, the classroom experience is now a *collaboration between teacher and students*. Minds come together, goals are talked about, hopes and dreams are expressed, personal interests are elaborated upon, skepticism is raised, questions are asked, opinions and perspectives offered. This is inquiry and discourse as a way of life. It is a way of saying to children, both verbally and tacitly, that personal growth is necessarily a personal, social, and communal creation, and that we trust them, and expect them, to take a critical role in making that creation happen.

Douglas McGregor specifically states that Theory Y is based upon a person pursuing "objectives to which he is committed." Once again, *purpose* is brought to the forefront. I absolutely accept the fact that we have to force our children into learning (or at least doing) what it is that most schools want them to do. That's because they aren't committed to or invested in those objectives. They aren't *their* objectives, they're strictly the school's and the teacher's objectives. If someone were to ask me how we can get kids personally invested in and excited about doing "daily oral language" and math worksheets and reading textbooks, I would tell them not to hold their breath. It is not going to happen. Children are voracious natural learners, but only with respect to what they see as being personally purposeful and meaningful.

I am not advocating here learning that is strictly a product of a child's own discovery. Remember, teachers have a critical role in the educative process. It is up to them to create an idea-rich learning environment, to offer suggestions, to challenge, to raise critical questions, to encourage risk taking, to nurture reflection, to invite civic participation, to be model learners. A Theory Y classroom is a democratic space that has the power and potential of being alive with ideas, talk, possibilities, and hope. The last thing it wants to do is hinder the freedom of thought. The first thing it wants to do is see everyone as being important creators of ideas and knowledge.

Where's the Structure?

School is obsessed with the necessity of classroom structure. I have no problem with structure, because an environment or a system with no structure is an environment in chaos. The problem I have is with how most people define structure in a school context. Structure in a classroom usually means silent kids, sitting neatly, doing and thinking and saying what it has been preplanned for them to do, to think, and to say. Expectations and class rules, both overt and tacit, have been made clear, and deviations from these have specific and sometimes severe consequences. Expectations, rules, and consequences are not necessarily bad. However, structure in the context of school is a highly *externally controlled* form of order. This control stems from the direct and indirect authority of the teacher, the principal, the parents, the report card, and the state.

Most parents, principals, and school board members like to *see* structure the moment they enter a classroom. Either the place is quiet and ordered or it is not. There is no social or moral element to this vision of structure; it is reduced to a physical act. What this conception ignores is that structure can also be an *internal habit of mind*, something that stems from *within* human beings, as well as a *social construct*, stemming from shared purposes and values. The difference is between structure that is conceived as an externally forced physical order and structure seen as a socially and morally created internal *responsibility*. With the former, structure emanates from the teacher, who creates and maintains the daily classroom order; with the latter, it emanates from the classroom community life and its culture, and structure is *taught* as a democratic responsibility.

The structure of a democratic classroom is an inherent part of the classroom life and should be frequently discussed. Like Dewey's vision of democracy, it involves a *way of life* inside the classroom, meaning that it is a natural and interwoven part of the classroom ecosystem. John Mayher (1990) wrote that this classroom structure or control "derives not from the role or positional authority of the teacher in and of itself but from the *meaningfulness of the activities in which everyone is engaged*" (131, italics added). This is the belief behind E. B. White's epigraph at the beginning of this chapter: *Make the work interesting and the discipline will take care of itself.* I hear an endless stream of suggestions for getting kids to behave in school and take their learning seriously, but hardly ever do I hear anyone suggest that what we really need to do is make what kids are doing in school personally meaningful and relevant.

Dewey wrote eloquently about this vision of a classroom in his short and very readable book, *Experience and Education* (1938/1963). As he expressed it, "It is not the will or desire of any one person which establishes order but the *moving spirit* of the whole group" (54, italics added). Dewey goes on to write, "The primary source of social control resides in the very nature of the work done as a social enterprise in which all individuals have an opportunity to contribute and to which all feel a responsibility" (56). He offers the analogy of a game, in which there are inherent and tacitly accepted rules. "Without rules there is no game" Dewey writes. "As long as the game goes on with a reasonable smoothness, the players do not feel that they are submitting to external imposition but that they are playing the game" (52–53). When I was a kid and my friends and I got together to play football or baseball, the rules of the game were never seen as an imposition. In fact, they were understood as a *necessity*. The idea of getting rid of the rules never entered our minds. We knew that without them there could be no football game. While Dewey and I are not equating classrooms and games, we are saying that just as rules are a natural component of games as a holistic social activity, order is a natural component of a classroom that is built around a communal context.

As I've said before, our classroom often looks more chaotic than ordered and structured. If that's the case, then our structure works—or strives to work—within that chaos. But again, this takes time and patience. After years of traditional schooling, with minimal self-direction and decision-making power, it would be unreasonable to expect children to walk into a democratic classroom and immediately know what is expected of them or how to be a responsible member of the community. Educator Ira Shor (1992, 1996) writes that students start in democratic classrooms from a "less-than-zero" position. They have been so profoundly shaped from undemocratic social and cultural (and school) experiences, that they actually start with what we could consider a negative position. I've come to see this as a form of dependency. Children have had so few opportunities in school to think for themselves, to act on their original thoughts, to freely ask questions, that they have come to depend on their passivity, on being fed their learning. The more you control a person's life (or a child's learning), the more they are going to come to depend on that control. Because of this it's not uncommon for some students to *resent* being given the responsibility a democratic classroom asks of them.

I see something similar happening with teachers. After being silenced for so long, after never being invited in on the official decision-making process of schooling and teaching, after being told what to teach and when to teach and how to teach, after being treated as if they were intellectually inferior, teachers have become submissive. Many teachers seem to believe that they are powerless, that their voices must remain silenced, that their ideas and their experiences have no value. So children are not the only ones who enter school from a less-than-zero position. What we end up with is a form of educational oppression, where those closest to the action, those with the greatest stake and emotional investment in the process, have the least power.

We must help children (and teachers) learn what it means to live and work in democratic environments. I'll repeat Hilton Smith's (1995) quote from earlier: "Schools in the United States have provided plenty of schooling *about* democracy, but very little *for* or *in* democracy" (63). We need to help kids see the value in putting the community good before the individual gain, in living a life of thoughtfulness and consciousness. We need to help children develop and use their voices, and to see themselves as being empowered to create change. They learn this vision of themselves only by *living* it. You can't come to know what it means to be a responsible, decision-making member in a democracy if you are not in a classroom or a school that practices democracy to begin with. It will get messy at times, especially at first. The communal structure that I wrote about above may crumble occasionally; mine certainly does. But this is a natural part of the learning process. When my niece, Melanie, was learning how to walk, she fell down a lot. But now she's five and walking has become second nature.

Helping kids learn how to live their structural parts in a democratic classroom involves talk—a lot of talk. As I will show in Chapter 8, there are different kinds of talk in our classroom. There is formal talk, undertaken in large and small meetings, and there is informal chatter. When things are going good, it's important to discuss it as a class. Why are things working? What are we doing that's yielding such positive results? How do we know that things are working well? And the same is true when things are not working well. We need to open a dialogue and ask ourselves what the problem is and what we can do about it. If things are not working at any given moment, I'll stop what everyone is doing and bring the class together for a class meeting. There's no purpose in continuing our activities if community has broken down. We need to talk about what's happening or what's not happening, and we need to do this collectively. One way of discovering what's going on is through class role-modeling and drama. Through "fish bowl" modeling, where a group of students play-act working as a group while the rest of the class observes, the dynamics of interpersonal skills can be revealed (Mayher 1990). Creating plays and skits about our behavior can not only be helpful, it can be fun as well. Unfortunately, there are no panaceas to make this vision of freedom successful. The only way to make it work is to struggle through it in your own context and in your own way.

There are times when talk does not solve a problem. When, for whatever reason, the kids and the community are just not able to function. There are a variety of reasons for this and teachers need to be careful not to jump to conclusions. I have to remind myself often to slow down, to look at a situation from the perspective of the students, to look beneath the surface, to be critical of *my own actions*. Far too often teachers (including me) blame their students when things don't work. Sometimes it's not the students' fault. I'm not offering this as an apology for bad or inappropriate behavior, which I get my share of. I'm saying that sometimes we're asking children to do something they're not ready for, we're forgetting that they're *kids* and that they're *people* and that that doesn't always mesh with our objectives and goals in school. Even adults have trouble at times completing their tasks. If something isn't working, sometimes the wisest thing to do is to simply move on to something else and try again tomorrow.

There are other times of course, when things aren't working because the kids are not acting responsibly or they're just plain misbehaving. If that's the case, I need to decide what action to take. First, like I said, I usually try to talk it out. It can help to have a private chat with a student or a small group of students. This is something I've done often over the years. Since our classroom is so active and social, it's rather easy for me to pull a student or a few students off to the side for a few minutes to have a short talk. Oftentimes that's all it takes to help them get refocused. But if talking doesn't work and the student or students continue to act inappropriately, I need to do something about it. The simple fact is that I have no magic formula. If one of my students continues to be disrespectful or misbehaves, I do the same thing other teachers do, I struggle. I have many options available to me. Maybe I'll have them stay in for recess and do some work to make up for lost time. If the problem is a select number of students, and if I can identify them (sometimes this is tough), then I'll mete out the consequences to just those kids. If the situation warrants it, I'll call parents, and this might result in having a meeting at school with the child. Having a democratic classroom does not mean there are no consequences for inappropriate behavior. In fact, it's just the opposite. One of the hopes of democracy—both in and out of the classroom—is for each of us to take responsibility for our actions, and sometimes that involves consequences.

As much as the classroom functions within a natural social structure, as the teacher I am still the final authority, the one with the most power. It has to be that way, and not only because I'm the one directly responsible for my students' physical and emotional well-being, but because, as John Dewey said, the educative value of a classroom is dependent on the quality of the classroom experience, and the person primarily responsible for creating that environment is the teacher. So what happens in our classroom, what is allowed or not allowed, what freedoms we have or don't have, what controls are implemented or not, are ultimately up to me. (Of course, what I can and cannot do is much too often up to someone else sitting in an office somewhere.) Even when I involve my students in making a classroom decision, something I do often, the final decision is up to me. I'm the one, in the end, who says yes, we'll do that, or no, we'll do this. That's my job. A democratic classroom does not mean that anything goes and that my authority as the teacher is compromised. The difference is in having authority and in being an authoritarian. It's not an issue of having or not having power. I have it. The issue is what I do with it.

What Knowledge? Whose Knowledge?

Notions of freedom and control do not apply only to kids' behavior and teachers' methods. It is impossible to seriously consider the ideas of freedom, schooling, and democracy without being critical of the *knowledge* that's being taught in school. Just like the classroom environment, the content that schools teach—the knowledge that children are expected to learn—is highly *controlled* in the traditional paradigm of education. Children rarely have any voice about what they can learn in school. Everything is dished out to them from a variety of external sources: textbooks, worksheets, videos, teachers. The same, to a degree, is true of teachers. When a teacher gets hired at a school, one of the first things they're handed is the "official curriculum," the collection of knowledge that they're expected to teach their students.

It is imperative that teachers ask critical questions concerning school knowledge. Here are some questions that I continually ask myself:

- What knowledge is most important to know?
- Does everyone need the same knowledge?
- Is it possible for everyone to learn the same knowledge?
- What knowledge are my students allowed or not allowed official access to?

- Who decides what knowledge gets taught or does not get taught in school?
- Whose interest is being served by having me teach children certain knowledge and not teach them other knowledge?
- How much control should children have in choosing the knowledge they learn in school?
- Where does knowledge come from, anyway?

These are not questions to be left up to curriculum specialists, legislators, school board members, parents, or education professors. These questions have a profound impact on who I am as a teacher and as a human being, and are crucial in shaping the kind of people my neighbors will be and the kind of society we have. As a teacher I'm not merely a technician whose job it is to blindly transmit knowledge that someone else hands me. Not only am I a creator of significant knowledge and ideas myself, but I recognize teaching as both a moral endeavor and a political act. I therefore consider it a professional and ethical *obligation* to be critical of the knowledge that I teach. This means that I'll deviate—that is, *consciously* deviate—from the official curriculum. I've made changes in the official curriculum from the first day I stepped into my own classroom. Remember, all teachers naturally teach the "same" content differently.

When it comes to curricular content, all is not as it appears. It may seem on the surface that we're just teaching kids to multiply and divide and read and write and know some history. It looks value-neutral. But it isn't. We must realize that *knowledge is power*, and what knowledge people get, or what knowledge people have access to, greatly influences how much power they can have or cannot have. Teachers are the ones on the front lines, so it is teachers who must accept the primary responsibility for the knowledge they teach or the knowledge they allow their students access to. Ignoring the issue is denying the responsibility and relinquishing the authority to people far outside the classroom who have interests all their own.

How can we claim to be schooling children for freedom of thought, freedom of expression and voice, freedom to think for oneself, when school knowledge is so strictly controlled, when there is what Michelle Fine (1987) calls a "silencing in schools," a silencing that "constitutes the process by which contradictory evidence, ideologies, and experiences find themselves buried, camouflaged, and discredited" (157)? It is very interesting that when we think of the controlled knowledge that Adolf Hitler dictated be taught to the children of Nazi Germany, we call it *propaganda*, but when we think of the controlled knowledge taught to children in American schools, we call it *curriculum*. Knowledge, no matter what political belief system it belongs to, is inherently ideological. We live in a political world, and the knowledge we're taught, both in and out of school, has tremendous influence on our role in that world. Seen this way, teaching Johnny how to spell is a political act. Teachers must see themselves as political actors, as people who profoundly shape children who will go on to shape the politics, the economics, the ethics, the culture of our nation.

School Knowledge and Textbooks

One of the most obvious and pervasive examples of selective school knowledge is textbooks. Textbooks are one of those paradigmatic rules of schooling. Their use is so entrenched that people automatically assume that if you go to school, you use textbooks, and if you don't use textbooks, then you're not doing "Real School." But schools' dependence on textbooks works against the basic ideals of democracy and freedom of thought. Within the vast majority of schools, textbooks drive the official curriculum. In very real ways they *are* the curriculum. By their very nature they emphasize the memorization of endless facts rather than encourage the creation of our own knowledge, a questioning and critical habit of mind, the seeking of multiple perspectives. I believe that if we were to get rid of textbooks tomorrow, school as we know it would largely crumble. Teacher and students would go to school and begin the day with—nothing. They would have to *create it themselves*, they would have to *seek out* knowledge themselves.

Textbooks tacitly teach us to ignore the ideological nature of knowledge. No matter how many pages a textbook has, no matter how many pounds they weigh in at, textbooks can't help but leave out more information than they include. It's simply not possible to write a textbook or even an entire curriculum that does not do this. From the start, it is the *idea* of a textbook that we must be critical of. The idea of a textbook is that it is possible to narrow down knowledge in a specific discipline or "subject" and officially sanction certain information. This is the information that someone outside our classrooms has determined that "everyone should know." But is that possible—or should I say moral—in a supposedly pluralistic, democratic, and free nation? Exactly whose knowledge and what knowledge is allowed in a textbook?

As Michael Apple (1993) and many others have shown, textbooks (as well as the rest of an official curriculum) are presented to children as being "truth," when they are anything but truth. There is no such thing as a "neutral" textbook. Textbooks are collections of specifically selected information that imply to the students—especially students who are not encouraged to be critical of what they read and what they are told—that what is contained in their pages is science or English or the real history of "what happened," *the* view or perspective. This is true for every subject in school, but is probably the easiest to see in social studies. For example, the idea that history is a living thing, an evolution of understanding, that it is highly subjective, is totally lost. I am not saying that the fact that "Christopher Columbus sailed in 1492" is untrue, but rather that the idea that we can look at the "facts" of Christopher Columbus or Andrew Jackson or the American industrial revolution from *multiple perspectives* and *multiple interpretations* is hardly ever considered, and when it is considered, perspectives that go against the popular interpretation are covered in a paragraph. I believe it was historian Howard Zinn (1995) that said history—meaning the history taught in our schools and the history that our culture accepts as truth—are the stories of the *winners*. Rarely do schools teach history from the perspective of the losers. Consider how long it's taken for the stories of Native Americans or African American slaves or women or oppressed labor groups to get into a typical school's curriculum at even the most rudimentary level.

James Loewen (1995) has done a fascinating study of twelve of the most popular American history high school social studies textbooks, exposing in historical detail their untruths, omissions, biases, and out-and-out lies. (We should, of course, be critical of Loewen's interpretations as well.) Loewen shows how the knowledge in textbooks is highly selective and takes—in the case of American history—a very pro-American stance. As he points out, textbooks' titles and covers can be revealing:

> The titles themselves tell the story: *The Great Republic, The American Way, Land of Promise, Rise of the American Nation*. Such titles differ from the titles of all other textbooks students read in high school or college. Chemistry books, for example, are called *Chemistry* or *Principles of Chemistry*, not *Rise of the Molecule*. And you can tell history textbooks just from their covers, graced as they are with American flags, bald eagles, the Statue of Liberty. (3)

Of course, the greatest value of Loewen's book is not in replacing one set of historical facts with another set of historical facts, but in helping people see that knowledge and teaching are not objective, even with science and math. Exactly what science and what math should we teach and who gets to decide? Do schools, for example, encourage kids to be critical of modern technology and industry and science, or do they directly and indirectly relate these to "progress"? And what about so much of the science writing (or knowledge) that is largely ignored in schools? Some of the most profound and provocative science writing by, for example, Edward O. Wilson, Stephen Jay Gould, Paul Davies, the late Loren Eisley, are not all "fact-based," but are equally about reflection, philosophy, beauty, *morality*. And should science, as it is so often taught within the dominant paradigm, advocate an anthropocentric view of the world, which places human beings and their experiences and values at the center of our planet and universe? Consider, for example, evolutionary biologist E. O. Wilson's (1996) point that it is really "the little things that run the world" (155). According to Wilson, the earth's millions of invertebrate and plant species (microorganisms, insects, flowers, etc.) can easily thrive without human beings, but humans would perish without them. And what about that mathematics can be manipulated to create certain "truths," in, for example, surveys, statistics, and economics? Suddenly the facts of science and math that fill our curriculums are not nearly as objective and neutral as they appear, because all of this knowledge is *selected*.

Year after year of reading textbooks and having learning directed at them in a lock-step, programmatic fashion sends a message to children: This is what "learning" is. This is the stuff that's important to know. If it's not in these books, if we don't cover it and study it and test it here, then it must not be important. Your job isn't to interpret knowledge, to see the power and the politics of knowledge, to create knowledge, to think and speak and act for yourself. Children are being taught that learning and think-ing means being a passive receiving vessel for facts that someone deemed important for them to know. This is the *hidden curriculum* of schooling at work (Apple 1990; Giroux 1983; Jackson 1968/1990). Besides what teachers want their students to learn, there is a seemingly endless list of *unintended* or "hidden" learning that results from the process of schooling. John Dewey (1938/1963) put it this way:

> Perhaps the greatest of all pedagogical fallacies is the notion that a person learns only the particular thing he is studying at the time. Collateral learning in the ways of for-mation of enduring attitudes, of likes and dislikes, may be and often is much more important then the spelling lesson or lesson in geography or history that is learned. For these attitudes are fundamentally what count in the future. . . . What avail is it to win prescribed amounts of information about geography and history, to win the abil-ity to read and write, if in the process the individual loses his own soul? (48–49)

The hidden curriculum is everywhere in school. It is embedded in how schools and classrooms go about their day-to-day functioning. It is in the curriculum, the teaching methods, the school and classroom rules and values, issues of gender, the attitude- and self-esteem-forming structures of school such as ability grouping and tracking, the hallways, the offices, even the lunchrooms. My school's lunchroom recently started selling donuts and cookies and potato chips, and every day now there's a long line of kids to buy them. What might our students be learning from our school's donut curriculum?

The end results of years of the hidden curriculum, especially with textbooks, are disastrous. Children who hate reading, children who don't want to think, children who continuously wait to be "taught to," children who lack the insight and the abil-ity and the courage to ask questions and take risks, children who see life and learning and school as being about memorizing facts and learning the single "right" answer rather than developing a critical and questioning habit of mind, children who do not see that learning and knowledge can be amazing, lifelong, and empowering. As James Loewen (1995) put it, "Because textbooks use such a godlike tone, it never occurs to most students to question them" (5). And the bigger result of all of this is even more dangerous: a nation paralyzed with apathy and ignorance.

We must remember that the primary purpose of a textbook is not for children to learn, but for publishing companies to turn a profit. California alone has a textbook market worth almost $300 million (Routman 1996). Patrick Shannon (1995) noted that there are five major textbook publishers of basal series in the United States: Houghton Mifflin; Harcourt, Brace; Macmillan/McGraw-Hill; Scott, Foresman; and Silver Burdett-Ginn. It should come as no surprise that these publishers also own the most popular standardized tests: Macmillan/McGraw-Hill publishes the California Achievement Test, the California Test of Basic Skills, and the SRA; Harcourt, Brace offers the Metropolitan Achievement Test and the Stanford Achievement Test; and Houghton Mifflin produces the Iowa Test of Basic Skills. What all of this amounts to is a corporate lock on the official knowledge in our classrooms. Publishing companies produce the textbooks that drive curriculums as well as the tests that "assess" children's knowledge, and those tests determine, as Lisa Delpit (1988) writes, which social and political "gatekeeping points" children will be allowed to pass through.

It really makes little difference which publisher a school chooses. Since no publisher wants to risk losing business, they limit their risks and produce the same colorful textbooks with the same dull writing and containing the same "basic" knowledge one after another. (Unbeknownst to most people, all textbooks are written and published for the two largest markets: California and Texas.) The point in all of this is not meaningful learning. It is the perpetuation of corporate publishing profits via the Game of School. It's important to see how the parts of the game fit together. The textbooks, the grades, the tests, the rating and ranking of children, the tracking of children via ability groups, the sorting of which children go to college and which don't, of which children go to better colleges and which children go to community colleges or vocational schools. Without these standardized, assembly-line, school-by-numbers programmatic materials, much of this wouldn't be possible.

What textbooks and all of their rigidly structured curriculums add up to is *knowledge control*. Rather than looking at knowledge as being highly selected and political, it is reduced to lists and books of facts and skills. Once again, this is one of Linda McNeil's (1988) "contradictions of control." Rather than allowing into the curriculum ideas that might question or upset the status quo, the classroom follows a set plan of instruction with controlled "official knowledge" in an effort to have every teacher bake the same cake at the same time with the least disturbance and the most efficiency. How can anyone be surprised, then, that going to school is so uninspiring?

The dominant paradigm of school does not encourage active inquiry or the raising of controversial issues in classrooms because free student inquiry often runs the risk of questioning authority. And whether this is the authority of the classroom, the school office, the state legislature, the White House, corporate boardrooms, or cultural and economic hegemonies, it is something that school wants to avoid. Asking questions and raising controversial issues also means moving away from strict scope and sequence charts and into *unplanned* areas. Not only could this mean entering a debate on a topic that a teacher knows little about, but it could seriously throw off the curricular timing, making it impossible to finish the textbook or the required units by June. As McNeil (1988) concludes from her research on four schools, teachers "wished to omit material, or perspectives on material, that would foster contradictory opinions and make students want to engage in discussion. Most teachers felt they could cover more material more efficiently if controversial topics were omitted" (174).

By eliminating children's freedom to think for themselves and ask questions that are relevant to their own lives, we are preventing them from fully developing their selves, from defining who they are and who they wish to become. This may be the ultimate control of knowledge in our schools. *We do not allow children to consciously expand and understand and improve themselves.* In the vision of Maxine Greene (1988), schooling with freedom in its heart is a place where people—children and their teachers—openly, consciously, and purposefully work to *create themselves* (134).

Becoming Critical Readers of Society

Schools and classrooms that seek to help children create themselves are trying to bring to life what Henry Giroux and Peter McLaren (1986) call "democratic public spheres," and what George Wood (1988) refers to as "free spaces," and what Maxine Greene (1988) calls "public spaces" and "spheres of freedom." It is here that democracy is not just spoken about but practiced. It is here that children are given the freedom to ask questions, the responsibility to be civic-minded, the opportunity to be empathic, and the encouragement to look beneath the surface realities of life and knowledge and become what many have referred to as *critical readers of society*.

This notion of being a critical reader of society is virtually ignored by schools. As we live our lives, things are not as they often appear to be. Words and images have the power to manipulate our thinking and our actions. A critical reader of society is someone who can see beneath social and cultural realities. During the 1996 presidential campaign, with great fanfare, Bob Dole resigned his seat and majority leadership of the U.S. Senate to invigorate his race against Bill Clinton. The day after his resignation he flew to Chicago to launch his "new" campaign. Dole got on the airplane in Washington wearing his standard suit and tie (his Washington "uniform") and emerged from the plane in Chicago wearing khakis, a blue sport coat, with his tie off and his collar open. Bob Dole transformed himself into a Washington "outsider" *just by changing his clothes*. For Dole to do this he would have had to think that the American public was so ignorant and blind that they could be manipulated, which is not showing a whole lot of confidence in the American people. George Bush did the same thing (with considerably more success) during the 1988 campaign, with the infamous "Willie Horton" commercial and visiting an American flag factory. By no means am I trying to be partisan. I did some volunteer work for Bill Clinton's campaign in 1992 and had the opportunity to see firsthand the intricate planning and staging of what looked like overwhelming and spontaneous rallies of support. Truth is not an issue here. What matters is very consciously working to *manufacture a reality*, and this pervades politics and government.

The necessity of having a citizenry that can (and will) search beneath surface realities goes far beyond politics and into nearly every facet of our lives, from watching the news to buying groceries. Neil Postman and Steve Powers (1992) explain how news programs create realities with their selection of what is "news," and with the specific language and images they use, how news shows are manufactured to keep people watching (and money flowing), and also how it's become so difficult to tell the difference between news, editorial content, advertising, and entertainment. They make suggestions to encourage viewers to be critical, such as "learn something about the economic and political interests of those who run TV stations" and "reduce by one-third the number of opinions you feel obligated to have" (160).

Shopping for groceries may seem like an innocent and "free" act, but in fact grocery stores are laid out in a way to unknowingly entice us to buy more. Five years ago when I went shopping my grocery store chain just had "sales," but now for me to get reduced sale prices I have to first give the cashier my "preferred customer card." On the surface this is putting me in a position of authority and prestige and getting me cheaper groceries, but beneath the surface everything that I buy is now recorded with my name and demographic information in the store's computer. My grocery store knows things about me and my buying habits that I don't even know. And those lists of data about me (and you) are sold to other companies.

In an advertising campaign, the drink Mountain Dew (which is owned by Pepsi) sold cheap beepers to kids with six months of free air time (Barboza 1996). The goal was to hook-up five hundred thousand kids to Mountain Dew beepers. Each week the company "beeped" thousands of kids to call a toll-free number to hear about chances to win prizes and product discounts. Of course the real purpose far beyond the "prizes and discounts" was to use a popular media item (beepers) to wire children to advertising at all hours of the day and night. In the words of a Pepsi spokeman, "This is the ultimate in one-on-one marketing." An important idea to consider in this discussion is *hegemony*, which is when people (or states or companies or industries or even *paradigms*) have power and influence over others, sometimes on such a grand (and invisible) scale that we feel powerless. Maxine Greene (1988) observed that "most Americans are convinced that they are free. . . . Even so, many are likely to share a feeling of subservience to a system, or to a faith, or to an Establishment they can scarcely name" (19). I agree with this for myself and I can't help but feel the same is true for so many people today. Half a million children may think they have power with a Mountain Dew beeper on their belts, but who really is in control?

A critical reader of society can see through these facades and become *empowered*. We cannot say that we are educating children to be conscious and thoughtful and free if we are not helping them to see and question the complexities of life. A friend and education professor, Bill Pink, stated this beautifully: If the surface realities of our lives is a stage then as critical and democratic educators we need to help our students go *back stage*. School, under the dominant paradigm, not only ignores the back stage, it teaches—even advocates—the stage itself. Two good ways of thinking about helping children (and adults) go back stage is through the two related fields of study called the *sociology of knowledge* and *semiotics*. The sociology of knowledge is largely about how taken-for-granted assumptions are created and transmitted to form social "truths" and "realities." As Berger and Luckman (1966) write, "The sociology of knowledge must concern itself with whatever passes as 'knowledge' in society" (3). Much of what we do in our daily lives we believe we do of free will, but in actuality many (if not all) of our actions are embedded in socially constructed "truths" (or rules) that dictate how we should act and can lead to social *conformism* rather than to conscious questioning habits of mind and *change*.

Semiotics is about cultural, social, political, and economic "signs." Jack Solomon (1988) explains that signs are "common sense" and "natural" everyday things and ideas and labels that really—beneath the surface—have not-so-commonsense and not-so-natural "hidden cultural *interests*" (10, italics added). Bob Dole's khakis, my "preferred customer card" (and that specific language they chose to use) and beepers are cultural signs with far more purpose and influence than what appears on the surface—which is one reason they *work* so well for their creators. Solomon suggests using six ways of knowing to see beneath what appears to be the common sense of everyday life:

1. Always question the "commonsense" view of things, because "common sense" is really "communal sense": the habitual opinions and perspectives of the tribe.
2. The "commonsense" viewpoint is usually motivated by a cultural interest that manipulates our consciousness for ideological reasons.
3. Cultures tend to conceal their ideologies behind the veil of "nature," defining what they do as "natural" and condemning contrary cultural practices as "unnatural."
4. In evaluating any system of cultural practice, one must take into account the interests behind it.
5. We do not perceive our world directly but view it through the filter of a semiotic code or mythic frame (such as gender myths, economic myths, historical myths).
6. A sign is a sort of cultural barometer, marking the dynamic movement of social history. (10)

These are excellent suggestions for helping children become critical of knowledge, information, and how they read society. As Solomon writes:

> Once you see behind the surface of a sign into its hidden cultural significance, you can free yourself from that sign and perhaps find a new way of looking at the world. You can control the signs of your culture rather than having them control you. (8)

These ideas may seem highly complex and to be reserved for the college classroom, but waiting until college is much too late—and unnecessary. The fact is that even young children can understand some of these ideas if they're presented in contexts that make sense to how they see the world.

Critical Pedagogy

I have referred to critical pedagogy several times, and although it is not in the scope of this book to do this topic justice, any discussion of democratic schooling would be incomplete without it. The roots of critical pedagogy go back over a century to the beliefs of *critical theory*, which is a social theory rather an education theory. Much of what I have been writing about in this section concerning official school knowledge, knowledge control, and access to knowledge is based on the beliefs of a critical, and what I like to call transformative, education. (For an extended introduction to critical pedagogy, see Giroux 1983; hooks 1994; McLaren 1994).

Critical pedagogy sees schooling as a political process and teaching as a political act, and directly relates both to social and economic inequalities and injustices. Critical pedagogy specifically sees our schools and their official knowledge as propagating injustices primarily within the scope of race, gender, and class. It is, in its heart, about issues of *power*—who has power and who is allowed to get it. Critical educators use the phrase *social reproduction* to point out how our schools play a role in maintaining social classes and social roles (the rich stay rich, the poor stay poor). Through its control of knowledge, its rating and ranking of children, its sorting, its unequal funding, schools have historically worked to maintain the social status quo rather than to consciously change and improve society and the lives of all of its people.

Critical pedagogy advocates schools and classrooms that are *transformative*; that work to empower people, to make equality a reality, to make our country and our world a better place to live. Since critical and transformative issues are central to the idea of "literacy," I'll have more to say about these topics in my discussion of literacy and what has been called *critical literacy* in Chapter 7. I'll add here, however, that I think traditional concepts of critical and transformative pedagogy are limiting, so we need to expand their meaning. There are many areas other than race, gender, and class where we could work to improve our communities and our world. Critical schooling and teaching, for me, includes issues such as violence, the environment, health care, the media, marketing, multiculturalism, and very simply how we get along with our neighbors. All of these can be transformative and empowering ideas to explore with children.

Knowledge Control and Henry Ford

To get a better picture of the knowledge control in our classrooms and how we can help children gain critical perspectives, it will help to look at an example. One of my students, Agustin, an eighth grader, was researching Henry Ford. It wasn't a major project, but we were constructing a world history timeline, and after a class brainstorming session, Agustin chose to research Henry Ford. He began his inquiry using two sources, an old biography of Ford that I found for him and the encyclopedia. (My school at this time didn't have a library, and this project didn't warrant a trip to a public library.) After a few days, Agustin told me that he had done some reading on Ford and had some information on his life. At that point I asked him one question: Did any of the sources say anything bad about Ford? At first he didn't understand the question, so I rephrased it. I told him I was wondering if either of the two sources he had read said anything negative about who Henry Ford was as a human being. Agustin said no, the information was limited to Ford's life and how he invented the Model T and so forth. What Agustin had done at that point is what most kids would do when researching a famous figure like Henry Ford. They study the "facts." In Ford's case, this would be where and when he was born and raised, a little about his parents, his work on the automobile and the assembly line and so on. Basically it's names, dates, and places.

The next day I brought in a copy of David Halberstam's 1986 book, *The Reckoning*, which is a history of the Ford Motor Company and Nissan. I gave the book to Agustin and asked him to go out into the hallway where it's quiet and read part of a chapter, which is a short biographical sketch of Henry Ford. Halberstam's book is not easy reading for most adults, let alone a seventh grader. The book is 752 pages long. But I gave it to him to read because there was knowledge in it that was important for him to think about if he was going to look at Henry Ford. I didn't really care how much of the reading he understood. More than anything I used the book so we would have a common text for us to discuss. That's what I wanted to engage in with Agustin, a dialogue about Henry Ford. I look at this as Vygotsky's (1978) zone of proximal development that I wrote about in Chapter 3. Alone, Agustin would perhaps struggle with the book, but I can help him make some sense of it.

After reading part of the chapter, he came back into the room. As I'd expected, he didn't understand some of what he read. I pointed to two specific areas in the chapter. The first dealt with Ford's notorious anti-Semitism. For example, Halberstam quotes Ford as having said, "When there is something wrong in this country, you'll find Jews." I brought up information that was not in Halberstam's book. I told Agustin that for years Ford financially supported the anti-Semitic newspaper *The Dearborn Independent*, spreading misinformation and prejudice. Before this day, before our dialogue, Agustin had had no idea what *anti-Semitism* meant.

The second part of the chapter that I focused on had to do with one of Ford's most famous acts, giving his assembly-line workers a five-dollars-a-day wage, which at that time was considered an enormous sum of money for a factory worker. Historically, it's safe to say that most people have seen this as a kindhearted gesture of Ford. But it was not benevolence that led Ford to give his workers a raise. He did it for two reasons: First, he believed the higher wage would get him the best workers, but more importantly he used the wage to keep his workers from organizing and joining unions, which were gaining in strength at the time. In the end, the higher wage had one primary purpose: it was a form of social control to get higher profits for Ford. And the profits certainly did come. According to Halberstam, in the first three years of the five-dollar wage, 1914, 1915, and 1916, the Ford Motor Company's after-tax profits were $30 million, $20 million, and $60 million. Within ten years, Henry Ford's personal wealth was valued at close to $1 *billion*. Remember, this was in the 1920s.

Agustin and I went to the chalkboard and did a little math. (It's worth pointing out the natural and unplanned subject integration that occurred here.) I didn't know how many days a Ford worker worked each week, so we went with a six-day workweek. At five dollars a day, a Ford worker would have made thirty dollars a week or $1,560 per year. I asked Agustin to compare this to the Ford profits, the largest portion of which undoubtedly went into Henry Ford's pockets. Fifteen hundred dollars a year compared to tens of millions. I asked him, "Is that okay? What do you think about that?" I wasn't trying to tell him what to think. I was helping him to see from a different perspective and then encouraging him to make up his own mind. I was not saying that Ford was evil. I was helping him to see that people and knowledge are more complex than the picture that a textbook or an encyclopedia normally paints. At that point Agustin said, "You know, this is like my dad. He worked for this company for a real long time, and they just let him go." Agustin's understanding and sense making of Henry Ford had suddenly entered a whole new dimension, and it did so by his relating David Halberstam's text and our dialogue to his own life by what happened to his father. Henry Ford giving his workers five dollars a day is a fact, but what it *means* to each of us is not. Agustin's work on Henry Ford was no longer about one human being, it was about *humankind*, and perhaps more importantly, it had relevance to his own life.

Helping children to be critical of knowledge and surface realities is central to democratic schooling and critical pedagogy. It nurtures in people what the late Brazilian educator Paulo Freire (1971/1990) called *conscientizacao* or a "critical consciousness." Freire equated traditional schooling with "banking education," where students are required to memorize (or deposit) specific knowledge rather than to nurture questioning and empowering habits of mind, the freedom to think for themselves, and the conviction to act on their thoughts. He wrote:

> It is not surprising that the banking concept of education regards men as adaptable, manageable beings. The more students work at storing the deposits entrusted to them, the less they develop the critical consciousness which would result from their intervention in the world as transformers of that world. The more completely they accept the passive role imposed on them, the more they tend simply to adapt to the world as it is and to the fragmented view of reality deposited in them. (60)

The development of a critical consciousness is all but ignored within the dominant paradigm of schooling today, which is all about banking knowledge and perpetuating an unconscious and antiintellectual way of life. Democracy demands much more than this; it needs people who refuse to live passive lives.

Freedom and Affective Knowledge

I draw no distinction between what is commonly referred to as "cognitive" knowledge and the many forms of affective knowledge. To me they are equally important parts of the whole of human life and experience. The knowledge that schools emphasize and test are facts and skills. These discrete bits of "technical knowledge"—once again, the stuff that people believe we need to know to get a job—have a virtual monopoly in school curriculums, while anything having to do with human affect is given negligible recognition at best. Knowledge in the visual arts, drama, music, human emotions and feelings, and interpersonal relationships are not seen as being "meaty" or "rigorous" or "academic." The assumption is that that's not what school should be about; it's too touchy-feely, it's not "real learning." This can be seen in how little time and money affective pursuits get in a typical school day, and in the fact that when budgets are tight, they're among the first to get cut.

But when schools do not nurture, celebrate, validate, and *teach* affective ways of knowing, official school knowledge is reduced to the hard "cognitive" facts and life itself is reduced to that which can be quantified. This seriously threatens our freedom of thought and imagination. Concepts like beauty, love, power, intuition, cynicism, freedom, oppression, hate, equality, caring, collaboration, goodness, and community are eliminated or ignored, since they aren't measurable absolutes in the sense that 2+2=4. Not surprisingly, none of these ideas are on E. D. Hirsch's (1988) list of "what every American needs to know." This is probably because such things can't be tested in the way that "Toledo, OH" and "Donald Duck" and "Taft-Hartley Act" (which are all on the list) can be and because they inherently hold different meaning to different people, which works against the straight-transmission paradigm of schooling.

Consider the subject of history or social studies, which school horribly perverts into lists of names and dates and places. Any respected historian would tell you that history is *interpretation* and constant reinterpretation. As James Loewen (1995) points out, history is really more about *questions* than answers; it can be seen "not as a set of facts but a series of arguments, issues, and controversies" (37). What frame these issues, what give meaning and purpose to all knowledge, are not facts that exist in a vacuum, but meaning, what this knowledge *means* to all of us, and what we do with it, and how it impacts our lives, all of which intimately rely on—even require—human affect. We can add to this the view of the great historian Barbara Tuchman (1981a), who equated the work of the historian not to the scientist collecting facts and seeking truth, but to the *artist* employing creativity and imagination. What did Tuchman consider to be the most lasting achievement of humankind? Not science or technology or our militaries or our economies, but our *art*, which "opens our eyes, ears, and feelings to something beyond ourselves, something we cannot experience without the artist's vision and genius of his craft" (1981b, 236).

Elliot Eisner (1985, 1994) has written a great deal about school's neglect of affective ways of knowing and its false separation of cognition and affect. One of his strongest points is that cognition and affect are actually *inseparable*. When human beings make meaning, when they create sense of the world, there is no separation between their cognitive ways of knowing and their affective ways of knowing, as traditional schooling would have us believe. Knowing, according to Eisner (1994), is *experience*, and within our infinite experiences affect and cognition "interpenetrate just as mass and weight do. They are part of the same reality in human experience" (21). And the psychologist Jerome Bruner (1986) has written extensively of the "narrative mode" of thought and making sense of life. It is through *narrative* that we make sense of art and are led to "good stories, gripping drama, believable (though not necessarily 'true') historical accounts" (13). Children do not leave their affect at home during the school-day; it's just that school largely ignores it.

A few years ago some teachers and I were looking for something we could do that would involve all of our students. We wanted to extend community beyond the walls of our classrooms. After bouncing a myriad of ideas back and forth, we came up with the notion of watching the sunrise together. From this particular school it was a twenty-minute walk to a Lake Michigan beach. We set a date and sent notices home inviting families to come along. It was 6:00 in the morning when everyone arrived at school. The place was alive with exhilaration and anticipation. There were over one hundred students, half a dozen teachers, and a handful of parents, some of whom had brought their dogs along. The sky was clear, with stars aglow, and the early morning autumn air was brisk during our walk to the beach. Once there, we spread out and waited. Maybe twenty minutes passed, but it seemed like forever. Suddenly, as the sun in seemingly slow motion cracked the horizon, everyone swarmed to the shore with screams of excitement. Together we stood and watched the sun rise. It was an experience that I'll never forget, and it was some of the finest knowledge that I've ever shared with my students.

The Importance of Freedom

Americans hold their freedoms dearly. The freedom of speech, the freedom of movement and association, the freedom of our "pursuit of happiness." This is typically how our schools teach freedom. Like their limited interpretation of democracy, it is a very physical freedom, leaving immense voids in how freedom can be moral, intellectual, creative, communal. Freedom just may be the most important element of democracy, and yet our schools have reduced the idea to little more than historical and political slogans.

Perhaps the gravest danger that a system of schooling based on control offers is the abject neglect of the *freedom of imagination*. Cultivating the creativity and the imagination of children should be one of the driving forces of our schools. Yet, with our schools' predetermined lesson-after-lesson factory-model curriculums and behavioristic structures, imagination has little chance of survival inside our classrooms. The Game of School is the opposite of creating and imagining: standardized, rote, mind-numbing thinking that is rewarded and perpetuated with good grades and gold stars.

Few people have written about freedom as eloquently as Maxine Greene. To Greene, freedom is a *verb*, not a noun. It is largely about being "the 'author' of one's world," creating a "consciousness of possibility" (1988, 22–23). For Greene, this is really a *moral* freedom, one that can help us shape ourselves and give meaning to who we are and how we live with others. With this freedom of "wide-awakeness" (1978, 153) is the idea—perhaps even the responsibility—of *action*, of choosing not to live isolated, passive, conformist lives. *This* is the freedom that our schools and our teachers must nurture in our children and in ourselves, so we can free them (and us) to live thoughtful lives of importance, free them to imagine, to create, to define themselves, to think and to act, to make a better world.

Six

Learning Through Projects

The word "project" is perhaps the latest arrival to knock for admittance at the door of educational terminology. Shall we admit the stranger?
—WILLIAM HEARD KILPATRICK

The project method is the application of the principals of democracy.
—JAMES FLEMING HOSIC

I don't know when I first started using the word *project*, but to me, it offers the possibility of truly breaking free from traditional schooling, of making learning a meaningful and democratic experience. Obviously, *project* is just a word and, in a learning context, exactly what it refers to depends on who you talk to. I've seen different language that gets at a similar idea. Chris Stevenson and Judy Carr (1993) use *integrated studies*; Garth Boomer et al. (1992) use *negotiated curriculum*, as do Ingram and Worrall (1993); and George Wood (1992) and many others use the word *thematic*, but with the proliferation of packaged and marketed "theme units," this word has quickly become as misused as the word *learn*. To me, projects are open, long-term, integrative inquiries done in a social setting that are created and/or developed with much student input and ownership. I strive for our projects to be as *authentic* as possible, meaning they're for real purposes, using "real world" sources.

I like to build our class around two project times, one in the morning and one in the afternoon. The blocks of time are at least an hour, and I try to have at least two days a week where we have a ninety-minute or even two-hour period, so we can get a lot done. Big chunks of time are an absolute for projects. The project time in the morning is for students to explore topics that they've chosen to study, either on their own or collaboratively with other students. I see this as being their time to ask questions about the world, having been given the freedom to explore their personal interests. Developing a lifelong love for learning is at the heart of our morning project time. Our afternoon block is for projects the entire class works on together, usually in collaborative groups. But this schedule is never set in stone. Flexibility is built into every day.

The important thing to remember about projects is that there is not just one way to do them. Each teacher needs to approach the idea of projects in a way that fits their own context and their own comfort zone. Of course, the way each of us chooses to do projects should never be finalized either. I'm constantly making changes and experimenting with new ideas. In fact, what's presented here isn't the one way I do projects, but rather, one of the ways that I've done them. I'm always asking questions, reading about new (and old) ideas, speaking to others, writing, observing, experimenting, conducting my own teacher "action research." The way in which projects are undertaken also changes with the students I have. All kids and all classes are different, and it's important to customize projects to suit the needs of each unique group.

What Are Projects?

I have never liked the image that the word *unit* brings to mind. *Units* are finite, predetermined, externally created, and "taught." There may be some freedom built into them (a unit on the American Civil War might allow a child to select a specific part of the conflict to study), but the strict, finite structure remains. The learning that takes place is usually not seen as being the result of social interaction, and the knowledge is usually highly teacher-, textbook-, and official-curriculum-directed. In units, as I have seen them implemented, the learning "outcomes," "goals," and "objectives," as well as all of the "lessons" along the way, have been preplanned down to the textbook readings, worksheets, and required final product or test. All of this leaves very little room for free exploration of a topic or idea.

Projects, in stark contrast, are *open-ended*. This means that I could not possibly predetermine everything that we will do or everything that will be learned, because most of the learning happens spontaneously as a natural part of the social interaction. The learning that takes place involves not just the content or topic being studied, but the *process itself*, the *totality of the experience*. This is where the true value lies. In studying a project topic, children and teachers interact with one another as a purposeful community. No longer is the process simply a means to an end. It is knowledge in itself. This vision not only offers different methods for teaching, it profoundly changes the *purpose of school*. The ideals and attitudes that are learned through the democratic process become an important part of the intended curriculum.

When kids are working on their projects, very few of them can be found sitting at their desks. Some are at tables, some are on the floor, some are sitting on a couch, some are working at a computer, some are out in the hall, and some may be in the library looking for resources. I rarely stand before them addressing them as an entire class at these times. I am bouncing from student to student, asking questions, making suggestions, challenging their thinking. Again, more than a teacher, I am a coach, a guide, a facilitator, a resource, and especially a fellow learner. The last point is critical. Since projects are open-ended I have no idea where any student's inquiry might lead. That means that I can no longer be the only expert. I'm an expert in a few things, and my students have expertise of their own, and together we'll seek out other experts. When a student is studying nuclear energy and no one in the room, including me, knows much about it, we are all learning about nuclear energy together.

The fact that projects are open-ended does not mean that I do no planning for them, or that I expect the children to "discover" their learning for themselves. Once again, I play a crucial role in the process. I am the one who is primarily responsible for creating the environment, for opening up the possibilities of experience, for helping my students learn how to learn. That means that I need to think about the directions my students can take, where they can go for information, and how they can best assimilate the new knowledge. I must also devise minilessons and discussions, and select common reading or journal writing for the class to do. Admittedly, there is not much formal planning involved in projects. I tend to scribble my ideas down on yellow legal pads. The "plan" for most project times is simply to "continue projects."

I adapted the project minilessons I use from Nancie Atwell's (1987) and Lucy McCormick Calkins's (1986) minilessons for reading and writing workshop. Minilessons are short, whole-class demonstrations or lectures, rarely longer than ten minutes, and often taking only five minutes, conducted at the start of project time. The idea is to keep my direct instruction to the class to an absolute minimum. My experiences, both as a teacher and as a student, have taught me that lecturing rarely results in meaningful learning. When I was in school and had to sit and listen to the teacher rattle on ad infinitum, my mind, as quickly as possible, went elsewhere. The less time I spend lecturing to the class, the more time we can spend actively working on our projects. I usually like to conduct minilessons with everyone sitting on the rug before me so we're together as a group. Minilessons can come from an official curriculum, but most of mine just come from me. I'm always asking myself what can help my students with their projects. Here are some project minilessons that I've done:

how to use an atlas	how to take notes	interview skills
how to use a book's index	ideas for projects	finding resources
what a quality project looks like	collaborative skills	using a telephone

The length of time that student-created projects last depends on the project a student chooses to do. Some have finished a project in two weeks while others have taken four months to bring theirs to completion. Whole-class projects are usually in the six-to-eight-week range. We take this much time because quality learning and quality work do *take time*. We also do this because as I've already written, *less is more*. Our schools try to teach so much stuff, it's not possible to meaningfully assimilate much of it. This is what Lynn Stoddard (1992) means when he refers to our schools' "curriculum worship." Schools are so obsessed with curriculum and adding more and more stuff, that all we do is keep watering down more and more knowledge, making it less and less meaningful. One good, long project is worth far more than an entire year of lockstep, bit-by-bit, textbook-filled curriculum.

Projects are also inherently democratic because they never rate and rank or sort children like the dominant paradigm does with ability grouping, tracking, and "gifted" schooling. One of the most beautiful and naturally occurring characteristics of learning through projects is that there is no such thing as "fifth-grade projects" or "high-track projects" and "low-track projects" and "gifted projects." All there are are *projects*, with everyone working at their own pace and at their own developmental location. Rather than forcing every child to fit the same mold, projects fit each child according to who they are and where they are. Because of this, projects perfectly lend themselves to Howard Gardner's (1983, 1991) theory of multiple intelligences. Rather than teaching everyone in the same way, or having them show what they studied in the same medium (such as written reports), projects allow children to learn in the ways each of them learns best and to show what they've learned via an unlimited variety of mediums. My students have written reports and stories and fictional diaries, made videos, danced, built models, worked with computers, conducted science experiments, performed plays and monologues, created posters and fliers and books, conducted interviews, created surveys, and more. Projects allow human imagination and creativity to soar.

Self-Directed Learning

Central to learning through projects is giving children the trust and the responsibility of directing their own learning. This means that for most of the day, students are working on their own, without me hovering over them. It's not unusual at all for students to work unsupervised in the hall, where they have more room. Understandably, the idea of giving children this freedom and inviting spontaneity into the classroom is scary to many teachers, since it so strongly works against the dominant paradigm of school that they themselves experienced, with its emphasis on order and control. I'm not expecting student freedom and classroom spontaneity to be top on the wish-list of most teachers. But then again, when we're doing projects, I am not freeing my students to go climb trees. There are expected purposes to what we're doing, and if it's not working for either one student or for the entire class, then we need to stop and talk about what's happening. Remember, one of the main purposes for giving my students the responsibility of doing projects is for them to learn responsibility.

When I speak to educators about projects, I often hear the same comment: "Different people learn in different ways, so this method won't work for everyone." I agree. But I do believe it can work for *virtually everyone*. I believe the primary reason some kids have trouble learning in a more active, self-directed, social, and osmotic way in school is because they have never been allowed to learn this way in school; their habits of mind are so entrenched, making the transition is difficult. How ironic this is when we consider how much these same children have learned in exactly this way from life outside of school! The vast majority of children are more than capable of learning in this way, because it is based on how human beings learn *naturally*. Project-based classrooms accept that most human beings learn best in the ways I described in Chapter 3. By nature we're social, active, and learning animals. That's what makes us human. John Dewey believed that the purpose of school shouldn't be to prepare children for later life, it should be life itself. That's the goal with projects. To tear down the walls of the classroom and to let life flourish.

I also accept that for some children, just like for some adults, functioning and learning in this type of environment, for a variety of reasons, can be difficult. For students who have serious difficulty during project time I make the necessary adaptations, including giving them more structure. I do what I need to do in each unique situation and with each unique student. But my goal is always the same: to help kids become self-directed learners by giving them as much freedom as they can responsibly accept.

Projects in a Social Context

Projects lend themselves perfectly to the kind of social learning that I advocated in Chapter 4. As Figure 6-1 shows, it's usually not quiet and orderly in the classroom during project time. People are moving and talking and doing. To demand quiet and stillness would be to work against the natural flow of the process. It should also come as no surprise that student talk during project time is not solely about their projects. Is the talk of adults during their time at work solely about their jobs? Of course it isn't. There's idle chatter about plans for the night or the weekend, there's talk of family and friends, of sadness and happiness, of last night's football game or concert, of our angst about our jobs and our bosses and our ambitions. This talk is natural. It helps the day go by. It satisfies our urge to be social. It's pleasurable. An honest teacher would probably tell you that they wish there was another adult in their classroom, someone they could communicate (and commiserate) with during the day. If adults make idle chatter a part of their own day, why does school make children's idle chatter such a high crime? When kids talk, they're only doing what comes naturally.

While students are at work on their projects, our room is alive with activity and thought. It's an exciting place to be. Children are talking to one another, sharing ideas and knowledge and language, and (hopefully) helping each other. Some of the talk is friendly chatter, but most of it concerns their projects, their thinking, and the process of learning itself. The learning that takes place is not a transmission from teacher-as-expert to student-as-empty-vessel, but the *meaningful and cumulative osmotic learning that we experience in our everyday lives.* This is so difficult for most people to have trust in. Wells and Chang-Wells (1992), who have done extensive research in classrooms that nurture learning in an active and social context, wrote:

> Learning that is concerned with understanding—rather than with the memorization of isolated bits of information or the application of a simple algorithm—is not an all-or-nothing affair. On the contrary, it involves the *cumulative construction of knowledge*

FIGURE 6-1 *Morning project time*

over many encounters with relevant problems, with the learner bringing what was learned on previous occasions to make new connections with the information presented in each new problem and thereby making more and better sense of the phenomena in question. (41, emphasis added)

This may be the key to understanding the values of a project-based democratic classroom. Our learning is not all-or-nothing. It's not about me teaching verbs on Tuesday and the students either getting verbs or not getting verbs. It is the cumulative and holistic experience over time: weeks, months, years. Our classroom is a rich, intellectually minded extension of the world beyond our school walls. Throughout the school year, with kids finishing one project, presenting it to the class, and moving on to the next, our classroom slowly creates a social ethos that lives and breathes life, because so many of the questions and topics of life are made a part of our collective classroom experience.

An Integrative Curriculum

Integrating curriculum has been one of the more successful progressive reforms of the last ten years. The idea is a rather simple one, and one that makes basic sense to a lot of people, especially teachers, which is why I think it's had success. Unfortunately, curriculum integration as it is usually implemented is a lot like cooperative learning. Neither innovation seriously questions or breaks away from the dominant paradigm of schooling. When teachers integrate curriculum, it usually means something like having students read *Johnny Tremain* while they're studying the American Revolution. This looks like we're significantly changing the way we teach. In the dominant paradigm, reading a novel is rarely connected with studying history, especially in elementary school. So curriculum integration certainly looks different from what's traditionally been done, but it really isn't. This thinking often continues to emphasize discrete, predetermined facts and outcomes, and the academic disciplines remain separate. There's usually one time period reserved for working on *Johnny Tremain* and its related assignments and another time period for working on the Revolution.

With projects, curriculum integration is built into the learning process with students working within a variety of disciplines at any one time. "Integration" is unnecessary, because the focus of study is already a whole. The idea of integrating curriculum is a falsely constructed one. In order for you to integrate something, it needs to be separate in the first place. The reason school needs to integrate curriculum is because *it falsely separated it from the start*. But with projects, we *start with the whole*. Therefore, there's nothing to integrate. When doing projects, the integration of multiple disciplines occurs naturally, just like it does in real life. There are no "subjects" in life. We're not involved with just one discipline or limited to a single way of knowing. In Chapter 3 I asked you to think of something that you always wanted to learn. I can't imagine that there is anything you could want to comprehend that would not encompass multiple disciplines. Whether you want to learn to play the drums, write romance stories, analyze the causes of the stock market crash of 1929, understand molecular structure, or build a barn, you will be constantly working within and constantly moving back and forth between a wide variety of disciplines and ways of knowing. Life is not divided into neat segments like it is in school. School compartmentalizes because of its factory and assembly-line roots, which dictate that teaching kids knowledge be done in a piecemeal fashion.

It is my job to make integrative suggestions to my students as they work on their projects. I do that by helping them *pull out* (as opposed to *put in*) various ways of knowing from the "whole" of their project. Most of the time my students are more than happy to incorporate a new idea into their thinking. For example, last year Nate was doing a project on his favorite cars, Volvos. I knew that he was struggling with his conceptual understanding of fractions, so I suggested he include some kind of survey in his project. Since he considered Volvos to be the safest car (a perception intended by the company's advertising campaign), he surveyed the class, asking them, "What car do you think is the safest?" He made a chart showing the fractional breakdown of responses as a part of his project. Nate didn't do this during math time, but during project time.

I get the word *integrative* (as opposed to integra*ted*) from James Beane (1992, 1993), who considers integrating curriculum to be a great deal more than simply reading *Johnny Tremain* while studying the Revolutionary War. To Beane, an integrative curriculum is as much about cultural awareness, practicing democracy, constructivist learning, and human dignity as it is about bringing multiple disciplines together. He writes:

> The process associated with the integrative approach involves continuous collaborative planning with young people as well as an end to authoritarian rule by adults. Moreover, the approach emphasizes inquiry, cooperative problem-solving, and the personal and collective construction of meaning. Clearly, this kind of process brings to life the concept of authentic democratic principles while dignifying the place of young people in school. (1993, 22)

Central to the process of the integrative curriculum is the involvement of the students themselves, engaging their lives, their ideas, their thoughts, their concerns, their opinions, their cultures, their realities. In this view, curriculum integration is more than merely sticking math and writing and history together, but rather, it is a holistic approach subsumed under a democratic belief system that values the life and the mind of the child.

Transformative Pedagogy and Projects

In the previous chapter I wrote of critical, or transformative, pedagogy, which involves bringing issues such as power, economics, race, gender, class, violence, and the environment into our classroom. It is certainly possible to make these issues an important part of projects. A student-created project on dolphins included their being killed by tuna nets; a video game project looked at violence; another project looked at the poaching of endangered species in Africa; and a project on Louis XIV included the class system of eighteenth-century France. Before I was familiar with critical pedagogy, I was less likely to nudge my students in those directions. In hindsight, when Barrie studied the U.S. presidents, I would have encouraged her to ask why they have all been white, Christian, and male; when Julia studied nuclear energy, I would have suggested looking at its potential dangers, including Chernobyl and Three Mile Island; when Ross researched army tanks, I would have suggested he ask questions about their cost and their role in war, and perhaps the idea of war itself; when David studied the

New York Stock Exchange, I would have suggested he ask questions about who owns stock in this country and who doesn't. When I make suggestions such as these, I'm not advocating certain political positions, but trying to help my students see the politics and economics embedded in so many issues that are a part of our lives.

Many student-created projects don't easily lend themselves to critical issues, and that's just fine. There's great value in learning about frogs simply to learn about frogs. Such inquiries can help build respect for the complexity and beauty of life; they can help children develop a love for lifelong learning; they can help kids learn how to learn; they can help them to interact purposefully and respectfully with other people; and they can especially encourage them to *ask questions*, to look around their world and ask why or how or when or what if? This is one of the greatest potentials of allowing students to direct their own projects. It can encourage inquiry to become a lifelong habit of mind. Of course, it can also help kids learn more about frogs.

Whole-class projects are the perfect opportunity to add critical components to a topic or theme being studied. For example, our class is currently doing a project on our own city of Chicago. Part of the project involves looking at the city's problems and considering what can be done to improve them. We've already interviewed people who live and work in the city, and have made a long class list of the problems we see Chicago having, such as poverty, potholes, ineffective schools, gangs, racial conflict, violence, teenage pregnancy, and pollution. We'll look into some of these problems, discuss them, and try to understand them better and consider how we might contribute to them ourselves. After that the kids will break into groups and write and perform plays to dramatize the issues and offer possible solutions.

The Project Plan

Before starting a project, a student must complete a project plan. Project plans are written on notebook paper. (Younger kids could use a prewritten form.) They must be neat with correct grammar and spelling. I explain project plans to my students by comparing them to the blueprints an architect makes for a building. Before you start the building, before you even dig the hole, you need to have a plan so you know what you're doing. Whether they're doing a self-created project or a class project, students need to decide on the following:

- a project title
- who will be working on the project
- questions they have about the topic
- possible resources
- possible final product (how they will show the class what they studied)
- three dates: when they'll start the project, when they'll finish their research, and when they'll present their finished project to the class

This plan is similar to the four questions Jon Cook (1992) suggests be asked and answered when selecting a topic as part of a "negotiated curriculum": "What do we know already?; What do we want, and need, to find out?; How will we go about finding out?; and, How will we know, and show, what we've found out when we've finished?" (21). These questions make perfect sense with respect to school projects, since these are the kinds of questions we ask ourselves (usually tacitly) when we're tackling a problem outside of school. Here's a project plan that Fran, a fourth grader, wrote:

Title: Endangered Species in Africa
Who's Working On It: I'm working on this alone.
Questions I have:
    How and why are species becoming extinct?
    What do they eat?
    Why do people kill them?
    What are they?
Possible Resources:
    the library
    zoos
    the World Wildlife Federation
    Ms. Deckert [a teacher who had been to Africa]
Final Product: Make a poster or a diary of someone in Africa.
Dates:
    Begin Research: Thursday, the 13th of October
    End Research: Friday, the 28th of October
    Present to the Class: Monday, the 14th of November

It's not uncommon for dates to change along the way. As students get into a project, things may take longer (or shorter) than expected or they may find an interesting new direction to head in. If a student can support a date change with good reasons, I'll go along with it. A terrific teacher I know, Brenda Krober, whose classroom is almost entirely based on student-created projects, has an additional requirement for project plans: a parent signature. This is a nice idea that I may add.

For student-created projects, once a student finishes their project plan they need to get it approved by me. Often I'll make suggestions, such as additional resources for them to check out, another question or two to ask, or I might disagree with them about their dates, saying that they've given themselves too much time or too little time. Whatever it is, we'll talk about it for a few minutes and they'll either redo the plan or I'll approve it as is. I also check it for grammar and spelling. Once their project plan is approved, they record their name and presentation date on a large sixty-day calendar that's posted on the wall. This way everyone knows when a project presentation will be presented. I allow two presentations a day. Typically, about three projects are presented each week.

Conducting Project Research

Most of the class time for projects is devoted to doing research in a variety of forms. While one student looks for a resource in the library, another might be at her desk taking notes; while one student is lying on the floor reading a book, another may be on the class telephone trying to locate someone who can answer a question; while one student interviews an expert on their topic, another is writing a letter to a company, requesting information. The best way for someone to become a better researcher is by doing research. As the students are engaged in their various research endeavors, I am moving from student to student, asking questions, nudging them in new directions, and teaching research skills. If a student needs to locate a city in Brazil, I am presented with a perfect opportunity to show her how to use an atlas, with its index and grid coordinates. If another student can't find information on uranium, it's my chance to show him a table of the elements. If I come across a student taking notes in full sentences and paragraphs, I can demonstrate to her how to take notes in an abbreviated and organized form, such as Dan did for his project on ants, shown in Figure 6-2 .

For most kids in school the primary sources for information are textbooks and the teacher, and the primary source for school research is the library. But when I have a question I need to answer as an adult, I rarely go to the library. It's there if I need it, but it's not usually my first choice. When I have a question that I need to answer (or at least supply with options), I start with the understanding that *the world* is my resource. Once I finished school, my primary source for information was no longer the library, it was the entire world. Anything less limits my access to knowledge and the possibilities available to me.

Kids spend so much time in libraries poring over reference books because this is what is expected of them in the Game of School. Fifth graders go to the library not so much to expand their minds as to prepare them for their required library work in sixth grade, in middle school, in high school, in college. It's a never-ending cycle: school prepares you for more school. Not that this is all bad. It's important to know how to use a library, and there are some professions that require a lot of what we could call book learning. But limiting school research to the library limits access to knowledge and limits our experiences. There's truly an infinite amount of knowledge to be gained beyond our school walls, and there's no reason why all children shouldn't have access to this information. Of course, schools are gaining ground with the introduction of the Internet and the World Wide Web into the classroom. But then again, computer resources require money, which a lot of schools don't have.

Before I put a computer in a single classroom, I would have a telephone installed for student use. After all, the phone is my primary research tool in life. I might use my computer to get information through the World Wide Web (which I recently did when I was looking to buy a car), but the telephone is where I usually start my inquiry. Our telephone directly connects our classroom to the outside world. On some days there's a waiting list to use the telephone. (The waiting list wasn't my idea. One day when there was a high demand for the phone, some students—on their own—posted a sheet of paper and started the list. That's problem solving in a real-life context.)

The classroom telephone offers a perfect example of how the project process helps us learn—communally (Figure 6-3). Using our telephone has led to some conflict. Now, conflict is not necessarily a bad thing. I consider it a natural and important

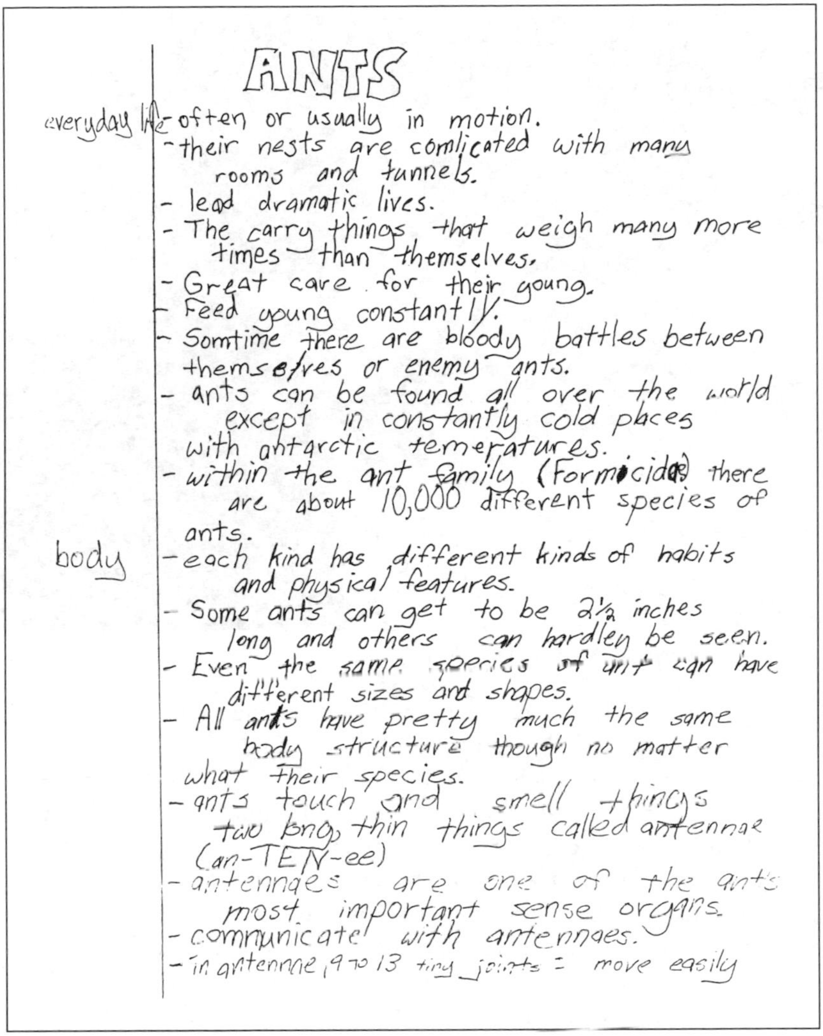

ANTS

everyday life — often or usually in motion.
- their nests are comlicated with many rooms and tunnels.
- lead dramatic lives.
- The carry things, that weigh many more times than themselves.
- Great care for their young.
- Feed young constantly.
- Somtime there are bloody battles between themselves or enemy ants.
- ants can be found all over the world except in constantly cold places with antarctic temeratures.
- within the ant family (Formicide) there are about 10,000 different species of ants.

body
- each kind has different kinds of habits and physical features.
- Some ants can get to be 2½ inches long and others can hardley be seen.
- Even the same species of ant can have different sizes and shapes.
- All ants have pretty much the same body structure though no matter what their species.
- ants touch and smell things two long, thin things called antennae (an-TEN-ee)
- antennaes are one of the ants most important sense organs.
- communicate with antennaes.
- in antennae, 9 to 13 tiny joints = move easily

FIGURE 6-2   *Some of Dan's notes on ants*

part of democracy and community. How we handle conflict is what matters. Do we let it hurt us or do we let it help us? When telephone-related problems come up, we sit in our circle on the rug and talk about them. We've had to discuss (and model) how to politely make a call and answer a telephone, which is knowledge that not all kids, even older kids, have. We've had to decide on the appropriate amount of time a student could talk for. We've also had to decide what to do if a caller got a busy signal or was put on hold. Do they go to the end of the waiting list? Do they let the next person in line use the telephone and then try again? Do they call the next day? And what if a student gets a call back after they've finished and it's someone else's turn to use the phone? These questions and issues do not have a single or easy answer. They all bring

FIGURE 6-3   *Hannah using the class telephone*

up issues of fairness and the common good. It's rather amazing how much we might learn about democracy from something as ordinary as a telephone.

I want my students to understand that the world is out there for them to learn from. I also want them to understand that the world is full of people who would love to help children (and teachers) learn. I remember when Michael was struggling with a project on human eyesight. He had trouble understanding what he was reading and didn't know what to do about it. The fact is that I don't know much about eyes and eyesight either; I'm not an expert. But there are experts out there. I reminded Michael that there was a hospital three blocks from the school. He immediately went to our telephone and by the next day he had scheduled a meeting to visit the hospital and interview an ophthalmologist. My students have rarely been turned down by someone for either an over-the-phone interview or a personal interview. I like the idea of class visitors too; rarely does someone turn down our invitation to visit our classroom and share their knowledge and experiences with us. Here are some of the experts that we've encountered either by telephone or in person:

- workers at animal-related organizations, such as the National Zoo, the Lincoln Park Zoo, the Shedd Aquarium, and the World Wildlife Federation
- other educators at our school, such as the science teacher and the computer teacher
- local university professors
- authors

- officials from local, state, and national government agencies, such as the City of Chicago, a water pumping station, the state conservation office, the Air Force, the CIA
- community members, such as residents of a local nursing home
- family members who have specialized knowledge
- employees of corporations and organizations, such as car dealerships, a candy manufacturer, hospitals, the American Cancer Society, local television stations, museums
- other professionals: a therapist, dentist, architect, doctor, horse trainer, meteorologist

When I first began to do projects, I adapted Nancie Atwell's (1987) "status-of-the-class" sheet, which she uses for writing workshop, to keep track of my students' work. The sheet is a simple one. The students' names go down the left side and the days of the week across the top. Lines are drawn to create a grid. Before project time I would conduct a quick roll call and each student would provide a short response (such as "take notes" or "call a doctor for an interview") on what they'd be working on. As each student responded, I would jot down their activity in the appropriate grid space. Even though this eventually took us only ten minutes to get through, I felt it was hurting our momentum. I wanted the kids to be able to get right to work. So, I decided to try something new. I've begun filling out a status sheet *after* project time by myself. I take five minutes and mark who I met with, record what we did, and note the students that I need to connect with the next day. There are advantages to doing this before project time, such as helping kids learn responsibility and to plan their time, but I decided to try something new. I can always go back to what I was doing before.

Project Presentations

All projects end with some form of exhibition. Once students finish a student-created project, they make a short presentation to the class as Daniel is doing with his project on gold in Figure 6-4. In the first few months of the year I conduct a few minilessons on creating a key-word outline. Students are asked to produce such an outline for each of their presentations. The purpose of the presentation is not for them to go over their entire project, because there isn't enough time to do that. I consider presentations to be more for the benefit of the presenter than the audience. Sharing a project is a formal public offering. It is the culmination of a student's thinking. Their presentations also give them experience speaking before a group of people in an organized, thoughtful, and respectful way. The goal is not for the audience to learn everything that the presenter learned—that's unreasonable given the amount of time devoted to the presentations—but rather for the final project to be made public, to become a part of our cumulative classroom experience. Audiences benefit from presentations by learning to respond respectfully and by being exposed to an infinite number of topics and ideas.

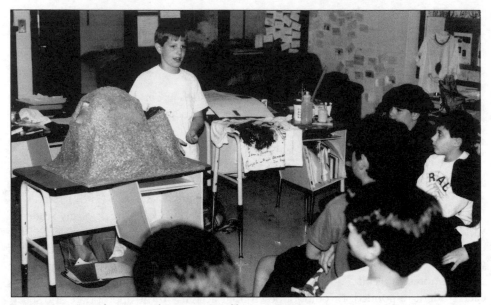

FIGURE 6-4   *Daniel presenting his project on gold*

Whole-class projects can result in a variety of final presentations. Students can either present their projects separately to the class or they can put them out all at once, in the form of a class show. Chris Stevenson and Judy Carr (1993) suggest that class projects end with a "culminating event," which I see as a *celebration*. This event is an acknowledgment not only of the fact that you finished, but that you finished *together*, as a community who shared and studied a common theme. When we brought to a close our whole-class project on Europe, we put all of our projects out for public display and had a celebratory feast cooked for us by Amanda and David, who studied Greek cooking for the project, and by Zac, who studied Italian cooking (Figure 6-5).

Project Assessment

Once again I'd like to refer back to Chapter 3, when I asked you to think of something that you would like to spend a year learning if you were financially supported the whole way. Now I have another question for you. The year is over and now I come to you and say, "Show me what you learned." How would you do that? Of all the possible ways for you to demonstrate your growth, what ways would you choose?

I've asked this question of many adults, and no one has ever said that they would take a test or write a report. If you learned how to fly, you would take me up in a plane; if you learned how to paint, you would show me your paintings, maybe the paintings of others that influenced you; if you learned about another culture, you would show me artifacts and tell me stories from that culture; if you learned about the Vietnam War, you would show me models and diagrams and pictures, and

FIGURE 6-5   *Our Europe feast celebration*

explain, possibly through stories and biographies, what the significance of the war is to you now.

My point here should be obvious. In the real world of learning, tests and reports and worksheets aren't the most meaningful way to understand a person's growth, they're just *convenient* ways in a system of schooling that's based on mass production. Frank Smith (1988) has written that the single greatest danger in education is our preoccupation with *evaluation*. Our schools are obsessed not only with curriculum, but with evaluation. This does not mean that assessment is bad. During project time I'm constantly evaluating my students, primarily through Yetta Goodman's (1978) notion of "kid watching." Since our classroom is so highly social, since I'm constantly interacting and talking with my students, I have a much clearer picture of where they are and what they need. When children are assessed within the dominant paradigm, the context is one of quantification. If there aren't any numbers, then the assessment isn't given credibility. Kid watching is the antithesis of a quantified assessment; it's about watching and listening and interacting with children in authentic learning contexts. It's about paying attention to the details of classroom life and the small connections children make.

Changing curriculum demands changing assessment. If you allow children and classroom culture to play an important role in curriculum creation, you can't fall back on prepackaged assessment. With projects, assessment is *authentic*. This means that there is no need for any external tool to evaluate how someone has done. Our projects are not only our projects, *they are also our assessments*. I assess my students by looking at their work, by talking with them, by making informal observations along the way. I don't need any means of appraisal outside of my own observations and the student's work, which is demonstration enough of their thinking, their growth, their knowledge, and their attitudes over time. This paradigm of assessment has been highly criticized for being unofficial, subjective, and touchy-feely. But there is no such thing as an objective assessment! *All assessment, even test-based, is subjective.* The difference is that when we assess children within the dominant paradigm, we end up with numbers and percents, but when we assess children within a democratic and naturalistic belief system, we end up with *human beings*.

To be honest, I've struggled with finding a practical and meaningful way to give feedback to my students about their projects. I've recently begun something new. I've created a simple "Project Feedback" form that I write comments on, in addition to offering my students short verbal comments after their presentations. Since there are a lot of projects, I keep my writing to a minimum, generally responding in three areas:

1. What I really love about the project
2. Areas for improvement
3. Questions that come to mind for further exploration

I don't think any more feedback is necessary. Most of my remarks will be in area number one, emphasizing the good. I'll also limit the second point to at most two areas for improvement. This way the student and I can focus their growth on just a few ideas or skills. The last question is my way of suggesting that we're never really finished learning about something. Answers to one set of questions should lead us to another set of questions.

I also have students assess themselves. Once finished with a project, students fill out a self-evaluation form, answering these four questions:

1. What have I learned from doing this project?
2. If someone was going to do this same project and came to me for help, what advice would I give them?
3. What examples of high quality are in my project?
4. How did I challenge myself doing this project?

Self-evaluations are a nice way to introduce the idea of *metacognition* to children. To be metacognitive is to be conscious of your consciousness, to think about your thinking. I don't see many adults being metacognitive these days, let alone children. But metacognition has great value for democracy and community. It can focus people and help them to see the world around them; it can help people have more respect for the details of life; it can nurture the idea of learning for the sake of learning and thinking for the value and beauty of thought; and it can encourage people to live more thoughtful, democratic lives.

Student-Created Projects

Students should be given a part of each school day to explore an interest or a question that originates in their own mind. The idea behind student-created projects is simple: kids are allowed to learn about what they want to learn about. This does not mean that they can do whatever they want. My expectation is that the questions they want to explore are purposeful and have value. This doesn't mean that they need to be purposeful to me, but rather that they contain some overall value to the growth of the child's mind. I also expect the students to work hard, to put a lot of thought into their work, to create a quality final product to demonstrate what they've studied, and to do all of this while being a caring member of the classroom community. All of these expectations form a kind of classroom-based set of standards.

Our projects, and especially our student-created projects, are based on what William Heard Kilpatrick (1918) called *purposeful acts*, which "[consist] of purposive activity and not mere drifting." Kilpatrick wrote, "As the purposeful act is thus the typical unit of the worthy life in a democratic society, so also should it be made the typical unit of school procedure" (323). To Kilpatrick, purposeful acts emanate from *inside a person* to bring a personally meaningful and relevant goal to its natural conclusion, especially within a social environment. Like Dewey, Kilpatrick also envisioned the classroom as being an "embryonic society." And note Kilpatrick's words, "not mere drifting." With projects, kids are not wandering aimlessly around the classroom trying to keep themselves busy. Their work has a clear direction. In response to the question of how much freedom children should be given to pursue their projects, I agree completely with Kilpatrick's answer: "As much as they can use wisely" (1925, 210).

In our morning project time kids can ask their own questions such as, What's a black hole? or What was life like for Native Americans? or Why are people killing elephants in Africa? or What's the life of a hummingbird like? or Who was Beethoven? Kilpatrick (1925) wrote, in the form of a light-hearted dialogue, about giving children the freedom to develop their own plans for their learning:

> "Don't you think that the teacher should often supply the plan? Take a boy planting corn, for example; think of the waste of land and fertilizer and effort. Science has worked out better plans than a boy can make."
>
> "And in such as case you would advocate furnishing the boy with the best plan the teacher could find or devise?"
>
> "Yes, wouldn't you?"

"It depends on what you seek. If you wish corn, give the boy a plan. But if you wish boy rather than corn, that is, if you wish to educate the boy to think and plan for himself, then let him make his own plan." (212)

Most of the time students come up with very clear ideas to pursue. But if a student wants to do a project that I see little value in, we'll talk about it. I'll work with them to create a meaningful project out of their original idea. That's a major purpose of mine in student-created projects: to help students bring clarity to their ideas and questions. I remember when a fifth-grade student, Jon, told me he had a new project. He wanted to "watch marshmallows go poof." Not surprisingly, I was skeptical. But I didn't immediately discount his idea, either. I wanted to know more. Here's how our conversation went:

ME: What do you mean you want to "watch marshmallows go poof"?
JON: I want to bring some marshmallows to class and hold them into a flame and watch them go poof.
ME: Why? I don't see a lot of purpose in that.
JON: Because it's a chemical reaction. What happens to the marshmallow.
ME: A chemical reaction? How do you know that?
JON: My mother told me.
ME: I think it's a great idea to study chemical reactions. But if that's what you want to do, Jon, then you should start with that idea: What's a chemical reaction?

And that's the question Jon explored. Once his project plan was done, he went to an expert in chemical reactions, the middle school science teacher, who pointed him in some directions that I could not have pointed him in. In his presentation Jon explained how rust is the result of a chemical reaction, and using the language of chemistry, he put its chemical composition on the board and explained it to the class. After that he actually showed the class a simple chemical reaction using materials given to him by the science teacher. All of this came from wanting to watch marshmallows go poof. The project may not have been what Jon initially intended it to be, but it did teach him about chemical reactions, which is what he wanted to learn. Working together, we shaped a project that fulfilled his interests.

Students have explored hundreds of topics, including historical figures and events, animals, scientific ideas and experiments, television and video games, inventions, sports, biographies, social issues, nature and the environment, poetry, computers, and careers. There are also personal opportunities presented by these projects. For example, for one of his projects, Andrew tutored a first grader in reading. His written assessment of his student was some of the best writing he had done all year. Offering children the freedom to explore their own ideas truly opens up limitless opportunities.

I usually begin each year by asking the class what they would like to learn about. We have a class brainstorming session, and as they call out ideas, I write them down on a large sheet of paper. For those who think children have no interest in learning about the world, I offer a list of students' ideas generated on the first day of school:

the Alamo	stars	mosquitoes	different solar systems
butterflies	twins	cowboys	the American Civil War
forests	bacteria	oxygen	electricity
airplanes	computers	politics	animal habitats
dinosaurs	horses	rain forests	black holes
architecture	fungi	our solar system	batteries
cars	gas		

Any one of these ideas could have been the subject of a very meaningful project. By the end of this year, students had done ten projects from this original list and had completed more than eighty projects in all.

When children are allowed to select topics to study, a classroom becomes an amazingly rich environment. Those eighty topics probably would not have been a part of our classroom and perhaps our lives if we didn't have this opportunity. By allowing a classroom to thrive on the unlimited ideas of the children, and fueled by a highly social learning environment, we become immersed in the language of learning and ideas. We are seeing, talking, and hearing the language, images, and symbols of black holes and bacteria, computers and rain forests, twins and the Alamo. To offer an idea of the richness of the social environment of the classroom, look at the student-created projects that were being worked on simultaneously in our classroom last year:

cheetahs	the CIA	box turtles
the history of pencils	Georgia O'Keeffe	becoming a teacher
dinosaurs	architecture	the space shuttle
bats	giant pandas	the court system
Ludwig von Beethoven	roof shingles	the history of the atomic bomb
jaguars	dolphins	artificial intelligence
the history of pizza	endangered species of Africa	
Northwestern Native American Indians		

Our class has a huge "Project Board" on one of our walls. At the start of the year, everyone (including me) makes a personalized name card that gets laminated and then stapled to the wall. On a cabinet nearby are blank four-by-nine-inch cards that students use when they start a new project. They write their topic on the card and pin it next to their name on the wall. This makes for a great visual presentation of the work we're doing as a class. (See Figure 6-6)

Following are short descriptions of three student-created projects. I've selected them because I feel they're representational of our classwork. Some projects work out better than others, and admittedly, these are three that turned out well. Just because students are self-directed doesn't mean they're always motivated to do their best. Student-created projects or not, school is still largely about work, and just like adults at times, kids aren't always excited about hard work. As I've already said, democratic

FIGURE 6-6 *Our project board showing all of our current student-created projects*

classrooms are messy places. This kind of teaching isn't easy, and can at times be frustrating when things aren't working smoothly. But for me, allowing children to create and pursue projects of their own choosing is life affirming. My job becomes so much more enjoyable and interesting and challenging. No two students are the same, no two projects are the same, no two days are the same. Every day I go into school knowing that I'll have many experiences that I didn't plan for, that arose out of the minds of children and the infinite spontaneous moments of a classroom community of learners.

Claude Monet

Susan, a fifth grader, did this project on the impressionist painter Claude Monet, one of her favorite artists. She loved Monet's paintings and wanted to know more about him. That's the beauty of student-created projects. They aren't primarily academic. More than anything, they originate from a simple curiosity or love that a child has. This can be seen in two other projects Susan completed, one on butterflies and the other on the history of pizza.

In addition to using the three books on Monet that Susan listed in her bibliography, she went to the Art Institute of Chicago with her mother to look at some of Monet's paintings (a nice example of using the outside world for our learning). Her

August 17, 1876

Dear Diary,

Today I start writing in you. I recieved you as a present from my Maman.

I am Blanche Hoschede.

I live here near Paris with my three sisters. Suzanne, Germaine, and Marthe. I also have a brother named Jacuas.

Monsiere Monet is an artist who paints impressionist paintings. My pa pa admires that kind of artistry, so he invited Monsieure Monet to come paint the panels of one of the rooms, and my pa pa will pay him. Monsieure Monet says that he is very grateful because his wife Camille is ill and he does not have much money left.

Au revoir,
Blanche

FIGURE 6-7 *A page from Susan's diary for her Monet project*

final product had two parts, a short report on Monet's painting and a fictional diary of Blanche Hochede (Figure 6-7), who knew Monet as a young girl and later married his son.

A number of students have written fictional diaries like this to communicate factual information. Brian wrote a diary of the mythological god Thoth for a class project on ancient Egypt; Fran wrote a diary of a girl taking a safari in Africa for her project on endangered species; Cindy wrote a diary of an Assyrian farmer for a class project on early civilizations; Naomi wrote a diary of a girl visiting Africa for a class project on the continent; and Katie and Rachel, who did a collaborative project on hummingbirds, wrote a wonderfully imaginative diary of a hummingbird's first two years of life.

Susan decided to include a traditional report in her final product. This contains pictures of some of Monet's paintings and her perspective on them. On one page she wrote:

> With the help of Monet's wealthy friend, Durand-Ruel, providing an income, and Alice (Monet's soon-to-be wife) looking after the children, Monet began a new series of paintings during the 1880s that took him away from home for long periods. He particularly liked the Normandy coast and made repeated trips to his favorite sites, like Pourville, Fécamp, Dieppe, Varengeville, and Étretat. He especially liked the aspects of nature during this period: the straight, tall cliffs that dropped suddenly into the channel; the "cote sauvage" (wild coast) of Belle-Île in Brittany, where great Atlantic waves crashed against the granite rocks; the dramatic Creuse valley in central France; and the sunny landscapes of Côte d'Azur.

When Susan presented her project to the class, she passed around books containing pictures of Monet's paintings. I'm sure that for some, if not most of the students, this was their first exposure to Monet's work. Susan gave that to them. During her presentation it was clear to me that when Susan looks at Monet's paintings she furthers her understanding and sense making of life itself.

Spiders

Patrick, another fifth grader, was struggling to find a project topic. He decided to flip through an encyclopedia to get some ideas. A little while later he had it. He came across an entry on spiders and decided to do his project on them. At first his research was limited to using some books and the encyclopedia. Pat took some notes on spiders and he made a small poster with four parts to it (Figure 6-8): the anatomy of a spider, three ways that a spider catches its prey, three different spiders' egg sacks, and finally, from a suggestion from me, a graph from a class survey on who would let a tarantula crawl up their arm (I said no).

As a result of Patrick's inquiry, my thinking about tarantulas would soon change. After Patrick had completed his project, I came across an article in the newspaper about one of the top tarantula experts in the country, who happened to be a professor at a local university. I gave the article to Patrick and suggested he give the professor a call. After writing down some questions he still had about spiders, Pat reached the professor on our classroom telephone. The professor was a great help to Patrick. For example, Pat knew that the thread of spiderwebs was sticky, but he was unsure why spiders don't stick to their own webs. The professor explained that the entire web isn't sticky, just certain threads, and that spiders know where to walk and where not to walk on their own webs. At my suggestion Pat invited the professor to come to our classroom and speak.

The class was bubbling with excitement (and a little fear) on the day the "spider man" came to visit. He wasn't only going to tell us about spiders and present a slide show, he was bringing some tarantulas with him, and if we wanted, he would let them crawl on our hands and arms. Pat and I both learned something with this demonstra-

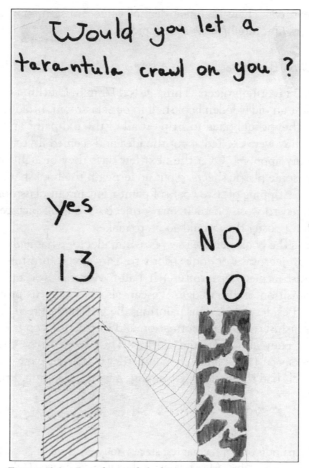

FIGURE 6-8 *Patrick's graph for his spider project*

tion: there are many myths about tarantulas, and the truth is that they're relatively harmless. As the professor put it, if you respect them, they'll respect you. And so, after initially saying no on Pat's survey, I changed my mind, and along with the other nine students who answered as I did, I soon had a tarantula crawling along my arm.

Patrick's project on spiders shows the unpredictability of this learning process. There was no way we could have foreseen an article about a spider expert being published in the paper. But once it came out, even though Pat was finished with his project, we extended his inquiry. Because there are no set time limits or limits on knowledge, we have the freedom to pursue information as it arises and to follow it in an infinite number of directions, some of which may be unimaginable before the project is begun. Pat's project also shows our reliance on experts. Throughout our lives we rely on people with expertise to help us. Doctors, car mechanics, gardeners, librarians, accountants—the list is endless. Experts from the outside world can serve as models for learners. There is a great deal of value in listening to a man talk passionately, lovingly, and intelligently about spiders.

Repainting a Class Bookcase

This is one of my favorite projects. Three girls, Hannah, Caitlin, and Katie, asked if they could repaint an old wooden bookshelf in our classroom. I told them how hard it would be. That they would have to strip off all of the old paint and sand down the bare wood. But they were excited about the idea and seemed invested in the project, so I gave them my approval. Over the next few days they brought in paint scrapers and I brought in some plastic sheets to put underneath the bookshelf, and they began the tough task of stripping off two coats of paint right in our classroom, while everyone else continued to work on their own projects. We took pictures of their work along the way for a poster they would go on to make.

In many ways the bookshelf idea serves as a model for what *authentic* projects can look like. This project was not done strictly to learn about furniture refinishing, but to actually refinish a piece of furniture. It had a very real (or authentic) purpose, beyond the acquisition of knowledge. We can also look at this project through an integrative lens. Besides the obvious painting, the girls had to read. They read books on furniture refinishing, and the information and instructions on the backs of primer and paint cans. They also did some writing. They wrote signs cautioning people about their workspace (wet paint, etc.) and they produced expository passages for their poster, which had six sections: Chipping, Zipstrip, Sanding, Primer, Latex, and Safety:

Chipping

Chipping the paint is one of the hardest stages. You may think it's easy but there are a lot of things to remember. Always go with the grain of the wood, always wear goggles, don't work too close to each other, and stay clear of the nails so you don't hurt the wood or chipping tool.

Latex

Latex is the finished coat. It is a lot thicker than the primer. The reason we got latex is because we called a hardware store and asked what kind of paint to use, and they said latex. We put on two coats of latex because after the first one we could still see white from the primer.

The girls also had to do math. They needed to estimate how much primer and paint they'd need to cover the bookshelf with two coats each. They also needed to think about cost, since they had to buy most of the supplies they needed. Finally, they had to think about time. They had to decide what they had to do and how much time they had to do it in. All of these are mathematical ideas that most of us use on a daily basis. And this math had more relevance to them than any textbook could offer.

They certainly did a lot of communicating. They made repeated phone calls to a hardware store for information, and had to listen closely to and ask questions of an expert. They also engaged in problem solving. After several weeks of chipping, they realized that there was some paint that they couldn't get off. I suggested using a chemical paint remover, but added that I didn't know much about them and that I was unsure if we could use them in the classroom, because of the fumes. Soon after, a school aide, Cody, stopped by our classroom. He had heard about the bookshelf project and wanted to take a look. It turned out that he knew exactly what to do.

Zipstrip

"Zipstrip" is a paint remover. We could not get all the old paint off, so we went to an expert, Cody. He recommended Zipstrip. He helped us most of the way. What you do is you put Zipstrip on the brush and apply it, then you wait five minutes for it to bubble up. Then you take a scraper and scrape it off.

It took the girls nearly three months to finish the bookshelf. The project experienced delays because they had to get various equipment and supplies from time to time, and they had to finish stripping off the old paint around Cody's schedule, which sometimes meant working during recess. (It's not uncommon for students to want to work on their own projects during recess.) Because they had to wait for Cody and eventually let the primer and paint coats dry for several days, they started other projects that they could work on during the final month when they couldn't work on the bookshelf. Above and beyond all of the more "content-based" learning that took place during their bookshelf project, the girls learned other, perhaps more important, knowledge. During one exchange from our parent-student-teacher conference that took place not too long after the bookshelf was finished, Hannah's father asked her, "Did you learn anything with this project?" Hannah looked at him and said, "Yes. I learned to believe in myself. I didn't think we would finish it, but we did."

None of these projects were done in isolation. When Susan was working on her Monet project, twenty-five other students were off working on their own projects; the same was true for Patrick when he was studying spiders; and for Hannah, Caitlin, and Katie when they were refinishing the bookshelf. This work is not always fun, and it's not always easy, and it's never problem free, but as we worked, we talked, we moved, we asked each other for help, we made suggestions, we taught each other. I'll never forget when Aliza, a fourth grader, presented her project on illegal drugs to the class. She wrote a survey on drugs and gave it to the upper-grade students in our school. For part of her presentation she showed the class several computer-generated pie graphs she made to show the results of her survey. The kids were really excited seeing her graphs. Within a week she taught half the class how to create their own graphs on the computer. This is what it means to learn as a community.

Being the Lead Learner: How Do Birds Fly in Sync?

Earlier I wrote about seeing myself as the lead learner in our classroom. To help demonstrate this, last year I worked on my own project. I wanted to show my students that I too have a lot of questions about the world, and that I'm always seeking answers and understanding. I selected a topic that I'd been genuinely interested in for some time. I wanted to know how flocks of birds are able to fly in perfect sync. I always saw flocks of birds swooping left and right in perfect formation, and wondered, How do they do that? How do they all know when and where to turn? (Schools of fish do this too.) I wrote up a project plan and presented it to my class for approval. They were tough on me, but they also had to acknowledge (begrudgingly) that the plan was well written. I taped a copy to the wall and got to work.

I admit here publicly that I missed my due date. But this was not an easy topic to study. (This sounds like an excuse!) In book after book, I read about why and how geese fly in V-formation, but I was stuck trying to find out how flocks of other birds fly in sync. I was about to seek out a bird expert for an interview, when I stumbled onto a wonderful book by Jerry Dennis, *It's Raining Frogs and Fishes* (1992) that had exactly the information I was looking for. The book itself is a testament to many of the ideas that I've been writing about. In fact, the book's creators, Dennis and illustrator Glenn Wolff, were inspired to write the book by their children's natural curiosity about the world:

> When our children began asking some very good questions about the world—Why is the sky blue? How can a flock of birds all change directions at the same time? Why don't blue jays go south in the winter like robins? Are you sure no two snowflakes are alike?—we realized our knowledge was far from complete. Inspired by our kids, we became more curious. Perhaps because we passed so much time as children ourselves laying on our backs looking at clouds and birds and stars, many of the things we became most curious about take place in the sky, and are studied by astronomers, meteorologists, ornithologists, and entomologists. Somewhere in the process of exploring those disciplines in an effort to plug the holes in our education, we realized we had a book to write. (ix–x)

It turns out that experts don't know how birds fly in sync. They have a few theories, including that of "bioinformation transfer," whereby birds exchange information through electromagnetic fields. Another possibility involves mathematical chaos theory; it sees birds as born with a set of "programmed rules"—since all birds have the same rules, they all fly according to them. These are complex ideas, but I explained them in my presentation as best as I could, and it was clear to me that the students were intrigued.

For my final product I wrote a six-page book called "Birds in Flight." I used my presentation as an opportunity to model a quality product and a quality presentation. I made transparencies of my book and showed them to the class for them to see a neatly typed, illustrated, and organized piece of work. I also wrote a presentation outline and showed that to class so they could see how I planned my presentation.

Admittedly, doing assignments like this is time-consuming; however, it's well worth the effort. Not only does the class get concrete examples of quality learning, but I get the formal opportunity to grow myself. And now, whenever I see a flock of birds flying in sync, I have new meaning and new understanding.

Getting Started

All teachers have different comfort zones regarding their professional practice. It's up to each teacher to decide what they're willing to try and for how long. But by starting slowly, a teacher can begin to experience the joys of learning and the freedom of thought right along with their students. A good way for a teacher to begin allowing kids to explore their own questions is to start small. Rather than looking at it as a new way to teach, try it as a one-time experiment. It doesn't need to be complex. It's good for the students to start with simpler ideas, conducted over the course of a relatively short period. A first-time project could last just two weeks, one week for research and one week for turning that research into a final product. This will also give the projects more structure. There's nothing wrong with bringing more structure to projects. Remember, there isn't just one way to do projects. And just because you start out with either more or less structure doesn't mean you have to continue that way. As your projects continue, as you learn, as you're willing to take more risks and perhaps give up more control, you make changes, experiment with different ideas.

One of the most important things to remember is that if there's a problem, if something isn't working, *take it to the class*. Sit around in a friendly circle, define the problem, talk about it, and try to solve it together. There are going to be bumps along the way. These should be expected. In fact, the road will never be entirely bump-free. The thought of students studying topics that you may know little or even nothing about can be threatening. But it is refreshing to break away from the vise-grip of a dictated, standardized curriculum and begin to live learning as an exciting and human endeavor.

Whole-Class Projects

As much as I believe that it's important to give children the freedom to pursue their own projects in school, I also believe that a part of the day should be planned by the teacher—*with student involvement*. This is our afternoon project time, and although this classwork isn't initiated by individual students, my goal is to base it on purposefulness, creating a type of *communal* purpose. When a class is working on the same project, when we're all working together toward the same destination, there is a coming together. This experience isn't possible when everyone is working on their own project, to a certain extent because we remain separate in our pursuits. Our whole-class projects close this separation.

There are two different kinds of whole-class projects, *class-created* projects, when the entire class, including me, chooses a topic to study, and *teacher-created* projects, when I select the topic. I like to alternate between the two. Teacher-created projects also allow me to fulfill my own requirements for teaching a mandated curriculum.

Class-Created Projects

There is nothing quite as exhilarating as sitting down with twenty-five children and creating a project together. But choosing a topic for an entire class to study is not done quickly. The process takes us about three consecutive days and begins with a class brainstorming session. This involves the students sitting on the floor before me, taking turns suggesting topics for our class to study. As they make suggestions, I write them down on a large sheet of paper. Since I'm also a member of our class, I'll make suggestions too. The goal here is *not* to make a list of topics and then have the class vote to determine a winner. The goal is to come to a *consensus* as a class. We're looking for a topic that everyone, or nearly everyone, can connect to personally. In order to accomplish this, as I record the kids' suggestions, I connect related ideas together with arrows. What we end up with is a large diagram that includes a wide variety of topics. Figure 6-9 is the diagram that resulted in a project called, "Our Urban Ecosystem."

Look at the wide variety of suggestions our class made during our original topic brainstorming session. By connecting related topics, we can create larger topics. Nuclear power is related to the atomic bomb and to people; drugs are related to our brain, the legal system, and Hollywood; stars are related to the sun, time, and aliens;

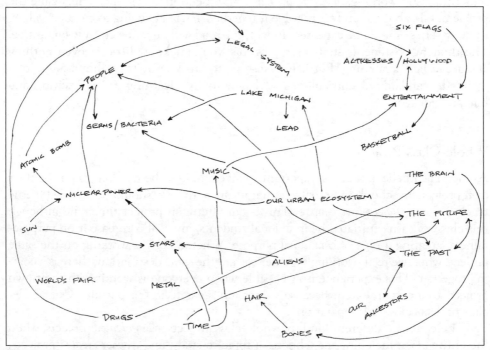

FIGURE 6-9 *Our topic web from selecting a new class-created project*

124

our ancestors are related to the past and time. We look particularly at the topics that have a lot of arrows either going from them or to them. These are the topics that the class has the most interest in and that can be joined into a larger single topic or theme. The project we eventually decided on, "Our Urban Ecosystem," is related to the sun, people, germs and bacteria, nuclear power, time, the future, the past, and Lake Michigan. Topics can also be related to literature. The idea for creating the ecosystem project from our topic web came from Gary Paulsen's 1990 book *Woodsong*, which I was then reading aloud to the class.

The next day we sat in a circle on the floor and discussed our diagram. We eliminated the topics that had few or no related ideas. Topics such as aliens, hair, bones, the sun, and the world's fair were crossed out. Suggestions that were too broad or too narrow were also eliminated. For example, the topic "people" is too general, so we eliminated it, and the topic "lead" is too narrow, so we eliminated that as well. We didn't entirely dispense with these concepts, however; both of them were merely subsumed under larger topics. At this point all remaining topics were circled and we began an open discussion, with everyone free to comment on why a certain topic would or would not be good to study. The hope is for the students to do most of the talking with me acting as facilitator. As the discussion continues, certain topics stand out as being more compelling. Discussions like this need to proceed carefully. Kids take their ideas seriously, and it's easy for feelings to get hurt.

Our discussions usually extend over several days. (Some topics are easier to decide on than others.) Everyone will be making a long commitment to whatever topic we choose, so the process can't be rushed. I also want to be sure that everyone has an opportunity to have their voice heard. Eventually the discussion is narrowed down to just a few topics. After extended discussion, the topic of our project finally emerges. Usually everyone can agree on the topic; sometimes there are one or two students who disagree. This needs to be anticipated. If a student is convinced that there is no subtopic of the chosen theme that would interest him, I meet with him to find a related topic that he would be interested in studying.

Next, we have another class brainstorming session to break the main topic into subtopics. This has already partly been done through the diagram we created. For example, the final subtopics for the "Our Urban Ecosystem" project were: Lake Michigan, wildlife, climate, industry, and pollution. Most class-created projects are studied in groups, with each group choosing a subtopic together. I mostly leave the question of which students will work together up to the students. However, because I want them to work with different students throughout the year, I'll often make suggestions about the makeup of their groups. When I give them both freedom and direction, they usually do a great job of making their own groups. If the students have difficulties creating good groups, I have no problem choosing them. Once the groups are formed and they have their assigned subtopics, each group sits down together and writes up a project plan.

Equality and Prejudice
We did this project some years ago, but "Equality and Prejudice" remains close to my heart, perhaps because it shows how willing children are to explore serious and critical

issues when given the freedom to do so. Here was a class of sixth graders that could have chosen to explore an endless number of topics, and they chose to look at the issues of equality and prejudice. That says a lot by itself to dispel some of the myths about children's lack of interest in learning about important ideas.

The project had five subtopics: anti-Semitism; African Americans and whites; the elderly; class cliques; and sexism. I don't remember the specific work undertaken by the students. I do know that the group looking at African Americans and whites researched demographics and statistics. For example, they looked at the differences in how the death penalty is meted out, noting that African Americans are given capital punishment far more (in relation to their population) than whites. They also looked at differences in income, education, and life expectancy. This information led to many "why" questions, such as, Why do African Americans have lower incomes than whites? There aren't any easy ,"right" answers to this question, which makes it perfect for kids to think about.

The group studying the elderly conducted interviews with local nursing home residents. This was a great learning experience for me, because I realized after the fact just how much help and preparation students need for doing quality interviews, and how much I didn't give them. "Real" people are a powerful primary source of knowledge for children. But to do interviews well kids need help. You can do mock interviews (or even real interviews) inside the classroom with the students observing. The students can also interview each other, family members, friends, or school employees for experience. For our class project on Chicago, I taught interviewing skills by inviting nearby high school students into our classroom for actual interviews. I suggest that students tape-record their interviews and possibly have them transcribed. Ellie recorded her interview with an Egyptologist at a museum, Nick and J. P. recorded their interview with an architect, Julia videotaped her interview with a horse trainer, and Jerry recorded his interview with a computer expert.

One group decided to study the cliques in our classroom and look at possible prejudice and exclusion right inside our own walls. This had to be handled delicately, but I thought it was an outstanding idea to be included under the larger themes of equality and prejudice. It brought the issue right into our own lives, encouraging all of us, me included, to confront issues of how we see other people. It also allowed our class to put the label of "prejudice" on what happens when children exclude other children (and adults exclude other adults). Far too often kids see excluding others as a "part of life" or just "being a kid." The group surveyed our class, asking questions such as, "What are the advantages of being in a clique?"; "What are some disadvantages of being in a clique?"; "Should something be done to stop cliques?"; What can be done to stop cliques?"; and "Are you in a clique?"

In her book *You Can't Say You Can't Play*, Vivian Gussin Paley (1992) writes how damaging it is when children exclude other children. She tells of an experiment she tried in her kindergarten classroom, in which her students were prohibited from excluding others. If someone wanted to play, they had to be included in the group. She hung a sign on their classroom wall: YOU CAN'T SAY YOU CAN'T PLAY. Since this was relevant to the class clique theme (as well as the topics of equality and prejudice), I read parts of Paley's book to the class each day for a week during our class meetings to discuss her ideas.

I don't recall what the groups on anti-Semitism and sexism specifically studied. I know that the sexism group (all girls) looked at the women's movement. I remember the group marching into the room for their presentation with posters and banners emblazoned with slogans demanding gender equality.

I took on a project myself in order to help the class see how pervasive issues of prejudice and equality are in our lives and society. For one month I cut out every article in the *Chicago Tribune* that had to do with these two issues and posted the articles on a hallway wall outside our classroom. By the end of the month there wasn't a single inch of wall to spare. An area of approximately seven feet high and twenty feet across was covered with newspaper articles having to do with equality and prejudice. In fact, there was a pile of articles left over that didn't fit. Even I was surprised as more and more of the wall was covered with the visceral reality of the lack of equality and the pervasiveness of prejudice in our world. At the end of the month, our class went out and sat in the hallway, looking at the wall of articles and discussing what we can do to stop this.

Teacher-Created Projects

There are two kinds of teacher-created projects. The first are projects that are not part of the official curriculum. Obviously, deviating from the mandated curriculum isn't something that all teachers would be able to do, but I bet a lot more teachers can do it than think they can, they just need to take the initiative. Second, there are what could be called curriculum-based projects, which derive from the official curriculum that I'm required to teach. So, for example, instead of teaching "plants" or "geometry" as finite units, or out of a textbook, I turn them into long-term integrative projects. For our project on plants, we took three months and grew dozens of our own plants right in our classroom, studying and observing them as they grew, and conducting controlled experiments on them. For a project on geometry, we took two months and each designed our "dream house," creating floor plans drawn to scale.

Although teacher-created projects result from my decisions, they are not solely my creations. I strive to involve my students in their development as much as possible, and I work to build into the project opportunities for the kids to have ownership over what they're doing. In our plant project, for example, the kids planted their own seeds, and then cared for their plants, then designed their own plant experiments. With our dream house project, all of the kids had fun creating the houses of their dreams. (I'll never forget Ross's dream house, which included a whale tank!) With curriculum-based projects, I do not simply take topics from the curriculum and teach them as they're given to me. If I'm required to teach medieval Europe or electricity or decimals, I devise the way to present these subjects to my class, I shape the information until I have something that I hope will be meaningful and purposeful to my students.

Africa

The topic of Africa was not part of the required curriculum in any way. Another teacher and I thought it would be valuable and fun to explore the continent with our mixed-grade classes of fourth- and fifth-grade students. My purpose in doing this project was *not* for my students to learn pages of facts about Africa. I have haunting memories of sitting in "Man and His Culture" in my freshman year of high school and having to fill in endless worksheets of factual questions on African Bushmen. About the only thing I can tell you today about African Bushmen is that they live somewhere in Africa. Our Africa project—like all class projects—was really about *broad ideas* and developing certain *attitudes* about learning and developing positive *habits of mind*, and doing so while *working as a community*. Here are some of the broad ideas that I hoped my students would assimilate during our exploration of Africa:

- Africa is a large continent with many countries inhabited by many people.
- The world is not our world, it belongs to everyone, including people in Africa.
- There are other cultures in the world and many of them are very different from our own.
- A culture includes religion, art, education, economy, home life, government, industry, food, holidays, and more.
- Other cultures are just as important to the people who live in them as our culture is to us, and our culture is not necessarily the best culture, it's just our culture.
- Respecting and thinking about other cultures can improve our own lives.
- African cultures have many myths, which are ways to explain the unknown.
- Myths are handed down from generation to generation through our cultures.

These ideas would be complemented by learning various research skills, including finding resources, reading for information, taking notes, analyzing information and knowledge, and summarizing, as well as by reading and writing skills. There is hardly a mention of a traditional quantifiable discrete fact in the list, such as names of rivers in Africa or the names and dates of African history. This does not mean there were no facts in this project—there certainly were—but they were embedded in the various subtopics the students chose to study and it was not the knowledge I wanted to emphasize. I added the ideas having to do with African myths to bring written, aesthetic, and dramatic components to the project. Throughout the project I read various African myths to the class. Eventually, the class broke into groups and spent several weeks creating and rehearsing short plays centering on a myth of their choice. Most of this content wasn't directly "taught," but was a part of the holistic experience of studying Africa. In addition to these ideas, other points were raised in class discussions. For example, we talked about the famine in Somalia, apartheid in South Africa, and the role Africa played in human evolution. Class projects, like student-created projects, are open-ended.

After we spent some days discussing Africa and culture, we brainstormed a list of subtopics. My purpose here was to give the kids the opportunity to connect with a specific area of study that they had a personal interest in. Since I didn't have a long list of predetermined "stuff" that everyone had to learn, it wasn't necessary for every student to study the same topic at the same time. (We did do some journal writing on Africa-related topics together.) Most of the ideas I listed above could be learned by studying nearly any subtopic having to do with Africa. By allowing the class to study a wide variety of subtopics, we're making the classroom experience that much richer. Instead of having twenty-seven children exploring African mythology, students are involved in a variety of inquiries including languages, wildlife, holidays, arts and crafts, and country studies. Here are the topics the students chose to study (some topics were researched by more than one student):

African myths	African games	Voodoo
the Mbuti tribe	African holidays	African jewelry
African wildlife	endangered animals	Madagascar
African art	African languages	South Africa
the people of Kenya	Somalia	African clothing
human evolution in Africa		

For her project on the Mbuti tribe in Congo, Samantha created a newspaper called *The Congo Tribune*. Under the headline of "Community," she wrote:

> Mbutis have the absolute best, purified, loving way of living. They live like they're one big family. All of the mothers and fathers treat all the children like their own. Blood hardly matters. They have community fires every night, they all move to a new part of the forest all at once, and they build things together, play together, work together, and almost completely live together. If the whole world lived like the Mbutis, I think there would be peace all around.

Samantha showed how the Mbuti people care for the members of their community in a comic strip she created for her newspaper (see Figure 6-10 on page 130). Zac's subtopic was African wildlife. For his final product he also created a newspaper, which he called *The Daily Drill* (see Figure 6-11 on page 131).

Our project on Africa offers a good example of the wide variety of final products a class can create. Here's what we ended up with:

various reports	various posters	a catalog of African art
three newspapers	a fictional diary	a game of African languages
an African meal	a children's book on Kenya	an "African" myth

To celebrate finishing our project we had an "Africa" night at school. I created a program listing everyone's contribution, and we invited family and friends. All of our work was displayed and we ate the food prepared by Shannon for her project on African food. To conclude our evening, each group performed an African mythology skit.

The American Revolution

Our American Revolution project was taken from the official curriculum of the Chicago public schools and was done during my first year teaching in a Chicago school. My students were seventh graders, mostly Latino and children of the working poor. It is my hope that this excellent work (and the work in the following project,

FIGURE 6-10   *Samantha's comic for her project on Africa*

which was done by the same class), can dispel some of the horrific myths about the abilities of urban, poor, and especially minority children. This is not to say that I didn't have to deal with unique difficulties in Chicago, because I did. I had more behavior problems, the kids needed more structure, many of them lacked certain "everyday" knowledge that most middle-class children have, and with a few of the students there was a slight language barrier, since I don't speak Spanish.

To begin our project I had the class break into groups of three and take fifteen minutes to write down questions about the Revolution. I took their questions home, narrowed them down, added my own, and passed out a typed sheet of questions the next day. The list was long to accommodate the specific nature of the questions, and

Dec 20 '94   **Volume 5.6000**

The Daily Drill

A ray of hope for endangered elephants in Zimbawbe

By Zachary Marloondia

In Gona-re-zhou National park in Zimbabwe two entrepreneurs named Clem Coetsee and Henry Hallward are doing something about the poaching problem for elephants. They are moving the elephants from Gona-re-zhou where they are hunted to, South Africa where they are protected.

ZIMBAWBE

How? You ask do they move eleven thousand pound pachyderms over one thousand miles? Here is how: first, they shoot the elephants with tranquilizers (that don't have any long term effect on the elephants) then they winch them on to trucks with pulleys and then drive them away.

These people have moved six hundred elephants this way and only twelve have died.

INSIDE
- (2) The Best Parks in Kenya
- (3) Endangered species
- (4) Letters to the editor
- (5) Imaginary Safari
- (8) Word Search

FIGURE 6-11   *The front page of Zac's newspaper on African wildlife*

was a way of incorporating structure into the project, which I felt this class needed, especially for our first major project of the year. Here they are:

1. Why did the American Revolution happen?
2. What countries were involved in the American Revolution?
3. What people were involved in the American Revolution?
4. When did the American Revolution happen?
5. How did England get to own the American Colonies?
6. What is independence?

7. What is revolution?
8. What's a colony?
9. What's a tax?
10. In your life, in what ways would you like to be independent?
11. Thomas Jefferson wrote the Declaration of Independence, which contains the phrase "All men are created equal." Did the colonists believe this? What about slavery, women, and poor people? Does our country believe this today? Do you?
12. All of the "founding fathers" were white men. Why was this? Why have every one of our forty-two presidents been white males? What roles did women, Native Americans, African Americans, Latinos, and children play in the Revolution?
13. Some people say that the American Revolution brought democracy to our nation. What is *democracy* and do we have it?
14. What "revolution" do you think we need today? What about our school, your community, your neighborhood, our country, your self, and our world, do you think needs radical change and why? How would you change them?

These questions formed the framework of our project. It should not be surprising that the students came up with the first five questions. These are good questions, especially number five, which involves issues of power and oppression, but they're all primarily fact based, reflecting what the hidden curriculum of schooling had taught these kids since first grade: when you study history, you study facts. (The students had many more very specific factual questions that I eliminated as part of our framework, but they remained important to the project.) Those first five questions are crucial to an understanding the American Revolution. But any notion of historical interpretation, any relation to the human condition, any reference to the present or the future, and any critical notions of political revolt are totally absent from them. If you're going to study the American Revolution, some facts are important, but what matters equally is what all of it means to each of us and to our world today.

I added the rest of the questions. Questions six through nine are all basic definitions that are necessary for a good conceptual understanding of the Revolution. Question nine, "What is a tax?," is a good example of that "everyday" knowledge that most of these kids did not have. Number ten was my way of beginning the project, which I'll explain shortly. The last four questions are all of a *critical* and *transformative* nature. They are about relating the underlying ideas of the American Revolution to our present lives and world, and considering what this might mean for making our world a better place. How, for example, can we ignore that the signers of the Declaration of Independence were all white males and largely wealthy, and that every president up to our currently "enlightened" modern times has also been a white male? (We can also ask why so many of our senators are millionaires.) I especially liked the last question. It removes the idea of *revolution* as strictly a thing of the past, and opens it up, relating it to our lives today.

After the class wrote their lists of questions about the Revolution, I asked them a question: "Have you ever been treated unfairly? Has anyone ever done anything to you that you thought was wrong and unjust?" Not surprisingly with a class of seventh graders, they let out a roar. So I had them break into small groups and make lists of their unjust experiences. Here's one group's list:

- teachers losing kids' work
- not being able to get a job until we're sixteen
- not being able to drive at twelve
- not being able to wear earrings in school
- not being able to eat in class
- grown-ups not taking kids seriously
- not being able to visit my aunt in the hospital until I'm fourteen
- not being able to sleep in school
- not being able to be president until we're thirty-five
- not being able to wear certain colors because they're gang colors
- not having freedom of speech
- not being able to go places by ourselves
- teachers not listening to kids

After some rather passionate discussion of their lists, I explained that the Declaration of Independence was also a text about unfair and unjust treatment. This lead to a lively discussion of the Revolution, including Howard Zinn's (1995) important interpretation of the Revolution being largely driven by the economic interests of wealthy (white) men. For homework I had the students focus on question number ten from our list: "In your life, in what ways would you like to be independent?" I told them to go home and write their own declaration of independence. One of the purposes here was to *situate* the idea of independence within the kids' own realities. Here's Adam's:

My Declaration of Independence
- to get to drive before I'm sixteen
- to get to own a gun
- to get to stay out as late as I want
- to get to have a good job before I'm fifteen
- to get to go to school for a month and take a month off
- to be able to own my own house
- to not have to do chores all of the time

Some kids included very personal hopes in their declarations. It's amazing the connections that were made between a concept from the American Revolution and their own lives:

- freedom from peer pressure
- to have a girlfriend
- to be able to be president even though I am a woman

- to have my mom and dad get along
- freedom to wear any kind of clothes without having a gang shoot you

Regular open talk and debate is critical to our projects. One of our discussions came from question thirteen, about the idea of *democracy* and whether or not we have it. For most of the students, *independence* and *democracy* were about *freedom*. I remember asking the class if they thought total freedom was a good thing. "It seems to me," I said, "that not many of you put any *limits* on your independence or your freedoms in your declarations. Should there be any limits on freedom?" Most of the class thought that once your freedom is limited, you're no longer free. Freedom, to most of the students, meant *no limits*. So I gave them my opinion: "I don't think total freedom would work, because with freedom comes *responsibility*. If everyone did whatever they wanted without thinking of others or the common good, the world would be in chaos. One person might want the freedom of peace and quiet and their neighbor might want the freedom to blast their stereo. How could it work if no one accepted any responsibility? If no one thought about anyone else?" I remember a quiet, pregnant pause in the classroom, as if the idea that freedom requires responsibility—and perhaps limits—had just dawned on them as making sense.

Most of the project involved groups of three students researching the questions and creating a board game that teaches its players about the American Revolution (Figures 6-12 and 6-13 are two of them.) I decided on the board games for three reasons. First, the class needed more structure, primarily so they could learn how to structure *themselves* for later projects. Second, I felt that they would like the idea of creating the games, which they did. And finally, to create a board game requires some

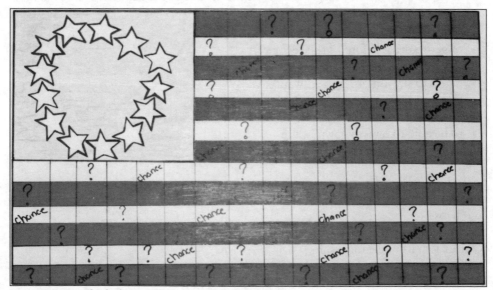

FIGURE 6-12 *Elizabeth's, Andro's, and Jose's flag game*

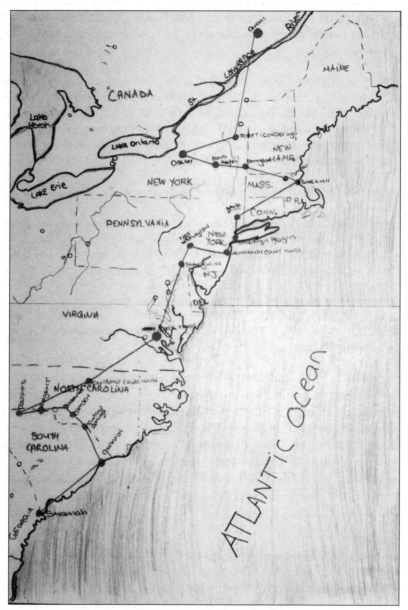

FIGURE 6-13   *Adam's and Esmeralda's thirteen colonies game*

logical thinking. You can't just throw anything together; the game has to *work*. Our research, as usual, using *no* textbooks or worksheets, took about four weeks and the board games took another three weeks, including time for each group to write a set of instructions for their games (helping them to work on their expository writing). From time to time throughout the project we also wrote in our journals about a variety of issues related to the Revolution and to the ideas of revolution and change.

As a culminating writing and discussion topic, we looked at the final question, "What 'revolution' do you think we need today?" We sat around in our circle and read our calls for radical changes in the world. Milena wrote about having a revolution for our own school:

> At Burley School we need some changes. The building is very old. I hope they will remodel the building. They could take the lead out of the building. They could clean the outside of the building. They could fix the roof. And I would like to see more trees near the school. I wish they would paint the school in better colors. If the students want changes they must form groups. They could try to change things. It might take time, but it might work.

And Jaime argued for a revolution to end violence:

> I think that this country should have a revolution against violence. Violence in this country is getting out of control. There is violence on TV, in the street, and in homes. When little kids see violence while they are growing up, when they become teenagers they are going to go out and do it. If it would be up to me I would put more police officers on the streets, put a limit of how much violence a movie can have or any other program, and I would also try to help families that have violence in their homes by giving them counseling. This is what I think this country should have a revolution against and why. Or should we let the cycle of violence keep on going until we have total chaos?

The revolutions the students called for were pulled from their own lives, thoughts, and experiences. Elizabeth and Reginald called for a revolution against racism and sexism and all types of discrimination; Edgar argued for a "sports revolution" because the players get paid too much; Danny called for revolutions against poverty and pollution; Pedro wrote about a revolution against war; and Jerry wrote about a revolution against gangs. When our research, our games, and our writing and discussions were finished, we celebrated by having an "American Revolution Gamefest," where we spread our games all over our classroom and spent the morning, literally, playing games (See Figure 6-14.)

Social Issue Surveys

This is another project that I created from an official curriculum, specifically fractions, decimals, and percents. As I mentioned, this was done by the same Chicago seventh-grade class that did the American Revolution project. Our "Social Issue Survey" project involved having groups of students write surveys on a variety of social issues, giving the surveys to various people, analyzing the responses, and communicating the results. The project began with the idea of a "social issue." What does the phrase mean? What is a social issue? Using newspapers, magazines, and personal experiences, we discussed various social issues. After several days of discussion and brainstorming, our nine groups of three decided to survey people on: poverty, gun control, television content, freedom of speech, racism, illegal drugs, the O. J. Simpson trial, prejudice, and women in the armed forces.

FIGURE 6-14   *Playing a game at our American Revolution Gamefest*

Writing the surveys took time. Although we had talked about many of these issues throughout the year in our class meetings, we needed to spend more time discussing them. I needed to help the class understand the idea of *opinions* and to see the power personal opinions can have. We agreed that school, family, friends, society, culture, religion, government, business, and the media all play a role in shaping our opinions. We did some journal writing too. For example, I asked the class to consider if it would be good if everyone had the same opinion about social issues. One perspective the class held was that we needed diversity; another perspective held that it would be easier if everyone had the same opinion—as long as the opinion everyone had was *their* opinion!

In their groups of three, students brainstormed possible survey questions. It was important to help the students be critical of their questions and to use the students' existing knowledge and opinions to help them further their understanding of the issues they were writing about. For example, when John, Adam, and Jaime were writing their survey on poverty (Figure 6-15), I showed them an almanac so they could see the national statistics on poverty, noting the differences between race, gender, and level of education. (I told them about Lyndon Johnson's War on Poverty and asked them if they thought we won the war.) And when Nick, Adrian, and Pablo were writing their survey on freedom of speech, I told them the story of when I was growing up in the Chicago suburb of Skokie in the 1970s and the neo-Nazi party wanted to march through town and it became a heated constitutional and moral issue. (Skokie has a large Jewish population with many concentration camp survivors.)

Poverty in America

Female _____   Male _____   Age _____

1) Do you think poverty is a big problem in America? YES __ NO __

2) What are your thoughts about poverty in America?

3) Do you think the government is doing enough
for the poor?   YES __ NO __

4) What can be done to end or reduce poverty?

5) Have you ever donated money to the poor?   YES __ NO __

6) About what percentage of American kids do you
   think are currently living in poverty?

          5%   10%   15%   20%   25%   30%

7) Do you think poverty in America is getting better or worse?

          WORSE ___   BETTER ___

   Why do you believe your answer in #7 is true?

8) Here are some approximate percentages of people
   living in poverty for the year 1990:

   White: 11%   African American: 32%   Hispanic: 28%

   Why do you think there are so many more minorities
   living in poverty?

FIGURE 6-15   *John's, Jaime's, and Adam's survey on poverty*

I also conducted several minilessons on survey writing. I explained the difference between closed-ended and open-ended questions, how the phrasing of a question, or just one word in a question, can mean the difference between getting a good or a poor response. We talked about the purpose of anonymity in surveys. And I showed samples of real surveys and passed out copies of survey results with graphs from newspapers and magazines. At times I used these to help the students understand how to create and interpret different kinds of graphs. The surveys we wrote went through multiple drafts and took at least three weeks to get into a final, typed form (Figure 6-16).

Television Survey

This is a social issue survey about TV. It can be an anonymous survey, so you don't have to give your name if you prefer not to.

Name _____ Male _____ Female ____ Age _____

1) Do you think there's too much sex on TV?   YES ___   NO ___

2) Do you watch shows that include sex?   YES ___   NO ___

   If yes, what are they?

3) Does TV have too much violence on it?   YES ___   NO ___

4) Do you watch violent shows?   YES ___   NO ___

   If yes, what are they?

5) What harm does TV do to people?

6) What good does TV do to people?

7) Place an X in the column to say what commericals should or should not be on TV:

	On TV	Not on TV
beer		
condoms		
drugs		
cigarettes		

FIGURE 6-16   *David's and Esmeralda's survey on television*

Once finished, some of the groups administered their surveys to other classes. I gave the students tips on conducting surveys in a respectful, professional, and effective manner. One group had to give their survey twice, because on the first time around they didn't come off as professional and their respondents took the questions as a joke. Other students gave their surveys to teachers and other adults in the building. When I did this project with a different class several years ago, one group sent their surveys home to be completed by parents. If I were to do the project again, I would take the surveys outside of school to be given to various populations in the community, which would make it an even more authentic project. (Taking our projects into the community is an important idea that I'm beginning to implement more.)

Analyzing the surveys also took time. For the groups to do the necessary math, I conducted minilessons on topics such as converting fractions to decimals and decimals to percents, on rounding off decimals, on how to use a calculator, and on graphing. I wasn't expecting most of the students to "learn" any of these from our minilessons. The most valuable mathematical growth took place while the students were actually *doing* and *applying* the mathematical ideas, symbols, and algorithms we had talked about. Most of my teaching of the math took place while everyone was spread out in the room working on their surveys. I moved from student to student or group to group to offer help and guidance wherever needed. As much of the current literature and research on math makes clear, math is just as constructivist and meaning driven as writing and reading (Burns 1992; National Council of Teachers of Mathematics 1989; Parker 1993). Because of this, as I worked with students individually, I encouraged them to create their own algorithms and emphasized their mental number sense and conceptual understanding, as well as helped with their computation skills—but did so within *real* contexts.

The closed-ended questions were obviously easier to analyze. These are the "yes/no" questions or the questions that are answered with a number or on a scale or chart. For example, on their survey on guns Maria, Javier, and Jose asked, "Does the Second Amendment give people the right to own a handgun, yes or no?" The open-ended questions were far more challenging. These are the questions that ask the respondents to write a narrative reply. On the same gun survey, the students asked, "What would you suggest be done to end or reduce gun violence?" With open-ended questions, suddenly the so-called objectivity and empiricism of math and survey conclusions fall away. Now they had to *interpret* people's meanings and language. We discussed that when we interpret someone's meaning, our biases and experiences and perspectives play a part in the results. In analyzing open-ended questions, the kids had to make decisions about how to categorize narrative responses, on the possible meanings those responses had, and if they should eliminate certain surveys because of confusing language or incomplete responses. Figures 6-17 and 6-18 are some of the graphs two groups created.

Our Social Issue Survey project, like all of our projects, was about much more than the traditional-minded school "content" that is imbedded within it, like fractions and graphs. Our projects are equally about learning other very important content. Projects help us to learn about working together; they help us to appreciate working together, to nurture the idea that our best learning—and living—is a social act. Our projects are also about learning as an active lifelong endeavor, not just a "school" thing. Projects are very importantly about learning to think for ourselves, rather than having our thinking directed for us. This requires classrooms with an ethos of freedom

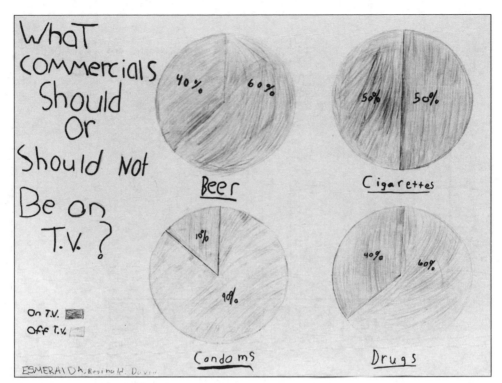

FIGURE 6-17 *Some of the graphs from the television survey*

and thoughtfulness. And our projects are not only about learning the topics themselves, but they encourage us to learn about *us*: who we are, where we come from, what we value, how we see and treat others, the people we want to become, the world we want to live in and leave to the future. Our projects help democracy thrive.

Moving Forward: Who Are We?

I want to take our projects in three directions. First, as I mentioned, I want to take our projects into our communities more. Second, I'd like to create more authentic projects with my students. By authentic, I mean projects that serve real-life purposes. Dennis Littky (n.d.), the principal at the innovative Thayer School in New Hampshire, has written about some of the real-life work his students have done: registering voters, working at nursing homes, writing a science book for the elementary school, creating a pamphlet about their town, building a nature trail. And there are the well-known *Foxfire* publications, founded by Eliot Wigginton (1985) and written and produced by high school students in Rabun Gap, Georgia. For more than twenty-five years these students have been interviewing and writing about the lives and livelihoods of the people of Appalachia. Like the bookcase-painting project three of my students did, all

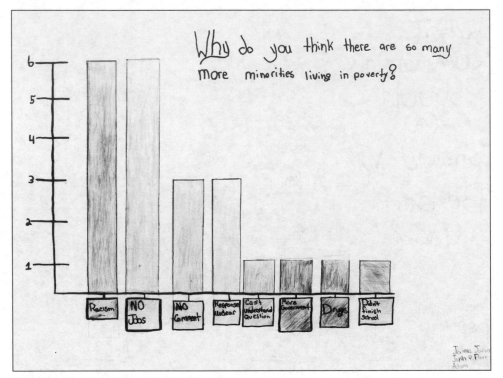

FIGURE 6-18   *A graph from the poverty survey*

of these projects resulted in some form of tangible product or experience. Bringing authenticity to a classroom—traditionally a "false" learning environment—is one of the most challenging tasks a teacher can undertake. Finally, I'd like to frame some of our projects within larger (and less literal) themes and questions. As George Wood (1992) and Deborah Meier (1995) have explained, the Central Park East Schools in New York City do this. For example, when the seventh and eighth grades study contemporary political issues with an emphasis on United States history, they have "essential questions" that frame their inquiry, such as "What is political power?"; "How does power change hands?"; and "What gives laws their power?" (Wood, 180). What this does is place the study of political issues and U.S. history—something that school usually sees as very fact-based—within the larger and abstract theme of "power."

I've recently started to adapt this idea in my own practice. This year the focus of our official social studies curriculum is Native Americans and the American Revolution. So, I came up with an all-year theme and framed it within a single question: Who are we? All of our work together will seek to answer this question. There are two primary reasons I chose this theme. First, many of my students have disciplinary problems, and I want our year together to encourage them to look at themselves critically, both to celebrate their qualities and to build their character. And second, I want our work to revolve around them; so that's what frames our work—who they are. The theme also works perfectly with our "A Thoughtful Life" (see Chapter 4), since that's about who we are, who we wish to become, and how we choose to live our lives. It equally fits our reading and writing (see Chapter 7) and all of our projects. I don't know if I'll like the results, or how successful it will be, but the important thing is that I'm going to experiment with something new and exciting and meaningful. Like I wrote earlier, how we do projects is never finished. I'm always asking myself how I can improve them.

It may be helpful to see how I envision this, at least in its embryonic stages. After I explained to the class what I wanted to do and why, we had a class brainstorming session to make a list of questions that could help us answer the theme question, Who are we? We came up with dozens of very thoughtful ideas: What do we watch on TV? Who are our ancestors? How do we communicate? What do we read? What problems do we have? What is a human being? From here the kids wrote our questions on large strips of poster board so we could hang them all around our room. After this I brainstormed some possible class projects, some small, some much larger:

- make "life graphs" (Rief 1992) of the good and bad events from our lives
- research and make family trees
- write oral histories from our families and publish a class magazine
- explore Native American history and culture:
    - research the history of Native Americans with books, movies, museums, etc.
    - have Native American historians, storytellers, artists, and musicians visit our classroom
    - interview the local Native American population in Chicago and create a publication (there are twenty thousand Native Americans in our own city)
    - relate oppression of Native Americans to oppression of African Americans, other minorities, women, "common" laborers, and the poor
    - experience a "real" Native American powwow
- write and illustrate children's books about our own cultures and neighborhoods

Hopefully you can see how I'm trying to intertwine the history and culture of Native Americans (a part of who we are) with the history and culture of my students. This is just a framework for us to start and to shape as we proceed. Within this we'll be doing other related activities: journal writing, class discussions, student-created projects. As time goes on, as we explore, as we ask questions, we might turn in a new direction. But that's okay. Our projects are collaborative experiences of discovery.

Seven

Democracy Through Reading and Writing

Once you learn to read you will be forever free.

—FREDERICK DOUGLASS

Writing is a way to end up thinking something you couldn't have started out thinking.

—PETER ELBOW

There is a particular part of Walt Whitman's (1855/1959) epic poem *Leaves of Grass*, that I can never forget:

> I believe a leaf of grass is no less than the journeywork of the stars,
> And the pismire is equally perfect, and a grain of sand, and the egg of the
>   wren,
> And the tree-toad is a chef-d'oeuvre for the highest,
> And the running blackberry would adorn the parlors of heaven,
> And the narrowest hinge in my hand puts to scorn all machinery,
> And the cow crunching with depressed head surpasses any statue,
> And a mouse is miracle enough to stagger sextillions of infidels,
> And I could come every afternoon of my life to look at the farmer's girl boil-
>   ing her iron tea-kettle and baking shortcake. (55)

It is some of the most beautiful language I have ever read. Not only has it always sent chills through my body, but his words and images give me a tremendous sense of freedom. They have come to represent for me the infinite power and possibility of language, and because of their instant accessibility, that power and possibility are open to all. This should not come as a surprise, considering that Whitman was a champion of democracy. When I read *Leaves of Grass* that's what I think about. The beauty and *importance* of life and freedom. I feel the same way when I read Thoreau's *Walden* or the writing of Annie Dillard or John McPhee.

There is a very special, multidimensional relationship between reading and writing and democracy. Reading and writing—having the freedom to choose *what* to read and write—are democratic acts. There is no doubt that our nation holds these freedoms as very dear. However, at the same time, with immense irony, our schools do not allow them to exist inside our classrooms. The most basic right of reading and writing, the power and control over what words and thoughts we will have, is strictly controlled against. Second, there is the process of reading and writing as a free act of *creation*. When I read Whitman or Thoreau or a novel I don't want to be told how to make sense of it, I want to make my own sense, I want the freedom to relate my being to their words and ideas in my own way. The last thing I want is to be forced to make certain meaning, to come up with the singular "correct" answers. And the same is true for my writing. Just like reading, writing is meaning driven; writing, as the Peter Elbow epigraph above says, is not about first determining our meaning and then jotting it down; writing *is the way* we create our meaning. This can't happen without democracy, both in our lives and in our classrooms.

Whole Language Is Democracy

Many people have defined whole language. Here's my own short version: whole language is learning naturally. Here's a slightly longer version: Learning—specifically *language*—naturally is about learning to read and write and speak and listen by reading and writing and speaking and listening in real and purposeful contexts. It really is that simple. The common belief is that children learn to read and write in school. I disagree. Children begin to learn to read and write and speak from the day they're born (and perhaps even before). School certainly enhances (or hurts) what they've already learned about reading and writing, but as I've already pointed out, kids know a lot about reading and writing long before they ever step foot into a classroom. They learned it from the same source they learned so much else: they learned it from life.

To be a whole language teacher does not mean to teach language in one specific way; it is not a "program." Any program calling itself whole language is not whole language. A "whole language program" in any way, shape, or form, is an oxymoron. Whole language is a philosophy of *learning*. As Louise Rosenblatt stated (Rosenblatt and Power 1991), it is not specifically about "language," but rather about *experience*. Language, she points out, just happens to be a part of experience. This is why the words *whole language* do the beliefs a disservice. Since it's a philosophy of learning and teaching as opposed to language, its beliefs apply to learning anything, whether it's reading, math, drama, or plumbing.

Learning language naturally begins with the belief that all people have an innate curiosity about their world. It begins with *trust* in the human organism, no matter if they're six or sixty; no matter if they're rich or poor; no matter if they're suburban, urban, or rural; no matter of they're American, Dutch, Japanese, or African. There certainly are cultural differences when it comes to learning language, but the thirst to understand, to make sense of the world, to know, to create, to learn, is a *human* trait that transcends all cultural and physical boundaries.

Through its constructivist base, whole language believes that all human beings are active meaning makers. We live our lives in a constant flow of transactions, consciously and subconsciously creating meaning from the world around us. This means, as I wrote in Chapter 3, that language learning, like all learning, is *meaning driven*, and that the learner is in charge of their learning, whether the teacher or the state legislature or the school board or the parent likes it or not. So whole language naturally does not embrace a transmission model of schooling, but classrooms that are built on learning as authentic transactions. Similarly, whole language teachers are also developmentalists. We do not accept that every second grader must be at the same place at the same time in their learning. In fact, we don't believe this is even *possible*, since all children are different people who develop at different rates and have different interests and strengths.

Whole language recognizes the importance of talk and listening in becoming literate. It puts a great emphasis on creating highly social classrooms that encourage speaking and listening. And because it believes that the best way people become better readers is by reading and the best way people become better writers is by writing, these classrooms devote large chunks of time to both. Rather than listening to a teacher talk about being a better reader and writer, students spend most of their time actually reading and writing. And since ownership and purpose is central to meaningful learning, children are given the power and freedom to read and write much (if not all) of what they want to read and write. This doesn't mean we throw kids in a room with a stack of paper, some pencils, and a pile of comic books and let them "teach themselves" as many critics of whole language claim (Groff 1993; Thompson 1992). That's not a literate or a learning classroom. Good whole language teachers take a very *active* role in the growth of their students—but their teaching looks very different than the traditional paradigm.

The whole language approach is against teaching skills in an isolated fashion, from the part to the whole, because that's not how people learn language naturally, and that's not how people experience language in their daily lives. A lot of people believe that naturalistic classrooms do not stress basic language skills, including phonics. This is probably the single greatest myth about whole language. I want to state emphatically that you can't be literate without reading and writing skills. You can't be literate without phonics. Skills have always been a critically important part of our classroom. Because whole language teachers do not present these skills in traditional ways, the automatic assumption is that they're not an important part of those classrooms. But they are! We just teach them differently—and we do that specifically because we believe that our students' learning will be far more meaningful as a result.

Whole language is against using mass-produced and marketed programmatic resources and materials because they falsify the learning process, foster disinterest in children, continue the corporate monopolization of curriculums, and because they simply aren't necessary for the vast majority of children. If you want children to become better readers, don't give them a basal or a textbook, give them the freedom to read books—real books—and read aloud to them. If you want children to become better writers, don't give them an English textbook or worksheets on how to use a comma or a semicolon, have them interact with language in a wide variety of contexts, have them write for real purposes. Put simply, the best way to get children empowered by language is to immerse them in language-rich environments.

These language-rich classrooms are about helping children become better readers and writers in authentic ways. That means that the teaching of skills is done in real contexts, from the personally relevant texts and readings of the students themselves, through short, one-on-one conferences during class. My students get far more out of a three-minute conference that's centered on their own writing or reading than they would from a forty-minute lecture that has nothing to do with where they personally are as a writer and reader. None of this prevents school from being a "rigorous" experience. Good whole language teachers have very high expectations for their students, just like good traditional teachers. We want them to work hard, to take their learning and thinking seriously, to be thoughtful, to produce high-quality products and ideas, to accept responsibility for their learning, and to do so while being caring classroom members.

The Politics of Whole Language

Whole language is not only a new way to teach or even a new way to think about learning. Whole language is also extremely *political*. Wanting children—*all* children—to become lifelong, critically literate readers and writers is threatening to many people who like the status quo. Whole language demands the sharing of power and control in the learning process with both students and teachers. So believing in and practicing whole language should be a conscious political decision on the part of the teacher. Helping children to become literate human beings is a key way to empowering a citizenry to participate in democracy and to make its highest hopes a reality.

Whole language is actually a term that has lost much of its meaning. It's been beaten up now for over a decade and it suffers terribly from misunderstanding, fear, misuse, and misinformation. I agree with Harvey Daniels (Daniels and Miner 1995) that most of the teachers and schools that claim to be practicing whole language are not. They certainly think they are, and they certainly use the nomenclature, but most of them don't really understand it and are applying it *within* the dominant belief system of schooling. The constructivist and learner-centered beliefs of whole language have the potential of turning at least part of the dominant paradigms of schooling and teaching on their heads. So a whole language teacher who has a good understanding of what that means cannot implement its beliefs while remaining entrenched in status quo schooling. Good whole language teachers are consciously aware that they're challenging the prevailing belief systems of school and teaching. So many teachers and schools are advertising themselves as "whole language practitioners," that when they don't get "results" (i.e., higher test scores or miracle students in a year) it's the whole language movement and philosophy that gets the blame. What's actually happening in all of those classrooms is rarely considered.

For some time now I have been hearing the death calls of whole language. The State of California, an "official" advocate of whole language, baled out recently. Why? Low test scores. But once again unquestioning perceptions, political ideologies, paradigmatic blindness, and an ignorant media are at work beneath the surface reality. Why did whole language "fail" in California? Looking at test scores is easy, but we need to look beneath the surface. According to Regie Routman (1996), California has the largest class sizes in the nation, ranks fortieth in state per-pupil expenditure, ranks near the bottom in public and school library services, has the highest number of ESL (English as a second language) students, and offers very limited professional development for teachers. This last point is crucial. Without retraining, without theoretical and practical understanding, how is something new ever going to work? As Routman writes, "What happened in California is being called the 'failure of whole language.' It was not whole language that failed. It was the implementation of a set of practices without adequate funding, staff development, community support, and understanding" (22).

To be honest, it didn't surprise me at all that California's whole language initiative failed. For me, California's foray serves as a perfect example of what happens when we mandate teaching, no matter if the mandates are progressive practices or traditional practices. Mandates don't work. Teaching is not about (or should not be about) making identical widgets. A top-down business or factory paradigm will not work. Teaching has a culture all its own. What matters is what's inside the hearts and minds of teachers, and how each of them translates that inside their classrooms. A state legislature, a governor, a curriculum guide, or even national standards isn't going to change a teacher's thinking—that needs to be accomplished through each teacher's professional and personal development. So, the ultimate failure in California isn't whole language, it's the idea of mandating teaching beliefs and practices. Every school district in the country would accomplish far more if they encouraged and supported (and expected) their teachers to pursue their own professional development rather than implementing mandates from above or wasting time on externally created "inservice." If teacher inservices were successful in implementing meaningful school and teaching reforms, our schools would be the envy of the world in terms of change and improvement. But they aren't. After a century of focused efforts at reform, our schools have hardly changed (Cuban 1993; Tyack and Cuban, 1995).

California hasn't been the only blow to whole language. It's been the target of a constant barrage of criticism from back-to-basic advocates, religious fundamentalists, political conservatives, classical humanists, and just plain ol' parents for years. It also suffers from a lack of serious and realistic commitment. To truly change an educational *paradigm* (as opposed to an educational *method*) is a long and complex process. Methods can be changed in an afternoon, but an entire belief system that's firmly rooted in social and cultural realities and assumptions would take many, many years, even generations, to see meaningful change on a large scale. Unfortunately, our society, with its empirically based scientific (or positivist) belief system, has very short expectations for change. We either get results tomorrow or we move on to the next idea.

I would say, however, that the reports of whole language's death are premature. For the very same reason that whole language failed in California, it is alive and well inside many classrooms throughout the country (even the world). Contrary to most educational reforms in history and to many reports in the media, whole language is going to stick around. Ken Goodman (1992) believes that it's here to stay for one profound reason: whole language was not mandated from above (except in California, where it "failed"), but was a grassroots movement. What fueled its growth wasn't a legislative or administrative mandate, but rather *teachers themselves*. Beaten, battered, and abused, there are far too many teachers who believe in the ideals of whole language in their hearts and minds to kill it off completely. That's what separates the philosophy from most other education reforms. Of all the people who are involved in the educational process, from legislators to administrators, from school board members to parents, from researchers and academics to other educational experts, the strongest voice advocating—and *practicing*—whole language has been teachers.

Whole language certainly has its limitations. First, it is by no means an education panacea. Ironically, in some ways it remains entrenched in the dominant paradigm of schooling. It is still very much classroom based. Although it could, it does not specifically move the students' learning outside of the school and into the world. It can also be so teacher-controlled that spontaneous interaction is lost. This may appear to be a contradiction, but it isn't. Although I consider whole language to be inherently democratic, not all see it this way. And because these classrooms are usually inside school systems that remain within the dominant behaviorist, empirical, and transmission paradigm, with characteristics such as separate classrooms, overcrowding, segregation by grade, ability grouping, standardized testing, grading, and strict curriculums, there are serious limits as to how far outside that paradigm these teachers (including myself) can take children. Learning language naturally is not going to eliminate our staggering dropout rate, end our horrendous financial inequities, raise the professional stature of teachers, or make critical reflective practice an important part of teaching. So whole language has a great deal to offer our children, but we can't look at it as the solution. Schooling and teaching are far too complex for us to do that. And even though a recent 390-page report (Steinberg 1998) claims to have finally ended the whole language/phonics debate ("Use some of both"), I agree with Frank Smith (1993), who calls this a "never-ending debate," because, Smith argues, "it is not based on 'evidence' but on ideology" (412).

I have to admit that I'm not enamored of the phrase *whole language*. Educators would do ourselves a favor by limiting our dependence on those two words and talk more about what they mean. The problem is that if we don't call it *whole language*, what do we call it? This is one of the most profound difficulties in education activism today. Schooling has become so much a business that unless you can package a reform, market it, and *name* it, you have a lot of trouble selling it, both literally and figuratively. After giving this much thought I've decided to do something quite radical for the remainder of this chapter. I'm going to call whole language *reading* and *writing*. Why is this so radical? Because school has destroyed these two words. Reading and writing in a school context mean something very different than reading and writing in an out-of-school, real-life context. School reading and writing have little to do with real reading and writing. I remember seeing a local newscast not too long ago. The anchorman was reporting about a school principal who told his students that he would eat a live worm if they read a certain amount of books in a certain amount of time. The news showed the principal sitting in his school's gym, eating the worm in front of his students. But never in the story did the anchorman use the word *books*. In fact, he said that the students had to read "works of literature." Why that language? I can only speculate, but this is what I think. In the context of school, "books" don't mean real books, like what we check out of the library or buy in a bookstore, they mean *textbooks*. The anchorman wanted the viewers to know what the kids read, so he had to use "works of literature" instead of "books." So, in the hope of bringing back the pure and simple meanings of the lovely words *reading* and *writing*, that's what I'm going to call it.

Critical Literacy

One weakness in the traditional practice of whole language is its almost complete neglect of the critical or transformative pedagogy that I wrote about in Chapter 5. In the context of language learning, this has been referred to as helping students gain a *critical literacy*. Although I've already touched upon some of these ideas, I think it's important to do so in the specific context of literacy and language. In repeating some of the themes from the chapter on freedom and control, critical literacy is about helping children become critical readers of language, life, and reality, by helping them to see and question the power, the politics, and the cultural assumptions of our everyday lives.

Two of the strongest advocates for bringing critical literacy to whole language practice are Carole Edelsky (1992, 1994) and Patrick Shannon (1995). Both of them see traditional schooling—as well as "traditional" whole language—as propagating a superficial, unjust, and unequal society that works *against* democracy. Edelsky writes:

> If critique were to be one of our main activities, and bringing down the barriers to democracy were to be a serious goal, we would have to re-theorize language education. That's because most of our current theories and practices—such as reader response theory; sociopsycholinguistic models of reading; transactional theory in reading; literacies as social practices; curriculum as inquiry; whole language practices; writing process practices; whole language as described theoretically by me, among others; and so on—can as easily support *avoiding* looking at white privilege, for example, as they support looking *at* it. Those progressive theories and practices are correct, I believe, but they don't go far enough. They don't actively and primarily—*as a first priority*—tie language to power, tie text interpretation to societal structures, or tie reading and writing to perpetuating or resisting. (1994, 254)

Patrick Shannon elaborates:

> Critical perspectives push the definition of literacy beyond traditional decoding or encoding of words in order to reproduce the meaning of text or society until it

150

becomes a means for understanding one's own history and culture, to recognize connections between one's life and the social structure, to believe that change in one's
life, and the lives of others and society are possible as well as desirable, and to act on
this new knowledge in order to foster equal and just participation in all the decisions
that affect and control our lives. Because subtle and direct competitions pervade and
influence our lives adversely, much of critical literacy is aimed at naming, analyzing,
and acting upon inappropriate competitions and their consequences on those lives.
Critical literacy helps us assuage the psychological and social damage not through
escape or denial but by allowing us to ask who benefits ultimately from these competitions, to forge bonds with our putative competitors, and to work symbolically and
physically to ensure more humane, just, and equitable civic lives. (1995, 83–84)

Shannon and Edelsky are both after a vision of whole language teaching that
goes far beyond reading and writing for pleasure, the development of skills in authentic contexts, nurturing lifelong literacy, and celebrating individual meaning making.
All of these are important. All of these are crucial to whole language practitioners.
But Edelsky and Shannon specifically advocate helping children explore how language and power can be institutionally, systemically, and politically used and abused
to create and perpetuate a society of winners and losers. It would be difficult to have a
classroom or a school that claims to be educating for democracy—for equality and
humanity—that does not have this as an important goal.

Here's something I did during the week of Columbus Day last year to help my
seventh-grade students see the ideology in language, text, and images, and develop
their own critical literacy. I got the idea from high school teacher Bill Bigelow
(1995). I began by reading to the class Jane Yolen's 1992 picture book, *Encounter*. It
tells the story of Columbus from the perspective of the Taino Indians. The story tells
of Columbus demanding gold from the Indians that they did not have, with deadly
consequences if they did not comply, and that he returned from his first voyage with
five hundred Indian slaves. Then I read a short part of Samuel Eliot Morison's (1942)
largely glowing biography of Columbus, *Admiral of the Ocean Sea*. Morison writes
(and buries deep in his 680-page book):

> The policy and acts of Columbus for which he alone was responsible began the
> depopulation of the terrestrial paradise that was Hispaniola in 1492. Of the original
> natives, estimated by a modern ethnologist at 300,000 in number, one third were
> killed off between 1494 and 1496. By 1508 an enumeration showed only sixty thou-
> sand alive. Four years later that number was reduced by two-thirds; and in 1548
> Oviedo doubted whether five hundred Indians remained. Today the blood of Tainos
> only exists mingled with that of the more docile and laborious African Negroes who
> were imported to do the work that they could not and would not perform. (492–493).

After I read these accounts, I borrowed copies of the social studies textbook my
students used in fifth grade. It had, as I expected, a romantic, one-sided story of
Columbus and his voyages (and that book was published in 1987!). I had the class read
the textbook's account of Columbus for homework and compare it in writing to what I

read aloud. The next day it was clear that this assignment was so out of the ordinary, they hadn't understood it. Needing a clearer and more structured assignment, I typed up some specific questions (some of which came from Bill Bigelow), passed them out and tried again. Some of the questions were, "What wasn't included in the textbook that should have been to give you a better understanding of Columbus?"; "What feelings come to mind when looking at the textbook's illustrations?"; "Who does the textbook get you to root for?", and "Are these ideas important to think about, and why or why not?"

Their thoughts about Columbus and history and what was missing from their old textbook and why it was not included led to a lengthy class discussion. We then divided into groups and role played some of the scenes of Columbus that we read about. My purpose in doing this was not to denounce Columbus and advocate a anti-European liberal agenda. It was to help my students understand that there is no such thing as *the* history of Columbus or *the* history of anything, so we must be critical of what we read and what we see and what we are told, and we must look beneath the text on the page and beneath the surface realities of our everyday lives.

Our lives are filled with the urgent necessities of nurturing a critical literacy. Life has become saturated with endlesss bits of information: images, soundbites, publications, histories, advertisements, products, political perspectives. A critical literacy empowers people to sort through these created realities and frees us to, in the words of Alex McLeod (1986), "take control of our own lives." For example, every day I see the effects that magazines, video games, toys, and movies (to name a few) have on my students. They play a significant role in creating specific ways of making sense of the world. The amount of violence in video and computer games, movies, and television is staggering. Just the other day our class was discussing violence at our daily class meeting. Soon, the conversation was about violence in video games. The next day, Chris, a fifth grader, brought in a copy of a very popular video game magazine, *Ultra Gameplayers* (April 1998), which became the topic for that day's class meeting. In reviewing the new game "Grand Theft Auto," the reviewer wrote:

> *Grand Theft Auto* sets the player up as the bad guy. Car-jacking, theft, speeding, murder, and cop-killing are just a few of the felonies asked of you. . . . The ability to beat the tar out of civilian drivers, then take over their car to perform your villainous duties is exciting at first, but this becomes monotonous. (70)

When I read this aloud to my class, very few of the students—in particular the boys—had any problem with it. To them it's just a game, it's fun.

It comes as no surprise that it is my male students who overwhelmingly see violent images as "cool"—an attitude that I continually see transferred to *real* violence. This is partly the result of violence and war and aggression being made a business and specifically marketed to boys. Go to a toy store and you'll see aisles full of war toys—which to me is an oxymoron—and other aisles full of dolls and "passive" toys. Take a kid to a toy store and they know their place. Recently I had a conversation with my students on what they wanted to do for a living later in life. Tiffany said, "I want to grow up and be the president's wife." I said, "The president's wife? What about being president yourself?" Much of the class (especially the boys) roared with laughter, demanding that girls can't be president. These kids were only eight and nine years old. They weren't born laughing at violence or stereotyping genders or seeing life as a competition. Our society and culture and corporations have indoctrinated these perspectives into them. In a very real way these perspectives control them—and us. A critical literacy works to stop this. It is about empowering people with insight, responsibility, compassion, *freedom*, the very qualities that help democracy thrive.

Reading

The Frederick Douglass epigraph at the beginning of this chapter connecting reading and freedom should not be taken lightly. We should not forget that slaves were prohibited from learning how to read precisely as a means to limit their power. For thousands of years women in many cultures have also been denied the right to read. And the vast libraries of the clergy and aristocracy were a specific target during the French Revolution (Manguel 1996). But still, school largely sees reading as merely a requirement for employment. Having people who can read is important for getting a job, but having people who are *readers* is important for democracy. We need to stop having school see reading as just a necessity for employment, and start seeing reading as a limitless means to enlarging our minds, encouraging discussion and debate, promoting personal and communal freedom, and making a better world. Reading can do that. And there is something else reading can do: it can give us endless amounts of pleasure and beauty. How often do you see either of those ideas on a standardized test?

Recently I saw a television report on a program in Boston called "Changing Lives Through Literature." The program involves groups of men who meet regularly to discuss novels they're reading. Who are these men? They're convicted criminals. According to the judge who runs the program, the key to personal change is *reflection*, which is what he helps these men engage in through their reading, especially about issues of character. The early results are very promising, with an extremely low rate of recidivism among the program participants. I hear about all kinds of "get tough" ideas to reduce crime, but how often do you hear about an idea like encouraging the men and women in our prisons to read and to think and to talk?

What does it mean to be a real reader? Well, real readers read real books and newspapers and magazines, not textbooks or basals or novel excerpts. Real readers also read for real purposes, not so that they can improve their comprehension or vocabulary. Both of these happen when we read, but neither are the *purpose* for reading, just some of the beneficial by-products the experience yields. Real readers choose what they read. Now that I'm out of school, no one dictates to me what to read. I read what I want to read, what has organic connection to who I am and what I enjoy and questions and curiosities I have about myself and the world. Right now I'm reading a biography of Walt Whitman, because I have an interest in the poet and in the time and culture in which he lived. After that I'll probably read a novel or a book on science since I like genre variety in my reading.

Teachers and schools feel it's absolutely necessary to assign "literature," often in an anthologized textbook format, to students because they don't trust kids to read good books on their own, because they believe they know best what kids must read in order to be "educated," and because school's dominant paradigm dictates that reading won't be beneficial for kids unless it's *taught*. Whether a child actually gets anything out of being forced to read something (or whether they actually even read it) seems to be a moot point. The purpose is to "cover" a book or a novel unit or a short story in a literature textbook the way fractions and geography are covered. The idea that children might get more—perhaps *much* more—from reading books that they select themselves doesn't occur to most people because it's not what the traditional paradigm prescribes.

Real readers read regularly and read a variety of texts and books. They don't read every book they see or didactic texts exclusively or the *New York Times* from cover to cover, but they do read consistently and from a variety of sources. Reading, to a real reader, is an important part of their life. Consider what the great writer Eudora Welty wrote in her 1984 autobiography, *One Writer's Beginnings*:

> It had been startling and disappointing to me to find out that storybooks had been written by *people*, that books were not natural wonders, coming up of themselves like grass. Yet regardless of where they came from, I cannot remember a time when I was not in love with them—with the books themselves, cover and binding and the paper they were printed on, with their smell and their weight and with their possession in my arms, captured and carried off to myself. (6)

Or consider Malcolm X (1964), who saw himself as illiterate before he discovered books and reading while in prison. At ten o'clock each night the cell lights were turned off and Malcolm would huddle with a book on the floor of his cell and read by the glow of a distant bulb:

> Anyone who has read a great deal can imagine the new world that opened. Let me tell you something: From then on until I left that prison, in every free moment I had, if I was not reading in the library, I was reading on my bunk. You couldn't have gotten me out of books with a wedge. (172–173)

Albert Manguel wrote an entire book about his passion for reading in his fascinating *A History of Reading* (1996). In explaining why he kept so many books, he wrote:

> I know that the main reason I hold onto this ever-increasing hoard is a sort of voluptuous greed. I enjoy the sight of my crowded bookshelves, full of more or less familiar names. I delight in knowing that I'm surrounded by a sort of inventory of my life, with intimations of my future. (237)

What a fabulous notion: our own small libraries being "inventories of our lives."

When I read, I savor the time. It gives me a tremendous sense of freedom. In a world that seems to be in never-ending motion, with constant demands, reading provides a respite. A lot of adults say, "I don't have time to read." For some this may be true. But for most it's really a question of priorities. They have time, they just choose to spend it doing something else.

Real readers talk about their reading. Even though the act of reading may be a personal one, reading to a real reader is often a shared experience with other real readers. Nancie Atwell (1987) envisioned her classroom reading workshop as the dining room table around which her family and friends gather to discuss ideas. That, she realized, was the direct opposite of what traditionally happens in school when it comes to reading. Real readers have literate, spontaneous, messy discussions about what they're reading. Recently I sat and listened to my wife and my mother discuss a book they had both read, Anne Tyler's *Ladder of Years* (1995). I don't want to give the story away, but it involves a middle-aged woman who leaves her family. Their discussion was wonderful, rich with ideas. They both loved the book, but had very different opinions about it. They disagreed totally about the ending, which steered the conversation into talk about generational differences. This is Nancie Atwell's dining room table come alive, and it can happen right inside our classrooms. About the dining room table idea Atwell wrote, "It is a literate environment. Around it, people talk in all the ways literate people discourse. We don't need assignments, lesson plans, lists, teacher's manuals, or handbooks. We need only another literate person" (19).

Real readers read at their own pace. School typically makes students read at the same pace, and this includes not allowing students to read ahead in the book, or at least not giving them specific permission to read ahead. I can't imagine a better way of killing a good book or a child's enthusiasm for getting into a good story. Imagine checking a book out of the library on the condition that you read only one chapter a night. This would be ludicrous, yet this is so often what school does. And of course, real readers are never segregated into ability groups. Life is full of books, and real readers just dive in. Ability grouping and tracking and "gifted" programs are such antidemocratic practices that they make our schools seem horrifically stuck in the Middle Ages.

Real reading is a lot messier than it's presented in school. Contrary to what school wants children to think, real readers don't finish every book they start. The truth is that there are far more lousy books in the world than good books. When I read a book, if I don't get into it, if I don't care about what's happening or what I'm reading, if I'm not looking forward to picking it up tomorrow, then I set it down and pick up a new book. Real readers don't always read every word in books that they do finish. Some people skim the slow part or flip past it entirely. That's the reality, the way real readers read. There are no laws about the correct way to read a book. People will read the way they want to read.

I've never met a real reader who looks up words they don't know in the dictionary. This is another reading killer. Making students interrupt their reading to jot down vocabulary words or look up words they don't know or answer comprehension questions kills the momentum and joy of reading. It turns the experience into a "lesson." Rather than getting comfortable for an hour and reading straight through, students are made to spend half that time setting the book down to complete an assignment. School simply has no trust in the act of reading a book. It's too simple. Learning, growing, and thinking just from reading. Where's the teacher? Susan Ohanian (1994), in her "plea for more disorderliness" wrote:

> Leaving a child alone to savor a book, to get from it what he will, and then holding one's tongue when that child closes the book requires a tremendous act of faith—faith in children and faith in books. Sad to say, school systems are not designed to easily accommodate acts of faith. They demand records: competency checklists and adherence to scope and sequence. . . . Trusting children and books is a revolutionary act. (161–162)

I remember being assigned three novels in high school, Howard Fast's *April Morning*, Hemingway's *The Sun Also Rises*, and Paul Zindel's, *The Pigman*. (There may have been more, but these are what I remember.) What I recall most about these books has almost nothing to do with their stories, their themes, their characterizations, their authors' style of writing, or any meaning the books may have had for me. What I remember most is the agony of having to read them. I've since reread Zindel's *The Pigman* and thoroughly enjoyed it, but chances are good that back in high school I didn't finish any of them. As Susan Ohanian (1994) also pointed out, what I did was fake my way through them. I faked my way through four years of high school reading by simply going through the motions. I read books because they were assigned and the only option I had was to fail. That's good incentive to fake your way through school. I'm not saying that I didn't gain anything from my high school reading. But being forced to read books that I had little interest in undoubtedly reinforced—through the hidden curriculum—one very powerful piece of knowledge: that reading was a deathly laborious activity that did not involve me in any way. I didn't graduate high school as just a nonreader, I graduated high school *hating* reading.

Last night I was talking with my wife, Laura, about how I've grown over the years. I believe I'm a *very* different person from who I was ten years ago, before we met. I see myself now as being more focused, more critical, less egocentric. I started thinking about who I am today and who I was ten years ago. I then realized that that was when I started reading. After twenty-five years of living the life of a nonreader, I had, on my own, become a voracious reader. And more than any single book I had read, it was my *cumulative experience* as a reader that had done the most in changing how I see the world and who I had become. Reading has taken me to a much higher level of consciousness and introspection. That may be reading's greatest value in a democratic classroom and to a democratic society. Reading helps raise our consciousness and our empathy to the details of the world around us.

I don't believe that everyone will want to be a reader just like not everyone will want to play football or play a musical instrument. But school today does little to get children interested in reading as a lifelong activity for growth, understanding, empowerment, inquiry, and pleasure. Reading has been perverted into little more than an economic necessity and a test score. I remember several years ago when I was in a workshop with a group of teachers. There were perhaps twenty of us sitting around a large square of tables. I don't remember why we were there, but the topic of homework came up. I told everyone that I thought homework was largely a waste of time. It took no time at all for nearly everyone in the room to denounce my statement as blasphemy. But then I issued a challenge. I said, "Wouldn't children be far better off if instead of doing all of the homework they're given now, they went home and read a book for an hour?" The room was suddenly silent. No one disagreed with me.

Quiet Reading Time

More than anything I could teach my students about reading, it is the act and experience of reading itself that has the most value. That's why we have "quiet reading time" every day. There's not a lot to be said about quiet reading time. That's exactly what it is. For at least thirty minutes every day, and some days longer, everyone, including myself, sits or lies around our classroom and reads quietly. (As a fellow reader during quiet reading time I become a model reader.) Some kids are sitting at their desks or tables, some are under their desks, some are on a couch (as in Figure 7-1) or lying on some big pillows or in a beanbag chair, or just spread out on our rug. One of the goals is to get comfortable. That's what I like to do when I read at home. If a student or even an entire class has difficulty reading quietly and respectfully then we'll talk about it. If that doesn't help I'll have them read in their seats until they can accept the responsibility. At the start of the year I use quiet reading time as a real example that with freedom comes responsibility.

FIGURE 7-1   *Quiet reading time*

There are other issues of freedom and control with our reading. Students choose the books they want to read. Ownership and meaningfulness is a priority here, and the best way for that to happen is to give children the freedom to choose their own books to read. I've always had an extensive classroom library with hundreds of the best in children's literature for the class to choose from, and I encourage them to bring books in on their own. A lot of people see it as politically dangerous to let children choose their own books to read. I see it as the exact opposite of this. I consider it politically dangerous to dictate to children that they can read only certain books.

As soon as a student finishes one book, they need to begin another. There are no guidelines for how many pages a student must read in a given night, week, or quarter. We're all different people with different reading speeds and vocabularies and reading histories, so all I ask is that everyone brings their book to school every day and for them to read at home every night for thirty minutes. (This is a good way for fulfilling school or district homework mandates.) If a student isn't reading, or isn't reading enough, and if my talking to them hasn't helped, then I'll assign them a mutually agreed upon book with a specific due date. Reading in a democratic classroom is not about giving children free rein to read whatever and whenever they wish. That may be a free environment but it isn't a literate one.

After finishing a book, students do two things. First, as Nancie Atwell (1987) had her students do, they record the title and author on a "Books I've Read" list stapled to the inside cover of their journal. It's wonderful to watch these lists grow as the year progresses. The second thing they do follows an idea I picked up from another teacher, Sharon Weiner. On a three-by-five index card they do the following:

- write down the book title in the upper lefthand corner
- write down the author's name in the upper righthand corner
- draw a small picture or image based on the book
- write a sentence or two in response to the book or a quote from the book
- record their initials in the lower righthand corner

This provides us with a succinct summary of the book. Granted, it's small, but it's a wonderfully simple way for someone to respond to a book. (When I finish a book, I make one too.) Once a student finishes a book card (they can do them during reading time) they deposit them in a book card in-box. I'll record that they finished the book in my own records, and then I'll tape the cards to the wall under a big "Books We've Read" sign. By midyear we have *hundreds* of cards on our wall, which is a great advertisement for visitors to our room that we're a classroom of readers. I've never seen kids get competitive with this. Our reading is not meant to be a contest, but a community activity. Last year I kept a running total on the wall, and the class felt a genuine sense of communal pride whenever we crossed a big milestone, such as one hundred books, two hundred books, three hundred books, read.

I allow my students to read only books during quiet reading time. This bothered me for some time, since books are certainly not the only valuable language medium. I struggled with the limits of freedom I was putting on their reading. So, last year I experimented; I conducted some teacher-research. At a class meeting, I explained what I was thinking and told the class that we would experiment with different reading materials and meet at the end of the quarter to discuss the results. For this quarter, kids could read anything they wanted during quiet reading time, but they still had to read their books at home each night. I brought two newspapers with me to school and some of the students split them up, taking different sections. Other students continued to read their books. A few brought in comic books. Some read from various magazines we have, such as *Time, National Geographic, Discover, Smithsonian, Sports Illustrated for Kids,* and children's literary magazines, such as *Stone Soup* and *Merlyn's Pen,* as well as magazines of student writing that my classes have created over the years. Others brought in their own magazines, including video game and sports magazines. I felt a tremendous excitement during reading time. No longer were we just reading, now we were reading a wide variety of texts from a wide variety of sources.

But something was missing. Over the quarter, I lost track of the books the kids were reading at home each night. While I read during quiet reading time, I also make informal observations of students reading. Sometimes after I've sat and read for ten minutes, I'll get up and quietly roam the room, reading my book and glancing at students reading their books, and maybe I'll even whisper a question or a comment. This may seem rather informal, but all of this "kid watching" (Goodman 1978) is a great help in maintaining a connection to each of my students and their reading. It's actually quite easy to see when a student is stuck or bored with a book, because they don't make much progress moving from page to page. This is not as easily gauged when kids are only reading their books at home. There was also a sense of community and shared purpose lost. Even though we were all reading, what we were reading varied so widely that I no longer felt the communal connection I feel with books. After the quarter was up we went back to exclusively reading books, and I simply accepted this as a necessary limit on their freedom.

Book Groups

When I started teaching in Chicago, I was confronted with a dilemma. For the first time in my career, many of my students were not fluent readers. Even from a developmentalist philosophy, it's clear that most of my third, fourth, and fifth graders are considerably behind in their phonics decoding, their fluency, and their comprehension. One of the primary reasons for this goes back to what I wrote in Chapter 3 about the sociocultural context of learning. The vast majority of my students in Chicago were not invited into Frank Smith's (1986, 1988) "literacy club" from the day they were born. These kids are not exposed to books at home, not involved in the discussion of ideas. It comes as no surprise to me that the handful of students that I've had in Chicago who are fluent readers do live in language- and reading-rich homes. I don't believe at all in blaming the parents, because schools (and hospitals and social programs and our governments) have largely failed to educate them about the crucial importance to children of an intellectual home life. (Of course, it would also help if our country was serious about fighting two of the root causes of illiteracy: poverty and prejudice.)

It took me two years to seriously start dealing with this dilemma. It was actually a good experience, since it forced me to confront some of my own assumptions, ask hard questions, and break away from my own status quo practice. I came to the conclusion that what we needed to start doing was a combination of quiet, independent reading, and reading from a common book in small groups. Reading in groups brings three powerful learning experiences together: reading, collaborative learning, and open talk and discussion. I decided to try three-week cycles. During the first cycle, the class would meet with their book group every day for about forty-five minutes. After three weeks, class members would read independently (from books of their choice) for the next three-week cycle. After that, they would return to their groups for another three weeks, and so on. After two group cycles (six weeks), the kids would then form new groups.

I had to decide how to structure the groups within a democratic belief system, giving the kids ownership over the book selection and avoiding any form of ability grouping or tracking. I ordered a lot of new books, in sets of four or five, for our classroom library. Since these kids represented a very wide range of current reading ability, the books went from about the first-grade to about the sixth-grade level. I let the students form their own groups, with one stipulation: they had to be mixed gender. I gave the kids this freedom because, first, it leads to their being invested in their reading, and second, I trusted them to make good decisions with respect to their groups, which most of them did. When they met in their groups, the kids took turns reading aloud, helping each other with their phonetic decoding and understanding, and especially *talking* about their books just like real readers. Some children don't like to read aloud in front of a group, so this has always been optional. It's important to me that none of the kids feel pressured to read aloud in front of their classmates.

I've made the differences in our reading ability an issue of democracy, and have included it in our curriculum. All of the groups are naturally heterogeneous, with a wide range of readers. Our book groups necessitated talking about this. Democracy and community means welcoming and respecting diversity, including in our groups of diverse readers. I explained to the class why so many schools have ability grouping and tracking (ours doesn't), and why I don't believe in them. I explained how everyone (including adults) is at a different place as a reader, just like we're all at different places with respect to playing baseball and cooking and public speaking. People who are highly developed readers have many, many areas that they aren't to highly developed in. (I spoke about Howard Gardner's theory of multiple intelligences here.) I also emphaiszed that even if someone is not as developed a reader, they can still make excellent contributions to book discussion and that their ideas and meanings are equal to everyone else's. My point in all of this was to help prepare the students to work collaboratively in heterogeneous book groups, knowing that we're all different, celebrating any differences, and being willing to help each other. Our book groups then are not only about enjoying books and growing as readers, they're about caring for others, respecting the common good, welcoming differences, and celebrating and sharing our unique meaning-making.

Our book groups have been a part of our classroom experience for about two months, and the early results are exciting. Most importantly, the kids themselves are excited. They really love reading in their groups. It didn't all go smoothly from the start (which I expected), but with some time and discussion we've come a long way. Some of the quality books the groups have read are *Sadako and the Thousand Paper Cranes*; *Harriet Tubman*; *A Jar of Dreams*; *Walking to Freedom*; *Number the Stars*; *Julian's Glorious Summer*; some of the "Amber Brown" and "Nate the Great" series. During each three-week cycle, the groups create one collaborative book-reaction project and present it to the class. For example, after one group read Lois Lowry's *Number the Stars*, they wrote a multiple-voice poem from the perspectives of the main characters, and after another group read the biography of Harriet Tubman, they wrote and performed a short play on her life. I've learned at least one very valuable lesson from our book groups too. The opportunities to share and talk about good books are important for all kids, irrespective of how developed they are as readers.

Reading Aloud

After quiet reading time, I read aloud to the class. Since everyone reads their own books during quiet reading time, reading aloud gives us a common text to discuss and react to as a class. I like to read with the class sitting in front of me on the rug as a group. This provides a nice feeling of community. When I taught seventh and eighth grade, we did the same thing. I usually read aloud for about twenty minutes. Right now I'm reading William Golding's classic, *Lord of the Flies*, and yesterday we were so much into what was happening, that before I knew it, forty-five minutes had gone by. A schedule with built in flexibility allows for us to get carried away.

I read many things to my students. Besides the book that I read aloud from each day, our communal text, I read excerpts from books that I happen to be reading. My students were fascinated to hear about Malcolm X when I was reading his autobiography earlier this year, and when I told them about David Mas Masumoto's book *An Epitaph for a Peach* (1995), referred to in Chapter 1, it led to an unplanned thirty-minute discussion that touched on farming, fruits and vegetables, grocery store produce departments, different belief systems, pesticides and herbicides, organic farming, and challenging the norm. My class of seventh graders *loved* me reading aloud parts of Luis Rodriguez's *Always Running: La Vida Loca: Gang Days in L.A.* (1993), which is a memoir of his younger gang life. The newspaper is an especially rich source to read aloud from. Virtually any paper has articles on politics, government, history, science, nature and the environment, business, ethics, prejudice, sociology, culture, and especially local news, which has special relevancy to our lives. Newspapers are a never-ending source for dialogue. I especially like reading and discussing editorial cartoons, which always encourages the kids to bring their own in for the class to talk about. I also point out to my students that newspapers present one interpretation of a story; they must be read *critically* like any text.

161

I also read picture books to my students, even my seventh and eighth graders. (I would read picture books to high school students if I taught high school.) Good picture books have everything going for them. They're exceptionally well written, they tell good stories with wonderfully imaginative illustrations, and they can be read in one sitting. So, if we're getting ready to start a project on the American Civil War, I might read Patricia Polacco's heart-wrenching book *Pink and Say* (1994) to the class to set the context of the Civil War. I did the same with George Littlechild's book, *This Land Is My Land* (1993) when our class was discussing the annihilation of the Native Americans, and with thirteen-year-old Nila Leigh's beautiful book about living in Africa, *Learning to Swim in Swaziland* (1993) when we explored Africa as a class project.

A few years ago I started "Friday Picture Book Day." Every Monday, two students volunteer to read a picture book to the class and lead a discussion about it that Friday (see Figure 7-2). At various times throughout the week, I let the two kids go somewhere to prepare. First they need to find a picture book they like (in the school library, in our class library, in a public library, or at home). They have to read it through a number of times, discuss its ideas, what it means to them, possible themes, and decide how they're going to present it to the class. When they read the book aloud, I sit with the rest of the class as just another audience member. Some of the best talk about books I've ever experienced has happened during these discussion times.

From time to time I'll have students react to books that I'm reading aloud from. These assignments are usually left open, to allow every student to respond to the book in their own way with their own unique voice. Usually I ask the students to give me their sense of a book or a specific part of a book, and I offer suggestions on how

FIGURE 7-2   *Ross and Ben reading to the class for Friday Picture Book Day*

they might do that. I want to free my students to *think* and *create* and *communicate*. While reading Gary Paulsen's (1990) book *Woodsong*, his account of racing in the Iditirod dogsled race, Julia created a collage from pictures and words she cut out of magazines (Figure 7-3). Her explanation of the images she selected offers a glimpse at the amazing and complex meaning she made from the book:

- I chose the backwards "R" because Gary Paulsen turned around at the end of the race.
- I chose the woman looking at the map because I think Paulsen found out things that he never had known before on this trip.
- I chose the dog because he owned lots of dogs.

FIGURE 7-3 *Julia's reaction to* Woodsong

- I chose the "To Boldly Go Where No Man Has Gone Before" quote because you wouldn't think of an everyday author dogsledding.
- I chose the phrase "an Incredible Voyage" because it *was* an incredible voyage.
- I chose the words "With Good Cause" because Paulsen had a good cause: he wanted to do dogsledding and he did it.
- I chose the word "toys" because it seemed that the dogs were Paulsen's toys.
- I chose the airplane made out of cans and stuff because in the book it seemed like when Paulsen found out more and more stuff about the dogs, he pieced them together and made sense out of it all.
- I chose the statement "The force is with you, like it or not," because once you start the race, you can't turn back.
- I chose the words "high risk" because Paulsen's risk of dying was high.
- I chose the picture of the boy playing with his toy airplane because it was like Paulsen was playing with his toys, only they were dogs.
- I chose the word "playground" because it was like he was playing on the playground and the dogs were the equipment.
- I chose the word "entertainment" because the book was like a movie theater and the movie was about dogsledding.
- I chose the word "teamwork" because you can't dogsled without the dogs and you can't dogsled without the musher.
- I chose the words "two cultures" because in the book it seemed like the dogs were one culture and Paulsen was the other.

By giving children the freedom to react to books in different ways, we allow their unique voices and talents and meanings to flourish. One day last week, after reading a very dramatic part in Golding's *Lord of the Flies* (1953), where the young boys (who are stranded on an uninhabited island with no adults) attack and kill one of the boys (Simon), I asked everyone to respond. It was a perfect opportunity to see what sense the class would make of what happened in the story. They were free to select their own way to communicate their thoughts. Elizabeth wrote a poem:

> Kill the beast, Kill the
> beast.
> That's all you hear is
> kill the beast.
> Kill the beast, kill the
> beast. Simon's not the
> beast.
> Kill the beast, kill
> the beast.
> Did you ever really
> see the beast?
> Kill the beast, kill the
> beast. How many beasts are
> there?

> Kill the beast, Kill
> the beast.
> Why do you want
> to kill the beast?
> Kill the beast, kill
> the beast.
> Can someone tell me
> who's the beast?

Nick made a drawing of Simon lying dead on the beach (Figure 7-4).

FIGURE 7-4   *Nick's reaction to* Lord of the Flies

And Jaime wrote to an imaginary district attorney arguing that Simon's death was no accident:

> Dear District Attorney:
>
> I think that what the kids did to Simon was wrong and on purpose. I think it was on purpose because it wasn't that dark and they could have seen him and known it wasn't the Beastie. I think that they made that up because they could have seen him from the light of the fire. That's what I think. That's a lie. I think that what they did was wrong because it is just wrong to kill another person, no matter who he or she is or how [old] he or she is. This is why I think that they should go to jail.

Responding to Personal Texts

Responding and reacting to what we read individually is as important as responding to what we read as a class. The purpose here is not to get students to react in the one "correct" way or to learn the one "correct" lesson from what they've read. Our responses to reading, like reading itself, entail a personal exploration. Reading invites each of us to ask ourselves what meaning a text had for us at a particular time and a particular place. Responding to reading in a *classroom* however, is really a *collaboration*. It allows everyone, me included, to share our meanings and grow from each other. These are all important issues of democracy.

There are a number of ways we might respond to our reading. One way is the book cards that I described above. We also use journals. I love journals. If there was ever a great and simple idea for schools to promote personal growth, journals would be it. But schools have been putting far too much faith in this one idea. A lot of schools are journaling kids to death. (So are preservice teacher programs. I've begun to hear preservice teachers curse journaling.) I know this, because I've done it myself as a teacher. Throughout the years, my students have kept many types of journals: reading journals, science journals, learning journals, math journals, personal journals, and social issue journals. Five or six journals at a time are simply too many. Three journals are too many. Last year I finally reduced my students' journals down to a workable number: one. That's it. Everyone, including me, has one journal they use for a wide variety of purposes.

As I mentioned earlier, each of us maintains a list of the books we've read in our journals. Here's a list of books that Charlie, a sixth grader, read one year:

Abe Lincoln Gets His Chance	*Bo Jackson*	*Sarah Plain and Tall*
Harlem Globetrotters	*Now is Your Time*	*Sabertooth Tigers*
Malcolm X	*Cracker Jackson*	*Julia of the Wolves*
Ben and Me	*Mouse Rap*	*Hatchet*
Don't Look Behind You	*Pedro's Journal*	*Michael Jordan*
Jump Ship to Freedom	*Mississippi Bridge*	*Rumble Fish*
Two Tickets to Freedom	*Picasso*	*The Outsiders*
There's a Girl in My Hammerlock		

These books cover the spectrum of genres—biographies, sports books, thrillers, books on history and social issues, historical fiction, and realistic fiction. What we see here is the list of a real reader. None of these books was assigned. They were readily avail-

able in our classroom library, reading was modeled and talked about as being important to our lives and our learning, reading was expected, and we had large chunks of
time devoted to reading each day. Both verbally, through me, and tacitly, through our
classroom culture, Charlie was invited to be a reader. This is, once again, what Frank
Smith (1986, 1988) refers to when he writes of the "literacy club." By making our
classrooms (and homes) literate environments, we invite children to be members of
the club.

Sometimes students use their journals to write a reaction to a book they've read.
This is fine, but I also encourage them to respond to their reading in different mediums. If one week I have the class write a letter to me, their parents, or a friend about
their books, perhaps the following week I'll ask them to draw a picture in their journal in reaction to their book. There are times I'll move away from the journal completely and invite the class to write a poem on their book or create a piece of artwork.
Last year, J. P. and Dan were both reading Brian Jacques's *Martin the Warrior*, a book
in his popular "Redwall" series, and they tape-recorded a conversation about the
book and gave it to me.

Our Reading/Art Project

A few years ago I came to see that encouraging my students to read as many books as
they could each year has its downside. Kids would go from one book to another book
and then another, for the sheer joy of being prolific readers. This is, of course, wonderful; it creates just the kind of literate classroom that I want. But it does not give
kids much opportunity to think about a single book for any great length of time. In
fact, reading like this can become rote after awhile, lacking any sustained thought or
insight. I realized that the idea of "less is more" applies to reading just as it applies to
the larger curriculum. So, I wanted to create opportunities for my students to slow
their reading down and consider a single book for a longer period of time. I wanted to
try to make reading a few less books mean more.

One of my favorite projects for doing this is what I call our Reading/Art Project.
I came up with the project after reading about a similar idea that teacher Linda Rief
(1992) used with her students. The project involves having everyone read a book of
their choice and then create a piece of symbolic visual art in response. Some powerful
ideas about reading and life can be learned when everyone focuses their thinking on a
single book for five or six weeks.

Everyone starts reading their book at the same time and finishes it within two
weeks. Because I want serious reflection about serious ideas, I approve the book each
student selects. I'm looking for books with thematic ideas, which eliminates books that
are written more for pleasure, such as mysteries, thrillers, and sports biographies. This
doesn't eliminate nonfiction, however. One year David read *The Final Days*,
Woodward and Bernstein's book about Watergate and Richard Nixon's resignation,
and created a powerful piece of visual art. (David's work also serves as a perfect example of the ridiculousness of the notion of "grade level," rigid curriculums, and manda-
tory reading lists. How many traditional curriculums would allow a fifth grader to read

167

a book like *The Final Days?* David's a very capable reader and thinker. By giving him the freedom to read, and by encouraging him to read, he did just that. He had a personal interest in politics and government, found the book on a shelf at home, brought it in, and read it. These are the limitless possibilities that freedom and democracy can nurture in children.)

At the end of the two weeks of reading, each student creates a symbolic painting or drawing based on their book. Because their images must be symbolic rather than literal, it encourages the students to think about the various meanings the books had for them, and to then transform these ideas into appropriate symbols. I begin by helping the class understand symbolism. This year I asked the art teacher to help, and she was more than happy to take time during art class to share the work of some of the great symbolic painters, like Salvador Dalí and René Magritte, and have the students create symbolic imagery of their own.

Students begin their drawings in class with "thumbnail" sketches, so-called because they're quick brainstorming drawings that are small, like a thumbnail. After a few days students have several pages full of small drawings, many of which vary widely. We share these with each other, discussing possibilities, while continuing our understandings of symbolism, which can be a difficult idea for kids (and adults). Over the course of the next week, we spend time each day revising our images. As kids work on their sketches, I'm bouncing around the room asking questions, challenging their thinking, talking about books and themes and characters and stories. When a student uses a particular color or shape, I'll ask why they chose that, to communicate that colors and shapes can be symbolic.

Eventually each student completes an eight-by-ten draft sketch of their final image. Once I approve this, they begin their final artwork. Students can choose their own medium. Most like to get a canvas from an art supply store and bring paints to class and create a painting. Others use posterboard and choose colored pencil or crayons or magic markers. Students have used a wide variety of materials, such as crepe paper, foil, cellophane, construction paper, even plywood. Several years ago, Abby read the book *Thunder Rolling in the Mountains*, which is about Native Americans, and she used a large piece of leather as her "canvas," burning her images into the surface using a wood-burning tool. Once finished with their final images, students need to write an explanation of their work as Samantha did in Figure 7-5 and Dan did in Figure 7-6.

Once all of the artwork is completed, it is hung along a hallway with the written explanations adjacent, like in an art gallery, and we have an art showing, inviting other classes and parents to come by. The project takes a good amount of time to complete, but it's an example that spending more time on less can result in so much more. This year I'd like to expand the idea into other mediums, such as drama, video production, and computer programs (such as Hyperstudio). It is important for me to remember, however, that no matter how successful these projects may be the most important act in reading takes place between each reader and the text and it is their individual meaning making that must be emphasized and celebrated.

FIGURE 7-5   *Samantha's artwork for* Ordinary People

Ordinary People, by Judith Guest

Ordinary People is about an ordinary suburban family with two teenage sons. One son died in a boating accident a year before. That son was the popular, handsome, athletic one. The other son tried to kill himself and has just returned from the hospital after eight months of rehabilitation. That son was the shy, insecure one. He blames himself for his brother's death. The mother can't feel any affection for people and acts cold to the living son because she liked the other son better. She cares more about how her family, house, and life look on the outside, than how they felt on the inside. The father is an ordinary middle-aged man, a tax attorney, who is trying to help his son feel better about his life. There is no communication going on between the three, and the family is falling apart! In my picture I created a beautiful house to symbolize the family. I then cut it up to show that the family fell apart, and under the broken house, the word TRUTH shines through to show that when they broke apart, they were forced to look inside each other to see their true feelings for one another. I found this a very powerful book.

One final word about reading. I don't think it's possible to teach reading and to help nurture a passion for reading if teachers themselves do not read. I'm not talking about reading educational literature, but reading a wide variety of texts: fiction, non-fiction, newspapers, magazines, poetry. Children model the adults around them, and I've learned, both as a teacher and as a kid myself, that children have a very keen sense of what's going on. Students can tell the difference between a teacher who

FIGURE 7-6 *Dan's painting for* Dragonwings

Dragonwings, by Lawrence Yep

Dragonwings is a book about a young Chinese boy who must move to a new land to meet his father. It is a strange new land, a land with prejudice and violence . . . the United States. My painting is symbolic. I'll go from bottom to top. First there is the earth. The earth basically symbolizes the earth. The dragon flying above the earth is a symbol of the Jade Emperor and how the soul takes a new form after the body dies. The two people in the sky are Moon Shadow and his father, Windrider. Windrider is pointing at an airplane representing his dream to fly.

teaches reading and a teacher who *lives* reading. A teacher who lives reading shares that passion. So, if a teacher were to ask me how they should teach reading, the very first thing I would suggest is that they be a reader.

Writing

Recently I shared with my class the story of Wei Jingsheng, a man who used to be an electrician at the Beijing Zoo in China, but who had spent literally all of the last seventeen years in a Chinese jail. Why? Because he wrote a wall poster essay arguing for political freedom for China and put it up on what is known as "Democracy Wall." China's leaders had launched the "Four Modernizations" to guide their country into the future: agriculture, science and technology, national defense, and industry. Wei Jingsheng, in his wall poster, added a radical "Fifth Modernization": democracy. He was sentenced to fifteen years in prison. Released after the fifteen years, Wei *continued* his writings for freedom and once again he was arrested. This time he was sentenced to fourteen years. I read a newspaper article about Wei to the class and showed them a picture of him sitting in a Chinese courtroom. (Just recently, as a show of good faith from China's president, Jiang Zemin, after his visit to Washington, D.C., Wei was finally released from prison and sent to the United States. A book of his political writings and letters has recently been published [Jingsheng 1997]).

As I expected, the class was shocked about this. All those years in prison for *writing something*? That was my point. Writing—real writing—isn't really about punctuation and grammar and spelling. Those things are all important in communicating what we want to say, but writing is really about *ideas* and *purpose* and *meaning*. Just as it does with reading, school reduces writing to a quantifiable act. It removes its meaning and its context and sterilizes it, presents it as merely a list of "abilities" people need in order to get into college or get a job. But it doesn't need to be that way. Classrooms can be created that actually live what writing is really about. The purpose then rises far above the writing-as-job-skill mentality and teaches writing as an aesthetic act, as personal meaning making and reflection, as empowerment and expression, as an act of free thought, as simple joy. Writing really can help make us better people and it can help make a better world.

When I teach various university courses, one of the assignments I give my students (undergraduate and graduate preservice teachers) is to create an original piece of writing. Some choose to write poetry, others write fiction or personal narratives or essays. During our last class I have everyone complete a self-evaluation, and one of the questions I ask is "What from this course (if anything) are you most proud of and why?" Of all of the activities and readings and projects that I have my college students do, virtually everyone says that they are most proud of their personal writing. Their writing touched a part of them that they had not experienced for years, and for many, their entire lives, including when they were in school as children. Writing that comes from within, writing that's done out of freedom, was a totally new experience for most of these adults. This is the case largely because when they were in school they didn't do much real writing, they did school writing.

Real writing is not done in order to learn writing skills, or grammar, or to improve one's spelling. Real writing, just like real reading, is done as a purposeful act, not just to learn how to use a semicolon or correct paragraph structure. Another way of saying this is that real writing is naturally holistic. When we write an authentic text, such as this book that I am writing as I type these words, all of those skills that school teaches bit by bit, and all of that language that school doles out as spelling and vocabulary lists, come together in the act of writing. I don't ever just do spelling or just do punctuation. I just write. Real writing (and all of its skills), just like reading, is meaning-driven.

Real writing is also not neat and tidy as is so often advocated, but is actually a messy, unpredictable, idiosyncratic business. When each of us composes text, there may be some similarities between us, but we all write from a unique internal process that works best for us. And although writing may be a "process," that process is by no means singular. There is not just one writing process, and writing cannot be reduced to the "cheeseburger" method of constructing an essay (the first paragraph is the bun, the second paragraph is the cheese, etc.). Recently I read my students a wonderful three-paragraph essay on the environment that an earlier student had written, and once I finished reading it, the class insisted that it wasn't an essay. "Essays must be five paragraphs," they told me. This is the kind of static, rote, learning-by-numbers thinking that the dominant paradigm instills in children.

My wife, Laura, is a social worker. Currently she's working with older folks with Alzheimer's, and before that she did therapy with people living with chronic mental illnesses, such as schizophrenia and manic depression. About six months ago she started writing poetry about her work experiences. She'd never written as an adult before this, and I doubt she would have considered herself a "writer." Here's one of her poems:

Isadora Duncan

Isadora Duncan, I've been reading her again.
Oh, to live life so tragic and romantic.

I got a new tattoo.
Let me roll down my sock. . . .
Oh, don't worry, it didn't hurt much.
But
     roses
          never
               do.

Isn't it cool?

Well, I'm still in love with Jack
who's still in love with Bob.
Some things never change.

I went to the graveyard again last night.
It was peaceful,
I never felt so understood,
in the still of the night,
beneath the glow of the moon

where nobody knew I was a freak.

Laura's poetry is real writing. You don't need to get paid to be a real writer. You don't need to get published to be a real writer. Real writing is text written for a real-life purpose from the perspective of the author. A grocery list is a more purposeful piece of writing than most of the writing that school asks children to do. I asked my wife why she decided to write about her work. This is how she replied:

I'm often left with so many feelings inside. All kinds, sad feelings, feelings of amazement, perhaps feelings of helplessness because I can't help that person enough.

Sometimes even feelings of awe. Writing can put me in touch with all of those feelings. It can give me perspective, it can reawaken things that I've gotten more of a distance on, it can get the feelings out, it can be very cathartic, it can help me gain a better understanding or empathize with a person's situation. I like to commemorate certain people in my mind. I know I will never forget them, but I want to, in some way, celebrate and honor them, and give myself closure in my own mind.

This is a real person giving real reasons why she took the time to put words on paper. Clearly, both the process and the end result add meaning, understanding, beauty, and peace of mind to her life. But writing does something more. As I quoted Peter Elbow (1973) earlier, writing is an act of *creation*. From a process of free thought, writing truly does allow you to "end up thinking something you couldn't have started out thinking" (15). Elbow says that writing is less about transmitting a message than about *growing* and *cooking* a message. This can happen inside a classroom with seven-year-olds and seventeen-year-olds. But for this to become a reality, we must value the experiences and the meaning children bring with them to school; we must trust their goodness and their willingness to create and their desire to learn; we must give them the freedom to write personally relevant and purposeful texts; we must cut them loose from the constant grip and direction of external sources, such as writing (or "English") textbooks and workbooks and punctuation worksheets, and we must give them a lot of time to write in school, to grow and to cook.

Real writing takes time. It can't be rushed. Of course, some writing is meant to be done quickly. Diary or journal writing is usually one-draft writing that constitutes rather immediate expression. And there's freewriting, where the (real) writer writes quickly and nonstop on whatever comes into their mind. Peter Elbow (1973) sees this as a good way for a writer to get to the essence of what they want to write about and what they want to say. But most good writing, as Elbow himself says, takes a great deal of time. That means encouraging—and expecting—students to put a considerable amount of thought into what they write.

Of course, just like with reading, I don't see how a teacher can honestly teach writing without writing themselves. This doesn't mean that teachers must write a novel. It means that teachers should do some of their own original writing so that they can experience it for themselves, and maybe even share it with their students. Granted, for most adults it would take a lot of courage to read their writing to a class of children, but what better way of showing kids that writing is not a "school" thing, but a very real-life thing? And this way, teachers will be able to empathize far more with their students about what it feels like to confront a blank page.

Writing Workshop

I basically follow Nancie Atwell's (1987) model of writing workshop, so I suggest reading her book *In the Middle*, along with some other excellent books on writing, such as Lucy McCormick Calkins (1986, 1991); Natalie Goldberg (1986); Donald Graves (1983, 1991); John Mayher (1990); Donald Murray (1990); Frank Smith (1986, 1988), and Peter Elbow (1973). In a nutshell, writing workshop is about giving children large chunks of regular time in school to write. Like with quiet reading time, the idea of writing workshop is a simple one. The goal is not to do "school writing," but to do real writing, to be a classroom of real writers, who draft, talk about, revise, edit, and publish their work. We usually have writing workshop four days a week for about an hour each day. Some days we may spend a little less time and others a little more. It's difficult to do much meaningful writing in a short amount of time.

Traditionally, in the dominant paradigm, children don't do that much writing. They spend more time filling in worksheets on punctuation and parts of speech and doing "writing exercises." When students actually do write, it's on specifically assigned topics and done as homework. But there is an enormous difference between having students write at home and having students write during class. Value must be placed on the *process* of writing. It is in the process of creating a piece of writing—the growing and the cooking—that the meaning making takes place and that the skills are used in a real context. It only makes sense that this process should take place in school. That's where the metaphor of *workshop* comes from. Writing time is a construction zone.

Virtually all of our workshop time is spent actually writing. Students work at their desks, on the floor, or on a couch: where they choose to write is up to them. Just as with quiet reading time, if a student abuses this freedom, I'll have them write at their desk or table. (But as with reading, it doesn't just stop there. We work on the problem, so one day they will be able to exercise this freedom responsibly.) On some days I'll do a writing minilesson before workshop time, during which I'll show the entire class something about writing, including at times a specific skill. Most of my direct teaching of writing ideas and skills, however, happens in one-on-one conferences that I have with students during workshop time. This way two things happen: First, I'm individualizing the teaching and learning of writing. I only go over with a student during a conference what that specific student needs most as a writer. And second, all of this teaching is done in context, using the student's own writing, which has a much higher chance of being meaningful and connecting to the student's existing knowledge.

Writing and Choice

I've never assigned specific pieces of writing for the whole class to do during workshop time. (I do assign journal writing several times a week, but this is single-draft writing.) One of the most important ideas of writing workshop is to give students the ownership of their writing, so kids are free to write what they wish. One of the common assumptions about writing is that if teachers don't give kids specific writing assignments they won't do any writing. Once again, it is an issue of control. But my own experiences year after year after year disprove this assumption. It is amazing what children are willing to do when they are given the freedom to express themselves. So, once again, this is an issue of trust. You have to trust that kids have important things to put into words. This does not mean that writing workshop is easy or that an entire class will dive right into their writing. This is another one of those "less-than-zero" (Shor 1996) positions, where kids have been told exactly what to write and when to write for so many years that most of them need time to learn how to write when given the freedom and the control and the responsibility to do so. So, starting writing workshop requires a lot of patience, a lot of time, and a lot of teacher reflection to help make it successful.

In every class I've had there have always been a few students who would not (or could not) accept the responsibility to direct their own writing, so I do the same thing for them that I do with students who struggle with directing their own reading. I have a short meeting with them and we agree on a specific piece of writing with a specific due date. But this is by far the exception. It may take them some time to get used to the idea of being a real writer, of sitting down before a blank piece of paper and creating from within themselves, but eventually they do great. If people want to know how I know that, I don't point to a single test score. I show them their writing. So, I use Pulitzer Prize–winning writer and teacher Donald Murray's (1988) advice on teaching writing as my guiding force: "The other day I found myself confessing to a friend, 'Each year I teach less and less, and my students seem to learn more. I guess what I've learned to do is to stay out of their way and not to interfere with their learning'" (233).

For me, Murray's advice means that to help my students with the *content* of their writing I'm not so much teaching as encouraging *conversation* and *reflection*, and that usually involves asking open-ended questions: Describe where this scene takes place; Tell me more about the girl; What's your favorite part? If the main character found a wallet on the street with a hundred dollars inside, what would he do with it? What make and color is the car that turns the corner? Why did the character leave home? Why did the character come back? What was she feeling when she came back? Your character is in the forest, when you're in a forest what do you hear and smell and think and see? The point here is that the person who knows the writing best is the author. My role is to help them cook and grow, to help them see their writing in more detail and clarity, and *yes*—to help build their skills. But the person who knows the writing best is the author, and that's true whether the author is ten years old or forty years old.

Journal Writing

About twice a week we'll write in our journals. Journal writing is a very real-life kind of writing. Many adults keep a journal, diary, log, notebook, or day book so the activity is less likely to be understood narrowly by kids as a "school" thing. It offers my students an authentic opportunity to develop their ideas on paper. Journals encourage us to reflect and gain consciousness. All of this, of course, applies for me too. When my students are engaged in journal writing, that's usually what I'm doing as well. In fact, I've noticed that the longer and more thoughtful my journal entries are, the longer and more thoughtful the kids' entries become. It's not uncommon for me—and some of my students—to write two-, three-, even four-page journal entries.

There are an endless variety of journal writing activities that we do, not all of which are done solely for the sake of improving our writing. Journal writing can be a way of exploring science, math, history, art, sports, movies, music, books, values, morals, politics, and democracy itself. The possibilities are truly endless. Writing in our journals specifically about social issues is a particularly important part of our classroom, one that I'll discuss more fully in the next chapter. Topics for journal writing usually come from me. I ask myself what would be an interesting and important idea to write about. I especially look for topics having to do with issues of democracy and the lives of the kids such as: What is a good person? Who are your heroes, and why? Write an evaluation of yourself as a classroom community member; If you could change anything about the world (or your neighborhood), what would you change and how would you change it? and What does equality mean to you? Sometimes we'll do creative writing; I'll have the class, for example, create a fictional character. And once a week we'll do freewriting, allowing us to write anything, a poem, a song, a speech.

Journals are an especially good way for me to learn more about my students as people and to engage in a private dialogue with them. Kids can put a lot down in writing if given the freedom to do so. Their concerns, problems, wonders, good times, bad times, funny times, struggles with friends and parents and siblings and teachers, can all come through in a child's journal. It is in our journals that our honest selves can appear. Walls are down, fear subsides, freedom and the space and distance to express ourselves takes over, and we're encouraged to use our voice on paper in a way we would not use it verbally in public or private. Some of my most introverted students have been the most expressive and prolific in their journals. Kids can also write to a wide variety of audiences in their journals, not just me. I've had my students write to their parents and their friends, and I often have them journal back and forth with my college students when I'm teaching an education class.

Writing and Voice

Writing, for me, is not so much about words as it is about voice. This is how I see the writing of my students, as limitless opportunities to let their voices be heard with paper and pencil. Through their writing, my students have tapped an exhaustive and eclectic list of genres, and none of it was assigned by me. Here are some of the things that they've written:

personal narratives	plays and scripts	comics
fictional stories	essays	songs
poems	advertisements	posters
newspaper articles	letters	reports
letters to the editor	children's books	myths

Lucy McCormick Calkins (1991) told a story about Mary Ellen Giacobbe, a former teacher who now works with schools on teaching and writing. As the story goes, Giacobbe was on her way to work with a school. When she arrived at the airport, she was met by a throng of anxious teachers who told her that they had a problem. They had given their students the freedom to write what they wanted, and everyone was writing about *farts*! They didn't know what to do. At that point

Giacobbe gives them the very best answer: *Tell them not to.* Allowing children to do real writing does not mean abandoning your sense of common goodness. In fact, being a teacher that's concerned about democracy and humanity *obligates* me to maintain my sense of empathy, caring, and justice, and to make this well known in our classroom. So, giving children the freedom to choose their own topics does not mean anything goes. If a student's writing is too violent, I'll question them on it; if a student's writing is sexist or stereotypical, I'll question that too; if a student's writing is purposely "juvenile" or thoughtless, then we'll talk about that as well. Children need to know that the words they write have power, and that those words and ideas are a reflection of the author. Real writers take responsibility for what they write.

Freedom Through Poetry

I love poetry. As I wrote earlier about Walt Whitman, reading and writing and sharing poetry is one of the most powerful ways to experience freedom and raise consciousness. I've written in the past (Wolk 1994b) why poetry is an important part of our classroom:

> I want to challenge [my students] to begin to see the world from different perspectives. If children begin to see the value in a flower or the wind or the pain of loneliness, imagine how this might transfer to their value and appreciation of people and life. Poetry is a terrific way of suggesting to adolescents that maybe there is more to life than VCRs and Nikes. (109)

From time to time we'll take an entire week of writing workshop minilessons, sit in our circle on our rug, and read the work of a single poet. I don't only want my students to hear great poetry, I want them to *see* it, so I make sheets with eight to ten poems and pass them out and we take turns reading them aloud. I have to admit that I'm discouraged by how poetry is usually taught in schools, especially to younger kids. There is very little trust in children when it comes to poetry. It's usually reduced to "format" poems written in shapes or strictly rhyming poetry. This does not even scratch the surface of what poetry can do. I like to share some of the great poets: Emily Dickinson, Robert Frost, Langston Hughes, William Carlos Williams, Gwendolyn Brooks, e.e. cummings, and of course, Walt Whitman. I've read and discussed this work with even my youngest students, third graders, and I wouldn't hesitate to do so with kindergarteners. I also like to use poetry in our class projects or within themes, such as oppression. We've read poetry of Native Americans, African American children of the civil rights movement, and poetry from victims of the Holocaust. Sometimes we'll read poetry out loud together as a group, which can be an extremely moving experience.

There are some wonderful books on teaching poetry, such as Ken Koch's *Rose, Where Did You Get That Red?* (1973). But probably the best thing to do is to begin by trusting *yourself*. Go and read some poetry. Kids who are afraid of poetry grow up to be adults who are afraid of poetry, and this is largely the result of how poetry is handled (or ignored) in school. But if poetry is anything, it is welcoming to all. Poetry begs to be read and savored. And no matter what anyone says, a poem does not have to mean the same thing to everyone. Just read some poetry and let it mean whatever it means to you, even if that's just the beauty of language and image. As Ken Koch suggests, don't get hung up worrying about meanings and symbols, just start reading poetry for pleasure. None of the student poetry included later in this chapter was assigned. Slowly, over time, in a classroom that celebrates poetry, children begin to write their own.

Publishing Our Writing

Our classroom produces literary magazines filled with our writing. Usually we'll put out a magazine every two to three months. Several years ago the students even went around the neighborhood, selling advertising space in our magazine to local businesses. Considering that a single run of a magazine could use five thousand sheets of photocopy paper, we used some of the money we earned to pay the school back for the paper and the wear and tear on the photocopier.

The democratic and reflective process we go through as a class community to create a high-quality publication that everyone can be proud of has a lot to offer. From start to finish, the process of producing a magazine takes about a month. We begin with a class brainstorming session on possible titles. As the students (and I) suggest titles, I'll write them on a large sheet of paper taped to the wall. We talk about the possibilities. I emphasize that the title of our magazine will be a reflection of our school, our classroom, and our writing, so it's a decision that needs to be taken seriously. Choosing a title can take a few days. It's a lot like choosing a class-created project. If we can eventually reach a consensus as a class, that's great; if not, then we'll vote. One year the class chose *Blade of Grass* as our title, in honor of Walt Whitman's *Leaves of Grass*, which we read parts of earlier in the year.

Once a title is chosen there is an open invitation for students to create a logo for the magazine. In perhaps a week all logos are brought in, they're taped to the wall in the morning to give everyone a chance to examine them, and at the end of the day the class votes. (When we vote on something, we usually cast two or three votes, so we don't have to pick just one.) Once the logo is chosen, other invitations go out. We'll need artwork for the front and back covers, three student editors, and two student production assistants. I select the editors. To be an editor, students must agree to work during recess and possibly after school. Even with these conditions, we've never had a problem filling these roles. In fact, there are far more interested students than roles to fill. However, since most magazines have multiple editions, most, if not all interested students, get a role at some point during the year.

Since our magazine isn't about competition, all submitted pieces of writing get published. We do set limits on how much any one student can publish. Usually this is two pieces of writing with a page total of five or six. The editors have three functions: to proofread all manuscripts and ask the author for revisions if necessary; to design the layout and the look of the magazine; and to assist in producing the actual magazines by helping to prepare the "camera ready" manuscripts. The production assistants are responsible for typing the copyright page and table of contents, and working out the page numbering.

Something wonderful can happen when a classroom devoted to democratic ideals nurtures and celebrates real writing. Oftentimes, it is the very notions of democracy itself that gets written about. What follows are a few selections of writing that have been done in our classroom. These are, of course, shorter pieces. Over the years I've had many students write ten-, twenty-, thirty-page stories and complete books written in chapters. Reading them, the democratic ideals of social justice, freedom, beauty, empathy, dignity, a critical consciousness, and the unique meanings and creativities of these children shine through. Who could possibly need a test score to understand a child as a writer? Just read their writing.

Voices with Meaning

Looking back into the past, I see myself standing next to my childhood idol, Martin Luther King Jr. As I look at his face, I wonder what he's thinking as he marches down the street? Is he scared, thinking that the police will catch us? Or, has he no fear, thinking, Just march on, who cares if they come? What was he thinking as he changed the future for all the black children in America?

Malcolm X. His words echo through the minds of so many human beings. His heart is within all of us. His mind is the mind that brought us halfway to freedom.

Rosa Parks. It was a little thing she did, but that little thing made history. It helped people find courage in themselves to sit down where they want to, to say "no" if they want to, and to stand up for what they think is right.

Now for a leader and a fighter we must not forget. The wonderful man, Nelson Mandela, the man who got put into jail for fighting for what he thought was right. A man who is now president of South Africa.

Now, to go back a couple of years when there was slavery in America. Go back all the way to Frederick Douglass. Looking into the eyes of Frederick Douglass, the man who talked to Lincoln himself, and talked about his plans. The man whose heart and soul itself will never withhold its stand. The "Black Lion."

Martin Luther King. Malcolm X. Rosa Parks. Nelson Mandela. Frederick Douglass. The voices from the past will make a difference in the future.
Sojourner Wright

Wall

The wall in my house
tells the story of my
life.

A picture of my Dad
holding a gigantic
fish with my sister smiling
and showing the gap in
her teeth.

My mother and father at
their wedding bending over
and hugging her brother.

My sister at Halloween
wearing a flapper dress.

My grandparents
hugging.

My whole family at my
uncle's pool having a
cannonball contest.

My brother and sister pushing
me on a swing.

My sister at the hospital before
her second heart surgery.

The wall in my house tells the
story of my life.
                    Peggy Moulton

Alone

She sits in a dark corner of a cold room alone. The only thing with her alive is a
small, brown puppy who is lying on a powder blue pillow on the bed at the other end
of the room. The puppy jumps off the bed and scampers to the girl who silently
strokes the animal's smooth, slick fur. The puppy lies there, whining; her whine is
almost a coo, a sound piercing the air above the whispering wind at twilight.

A stream of light comes in the window from a corner that is not shielded by a
shade. It's from a streetlamp that has just been lit. She listens to the mothers who
are now calling their children in from the outside for supper. "Charlotte! Jimmy!"
and other names and voices she doesn't know, ring out into the crisp air of the
night.

And she sits there, wondering, just wondering, How this world she lives in began.
Becky Swartz

Dear Father

I don't want you to think
that I am not thankful
for giving me
my life.

I just wish I
was born again.

Just one more chance.

I wish things wouldn't
have happened
the way they did.

I wish I could be
in your arms holding you
tight and never separating
like we did.

There's no day that
passes my mind that
I
    (regret) still being
mad at you.
        Esmeralda Dearmas

Another Day's Case

A normal day. No smell of flowers, no fragrance of perfume, just the regular fragrance of trash and my least favorite of all, the smell of crime. Today was a slow day for a detective like me. My only case to solve was of a missing train; a toy train that is. I couldn't let a boy down giving me a puppy face look. I had to find his toy train. Anyway, he's my son and I knew I'd regret if I didn't find his train. And I also paid thirty bucks for it.

My first plan: look for fingerprints on each thing in his room. Clothes, marbles, stuffed animals, toy guns, woopie cushions, video games, baseball caps, baseball cards, etc. It was a messy job but someone had to do it. I found nothing but his chocolate fingerprints. (Now I know who ate the candy.)

Second plan: suspects. My first suspect was my son who claims to be the victim of this ugly crime. I had to make him backtrack to the last sighting of the train. My next suspect was the mom. She complained about dirty dishes, cleaning windows, fixing doorbells, and other junk, so I held her off as a suspect. I talked with friends, neighbors, and dogs. This plan was useless.

I thought for a while and finally knew where the train was. I went up to the victim's room. I brought a machete to tear through the clothes and the toys on the path to the bed. The boy looked on as I went to my knees, glanced under his bed, and there it was, the toy train.
Ajay Mehta

Staying on the Path

My feet made no sound as I traversed the winding trail through the woods. Bright sunlight streamed through the treetops, making leafy patterns of shadow on the well-worn dirt path. Beautiful trees and flowers bordered the path, trying to lure me into the uncharted wilderness, but I remembered the warning that I'd been given—stay on the path. . . . You never know what will happen once you've strayed off of it.

There were stories of people who had disappeared into that forest, people who never returned. They were hard to believe in the bright sunlight, but when it got dark, I found myself believing these sinister stories with ease. . . .

But yet I wondered what evil could possibly be hiding in the lush forest. What was it that snatched people, holding them captive forever? It was so pretty. . . . But then, looks can be deceiving.

One thing to say about the path—it held a certain degree of safety. That was the allure of the wild beyond—the thrill of danger that lurked under the carpet of thick leaves on the forest floor. . . .

Leaves crunched under my feet as I struggled to find a way through the dense untraveled forest. The adventure of it was certainly satisfying after long periods of staying on the path; abiding by the rules, like so many generations before me. But I'd broken the chain, shattered the pattern.

The forest held danger, risk, surprise. Piercing thorns, unexpected bumps on the ground, thick foliage hard to penetrate. Where had those stories originated? Yes, it was hard, but I was sure that the work would give a well-deserved reward. I enjoyed the difficulty.

Except for the times at night when I heard soul-chilling howls from wolves . . . footsteps echoing in the deep, silent blackness . . . something unknown sneaking up on me . . . only then did the strange, twisted stories I'd heard flash back to memory. This was how they had originated—people who had strayed from the path but turned back—people who wouldn't live without a safety net. In the end, they didn't have what it took.

But there are some people who do—people who are adventurous, tough. I am one of those few, the rare who will risk safety for a chance at wonderful happiness.
Kristi Rakowski

Where

Where does this trail
lead to?
Where were all the
people who were staring at me?
Where did they go?
Where am I
going?
Where is my life?
Maybe it is
in heaven resting peacefully.
Cindy Yee

Injustice

(Inspired by the events in
Los Angeles in 1992, and
shortly after I suffered an
injustice of circumstance.)

To suffer Injustice,
Is to be wronged.
Oh, to be wronged.

To be caught
In a web
  so foul,
An Injustice.

To be hurt,
To feel the pain.
Oh, the pain of hurt.

We all must bear
The hurt,
  and pain
Of Injustice.

So hold not
  your tears.
Let them run free.
Oh, let them run free.

For I will understand
  your tears.
  Franco-Magno P. Deleon

Glory

How can I?
                        How can I
define   such beauty from
      they self.
As I gaze upon the
                  open, savoring earth,
I look,   not at the
shape, not at the size,
                        but at this
      wondrous enchantment
before me in
                  the meadow.
      And standing in awe
  looking at the   grand
      purple petal
upon the
            Iris.
            Jon Ungar

Ashley Megan Foley: A True Story About One Tiny Child and a Miracle

My sister, Ashley, was born two months premature and she weighed three-and-a-half pounds. Besides being small and having underdeveloped lungs, she had beta strep pneumonia, which made it impossible for her to breathe without the help of a ventilator.

On December 24, 1987, Ashley's bilirubin (which is the amount of jaundice in the blood), was too high. Some babies die because of this and some doctors think brain damage occurs with a bilirubin level of fourteen.

To bring down the amount of jaundice in her system (which caused her skin to look yellow, then orange, then black) the doctors had to give her four-and-a-half complete blood exchanges. A complete blood exchange is different from a transfusion because with a blood exchange the doctors remove a little blood at a time, while at the same time adding blood. Ashley's heart stopped beating during that horrible night.

Ashley was born with spinal meningitis, a hole in her heart, and a vein bleeding in her brain. She was a very, very sick baby and I wanted her to live. It was Christmas but everyone was sad and crying. All I wanted for Christmas was for Ashley to live. I prayed a lot and she fought for her life. She was tough. She even pulled out all the tubes a couple of times.

On Valentine's Day Ashley was transferred to Children's Memorial Hospital. I got to see her more often because Children's allows kids to visit their brothers and sisters, even in the Intensive Care Unit.

When she was at Children's Memorial Hospital, Ashley had to have an operation called a tracheostomy so that they could remove the tubes from her nose and throat. The doctor had to make a hole called a "stoma" in her neck.

Ashley started growing and breathing better and better. The doctor took her off the ventilator on May 22, 1988, and she came home six days later, five months and nine days after she was born.

Ashley will be five years old this December. Her health and her intelligence are miracles. She drives me nuts sometimes, but of all the Christmas gifts I could ever want, Ashley will always be the best gift of all. I really love her and I thank God for her.

Rory Foley

Elephant

An elephant
tiptoes across a dry, open field.
A dancer
skips across the stage.
His trunk
flares up,
a note rings free.
An opera singer
sings her highest concerto.
A hunter wakes up.
The elephant's tail
whips his sides,
conducting an orchestra.

In the city
The music begins.
  A shot rings out,
The opera continues.
But for the elephant
  The music is no more.
  Jess Clancy

Eight

Developing Our Voices

An education that creates silence is not an education.
—ROGER SIMON

Education is dialogue.
—GORDON WELLS AND GEN LING CHANG-WELLS

If I had to choose the most important characteristic that makes our classroom live democracy, meaningful learning, and community, it would be *talk*. Talk is not only allowed, it is *encouraged*. It's what I look forward to most each day. It's what, more than anything, brings *life* to our classroom. And through our talk, through our communal reflection and sharing and sense making, our voices are developed and our courage is strengthened. The single greatest necessity for that to happen in a classroom is to allow the voices of children to flourish.

Voice, of course, is not simply about talking. When I write of voice I am referring to developing our *conscious selves*, defining who we are, who we want to become, how we see our role in the world. All of us have a voice. The question is, What do we do with it? And to what *conscious* degree have we developed it and continue to develop it? These questions are central to creating and constantly recreating a democratic and humane way of life. What creates that life, what serves as its lifeblood and spirit and drive, are the infinite voices that make up all of our communities, from our backyards to globally. Although people and cultures express themselves in many mediums other than talk, such as writing, visual art, film and video, music, and drama, it is primarily the sharing of our everyday talk that makes those voices heard. I see few better ways of encouraging our voices to flourish in our lives than by encouraging them to flourish in our classrooms. This is a radical departure from the dominant paradigm which values—usually demands—silent children.

Talk in our classroom comes in many shapes and sizes. The spontaneous stream of small, informal conversations between students and between myself and students, run virtually unstopped throughout the day. During our project times, I engage in dozens of dialogues with any number of students. And the students, because we thrive in a social classroom environment, take part in conversations among themselves many times that in a single day. Although most of writing workshop is made up of time to write, the short conferences we have, our talk about our writing and about the act of writing itself, makes talk and voice an integral part of the writing process. The same is true for our reading. Not only do we engage in Nancie Atwell's (1987) dinner table talk about the books we read, but the act of reading itself plays an important role in developing our voices.

There are other times, more formal times, for talk, and that is what this chapter is about. Giving children the freedom and the opportunities to talk is so important that chunks of time each day are specifically set aside for the class to engage in dialogue. Once again, human beings are *social* animals; we *thrive* on social interaction. This is, as I explained in Chapter 3, how we learn most of what we know. So, it would seem obvious that schools should not only continue this natural learning through talk inside our classrooms, but that it should be one of the primary modes of learning. It is important to emphasize that this more "formal" time for talk and debate is equally driven by *spontaneity* and *freedom of expression*. When student talk is allowed in most classrooms (under the dominant paradigm) the result is far more what someone once called an "oral workbook" than it is the free and open expression of ideas and meanings. To nurture the voice of democracy we must *live* the voice of democracy.

Arthur Applebee (1996) offers a new way to think about curriculum: curriculum as *conversation*. Rather than seeing curriculum as a predetermined, static, written, external thing, he suggests we see it as a *living* thing, as the unplanned, limitless, and constantly evolving knowledge that grows naturally out of meaningful conversation. Applebee writes, "The knowledge that evolves is knowledge that is socially negotiated through the process of conversation itself; it is knowledge-in-action" (40). Needless to say, this is a profoundly different way of envisioning curriculum. You can't hold this curriculum in your hand, you can't bind it and package it and sell it, you can't hand it to a teacher to teach, you can't teach the same one to class after class after class. It's unique to every group of students and their teacher. And to do this you must *trust* children; you must believe that their voices are just as important—if not *more* important—than the teacher's voice. And you must trust that the experience and the process of talk leads to powerful learning.

The talk in our classroom is not just about being verbal. There is a better word that describes our talk: *discourse*. Discourse is about engaging in thoughtful and respectful debate. This is what I'm after during our formal discussions. I'm not interested in facilitating a discussion about anything that happens to cross our minds. We engage in informal chatter a lot and it's important. But the focus here is on purposeful dialogue about important topics; the point is to share our *questions*, our *ideas*, our *thoughts*, our *opinions*, our *concerns*, our *lives*. This is exactly what constitutes democracy in the Deweyan sense. This is what it means to be a free and empowered human being. We must ask ourselves what we want our children to learn from the process and the ethos of schooling. Do we want them to learn to be silent? Do we want them to learn to be passive? Do we want them to learn that their voices and their ideas don't matter? These are the attitudes that shape our daily lives and our world, and they don't begin after a child graduates, they begin once a child is born.

My role in our talk is critical. The purpose is not for me to teach a predetermined agenda. If there is an agenda then it's to encourage my students to think and express themselves. What is said, what is discussed, the content of our dialogue, must grow from the words and the ideas themselves. More than anything I need to encourage children who have not been invited to share their voices in school to do so. I need to encourage everyone to see multiple perspectives and not rest on easy, convenient answers. Herbert Kohl (1984) has another word for discourse, *Sprache*, which he says means *thoughtful speech*. His description of his role in a class discussion is illustrative of how a teacher can be less of a transmitter of knowledge and more a facilitator of talk and the construction of new meaning:

> My role in the discussion was to keep the questions going, to help the students think about their answers and imagine other possible answers. It was also occasionally to provide information or change the subject when fatigue set in or a dead end seemed to have been reached. I was trying to awaken dull minds, to find ways to focus thought and energy and encourage the expression of ideas. The goal was not to reach agreement about answers to my questions. It was to have students develop the habit of raising questions and entertaining a variety of answers. (114)

Just as Herb Kohl writes, I have found over the years that it is not easy to do this, to be a facilitator who guides and orchestrates, rather than a teacher who leads and dictates. First, as a teacher, once again I must fight the urge to talk and lecture, that urge "to teach." And second, children are much too used to being told what to do and what to say in school. In discussions, they want to be *told to*, rather than tell themselves. At the start of the year our discussions will often begin with a lot of silence. I'll invite the class to talk and everyone will wait. The students will be waiting for each other to talk—and especially for me to talk—and I will be waiting for the students to talk. People start looking at each other. The students think—they actually *believe*—that they have nothing worthwhile to share. If they did, wouldn't they have been encouraged to share it years ago? And besides, that's not what school is; school to most kids is about being well-behaved and silent. So good talk takes time. We need to build trust, we need to develop courage, we need to learn how to listen to each other, we need to begin to believe that who we are, what we have experienced, what we think, and the questions we have about the world are valuable and worthwhile.

Morning Meetings

We begin every day with our "morning meeting." From the first day of school, the kids know that once they enter our classroom and set their notebooks down, they have a seat in a large circle on our rug, where I sit too. It would be difficult to have an open discussion as a democratic classroom community if they're on the floor and I'm sitting in a chair, above them. Morning meetings are a great way to kick off the day together as a community. They usually last about twenty minutes. First we do our morning business, like attendance (which a student usually takes), and then we'll quickly go over the day's schedule, which another student writes on the board. Our business takes five minutes. Then our first formal talk of the day begins.

On some mornings we'll have "news of our lives." This is an opportunity for the kids (and me) to share personal experiences. This does several very positive things. It shows children that I value their lives; it brings rich content into our class; and it allows everyone, but especially me, to keep up on important happenings in my students' lives. If a student's dog was hit by a car, they'll probably mention it at our morning meeting; if their mother is in the hospital, they might share that; if they saw a movie the night before, they'll mention that. All of this information makes for lively and meaningful discussions on an infinite number of topics. If, for example, someone's relative is in the hospital, this might extend into a conversation about hospitals, illnesses, injuries, doctors, fear, worry, empathy, and even medical insurance and the rising cost of health care and what we could do about it. Allowing kids to talk about the movies and television shows they've seen may seem like a frivolous waste of school time, but movies and television are very powerful cultural mediums, so they're perfect for classroom discussion. Patrick Shannon (1995) writes about how he engaged in critical dialogue about the movie *Free Willy* with his young children, encouraging them to look beneath the surface of the film and to ask critical questions about its content. Our morning meetings allows us to do that as a class.

Morning meetings also allow me to express myself in class. I might share a happening in my own life, which helps to tear down the "teacher" and "student" walls, so the class can see me as a human being first and their teacher second. If my students see me as a complete person, with emotions, feelings, frustrations, passions, and a very real life outside of school, they're much more likely to treat me as a fellow community member, and even—dare I say it—a *friend*. A teacher saying they see themselves as their students' friend is usually seen as professional anathema. Many believe that if a teacher has a "friendly" relationship with their students, the students won't respect them as the adult authority figure. But the fact is that I do consider myself my students' friend. I certainly don't see myself as their peer. That's a very different relationship. But teachers and students can be friends, because more than anything else, friends are people who care about each other.

I bring a newspaper to every morning meeting, and on some mornings I'll share some news. I've already stated the value of newspapers. Newspapers offer a limitless array of topics for short discussions. Besides the current social and political news, I especially like using them for dialogues on history and science to show the class that these subjects aren't something limited to school, but affect all of our lives. For example, when a big hurricane hit the East Coast, the paper had a large diagram of the anatomy of a hurricane which I shared at a morning meeting. I also read an article on the discovery of a five-thousand-year-old man preserved in the ice in the Andes Mountains. And we discussed two terrorist bombings, one in England and the other in Israel, which resulted in discussions about the conflicts in Northern Ireland and the Middle East. It's worth noting the more traditional content contained in these discussions. All three of these stories required me to pull down a wall map and give the class some geographical information. I showed them the East Coast of the United States, where the hurricane hit, I showed them the Andes Mountains, and I showed them Northern Ireland and Israel. This is factual knowledge put in a real context, as opposed to a worksheet or a textbook that's usually completely devoid of any authentic context.

On some mornings I'll ask the class what news they've heard or read. This does several things. It encourages them to keep informed. Some kids start watching the news or reading the newspaper to participate in these discussions. And if kids just happen to be sitting in front of the television when their parents are watching the news, maybe they'll pay closer attention. It also opens up our discussion to news and knowledge from the perspectives of the students. When I asked the class this the other day, Constance (a third grader) said that she saw some film on the news of three women in a toy store fighting each other to buy a doll. This led to a great discussion. All of the kids agreed with Darren, who said, "Fighting over a doll. They're acting like *children!*" I asked who in our class fought over toys. Nearly everyone raised their hand. I asked, "Do children *have* to fight over their toys?" Everyone thought they did. The class thought fighting over toys was just part of being a kid. So I said, "If fighting over toys is wrong for adults, isn't it wrong for kids too? Couldn't kids just share their toys?" No one agreed with me. As soon as the meeting ended and it was time for quiet reading, two students got into a fight over a pillow, literally pulling it back and forth. It was the perfect opportunity to walk over and ask, "So, you're fighting over a pillow?"

It's important to stress that these conversations can't be planned in the traditional sense. Oftentimes I don't know what the length or the topic of a morning meeting will be until the meeting itself is under way, and many newspaper discussions can't be planned until I see the morning paper. And many, if not most, of the topics that come up during our morning meetings, as well as all of our other discussions, I know little or nothing about. I don't know much about hurricanes or five-thousand-year-old mummies, and I'm certainly no expert on the conflicts in either the Middle East or Northern Ireland, but this didn't keep me from bringing them up. If I limited our dialogue to only what I considered myself to be knowledgeable in, we wouldn't have much to talk about. Besides, it's quite possible that a student knows something about hurricanes or mummies that I don't. Just as with our projects, our reading, and our writing, when it comes to our talk, I'm just as much a learner as my students are. We learn together.

Morning meetings serve one more very important function. They set the tone for the day. There is something calming about beginning our days sitting together in a quiet circle on the floor. It helps to create a smooth transition from the rush to get out of the house in the morning and the incessant chatter on the bus, to a day of focused thought. I found this to be especially helpful with my students once I started teaching in Chicago. A sense of self-discipline was foreign to some of these kids, and our morning meetings helped tremendously to focus and relax them.

There is another very important point to be made about not only our morning meetings, but also our class meetings, which I'll discuss below. I believe that we must help children learn how to listen. The willingness, and perhaps even the ability, to listen to other people is a shocking void in our society, and this is true for both children and adults. How healthy can a democratic nation be if we all spend so much time talking and so little time listening to one another? So, I look at our meetings as opportunities to teach better listening. The primary way I do this is through *restating*. The way it works is simple. Before a student can talk they must summarize—or restate—what the student before them said. This brings an almost palpable sense of focused listening to many of our meetings. If a student doesn't know or understand what the prior student said, they politely ask them to repeat it or explain it. Restating may seem like an inconvenience, but it isn't. It can take some time for the class to learn how to engage in open discussion, but most of our meetings work nicely.

Class Meetings

Just as we begin each day with our morning meeting, we end each day with a "class meeting." These also take place sitting together on the rug, which gives our days together a nice bookend structure, both beginning and ending in a circle of talk (see Figure 8-1). Before each class meeting, we've already cleaned up the room, passed out any necessary take-home papers, and gone over homework. This way all of our end-of-the-day business is finished and we can concentrate on our dialogue, which is usually for the last thirty minutes of school. I also limit topics for any given meeting to one or two. Good talk takes time; it's important that we aren't rushed to finish one topic in order to move to the next. If no student offers a topic then I'll pose one. Class meetings happen whether students have a topic or not.

I first became aware of class meetings in William Glasser's (1969) book, *Schools Without Failure*. Class meetings are very different from our other times for talk. First, they usually have a specific agenda, and second—and most importantly—*the students have control over that agenda*. I want this talk to be situated in the lives of my students, so this means that from our first class meeting, I invite the students to bring up topics for discussion. I want all of my students to know that they have time set aside nearly every day to bring up something for the class to discuss. This means that the students' topics usually have precedence over my topics. This does not mean that I can't bring up topics for discussion, because I can and I do. It also does not mean that we discuss anything that a student may want to discuss. The expectations and purposes for class meetings are the subject of our first meeting, so the topics that are brought up usually fall within two categories, problem-solving meetings and meetings focusing on more general concerns.

FIGURE 8-1   *Naomi makes a point at a class meeting*

Problem-solving meetings are rather self-explanatory. The purpose of these meetings is to try to solve a problem. The problems we discuss have no boundaries. They can involve our neighborhood, our city, our nation, our world, and especially our own school and classroom. Since most of the problems come from the students themselves, they are naturally situated in their own lives, which gives our discourse meaningfulness and relevance. The purpose of problem-solving meetings is not to find blame or to punish, but to use thoughtful dialogue to define a problem and work toward solving it. Once again this is exactly how we would want children to solve their problems outside of school.

Students have brought many problems to our meetings for discussion. We've discussed problems on the playground during recess, such as certain kids excluding others; we've discussed local businesses that treated neighborhood kids unjustly; we've discussed students being called derogatory and racist names by other students; we've discussed students not respecting the property of other students, such as notebooks and book bags. One time two students brought up the fact that someone was breaking their pencils. Half the class moaned; they had had pencils broken too. After a short discussion, two students admitted to having broken the pencils, and they agreed to replace them, which they did the following day. Another time an East Indian girl told the class that being called "Gandhi" by other students was painful and offensive to her. Some of the students had not realized the pain they were inflicting. Children can get a much better understanding of the human toll their actions cause if they're directly confronted with them. Our culture does not do a very good job of encourag-

192

ing children to be honest with their peers about their feelings. Many see it as a sign of weakness or not being "cool," and fear being excluded because of it. I know that when I was a kid, I saw so many of my peers as being beyond my angst and fears. It wasn't until I got older that I saw that we all deal with the same feelings. Class meetings can encourage us to share those feelings.

Many of the problems we discuss are right from our own school and classroom, especially at the beginning of the year when I like to use our class meetings to discuss problems we're having as a classroom community. If there's not enough focus on our writing during writing workshop, we'll talk about it at a class meeting; if the room isn't being cleaned up after project time, we'll talk about that too; if kids are abusing the freedom to go to the bathroom or get a drink of water when they want, we'll talk about that; if the class is being too noisy and disrespectful going through the hallways, we'll discuss that; if there are problems during recess we'll discuss that. All of these problems can usually be solved or at least improved if those involved are given the opportunity to talk about them. Far too often adults and teachers want to "discipline" someone to solve a problem, when what's really needed is the opportunity for good talk.

It's not unusual for a student to bring up a problem they're having with *me*. Understandably, this is difficult for most teachers. To be honest, it's not always easy for me. However, there is no way I can tell my students that class meetings are for us to discuss topics that are important and relevant to them, and not allow them to question me, especially considering that many of our discussions are about *them*. If I did, it would be a glaring double standard and they would know it. So, there are times when a student or a pair of students will question something that I've done or something that I've said. Maybe I didn't keep a promise to the class, or maybe our writing workshop minilessons have been too long, or maybe I was disrespectful to a student. Being human, I accept that all of these things can happen. I make mistakes, poor judgments, abuse my authority. Being able to admit and talk about my errors and my humanness helps my students see that even though I'm an adult, I make my share of bad decisions, and that I'm willing to accept responsibility for my actions. Of course, if I feel their problem is unjustified, I'll tell them exactly that.

Not all problems can be solved, at least in the traditional sense. This is something that's come up numerous times. Students have said, "We can't solve violence or prejudice, so why discuss it?" This, to me, is exactly why we *must* discuss it. Problems such as these have become such an everyday part of our lives, that more and more people believe we are powerless over them, that they're a natural part of life. If it comes up I explain my view on this. I agree that these are not easy problems to solve, and that we can't solve them tomorrow or next week or next year. But this doesn't mean they aren't solvable; it does not mean, for example, that we can't consciously choose to live a nonviolent life, or live life seeing everyone equally and treating everyone with dignity. All problems can't be solved overnight or in a single discussion, but we can certainly think about them and use them to shape who we are and the lives we lead.

The other type of class meeting is what we could call a general concern or question meeting. These meetings are very open for students (and me) to bring up any topic or question about the world that lends itself to thoughtful discussion. This way something doesn't have to be a "problem" for us to discuss it. It's at these meetings that our class can get into heated debates about controversial issues. I try not to suppress the heat; that's the kids' passion talking, and that's exactly what I want. I am, however, the facilitator of respect. Heat is good, disrespect is bad. You can rebut someone's opinions and beliefs and arguments, but you can't attack the person.

Some of the topics discussed over the years have included the death penalty, prejudice, gun control, violence, gays in the military, apartheid, gangs, television, movies, music, stereotypes, sexual harassment, the environment, the Rodney King beating and the resulting riots in Los Angeles, black-on-black murder, and animal rights. The possibilities are endless. These discussions become a part of our classroom life and culture, so the ideas we discuss can turn up elsewhere. For example, for the thematic mural project that I wrote about in Chapter 2, a group of students, completely on their own, chose to create a mural about violence. One section of their mural came directly from our class discussion on the Rodney King beating (Figure 8-2).

FIGURE 8-2 *The Rodney King beating in a student mural on violence*

Class meetings are not restricted to being held at the end of the day. If at any time during the school day I feel we need to talk as a class, I'll call a class meeting. We'll stop whatever we're doing, sit on the rug, and talk. Just yesterday I stopped quiet reading time and called a class meeting. The kids came into our room much too noisily and could not settle down and read quietly. So we needed to talk about it, and I needed to tell them how I felt. Sometimes these instant meetings are only five minutes, sometimes they're twenty minutes, and sometimes we can go right back to what it was we were doing, and other times we cannot. Class meetings don't have any magic. There are times when we could discuss a problem we're having for hours and get nowhere. We just do what we can do. But still, I can't imagine a better way to spend this time. Every day our class meetings remind me that the power of talk opens up endless possibilities.

Social Issue Writing

There is another type of class meeting that we have, which I call "social issue journal writing." I stole the idea from a terrific teacher I know, Vikki Proctor. Vikki has her seventh- and eighth-grade students keep what she calls a "social justice notebook," where they write about a wide variety of social issues (Proctor and Kantor 1996). I've only been doing this more structured social issue writing now for a few years, so there's a lot I have to learn on how best to help kids write about these complex issues, but it has still led to some of the most passionate and intellectual discussions our class has ever had.

Our social issue writing usually begins with the newspaper. I'll cut out an editorial, an article, a column, or a cartoon, photocopy it, and pass it out to the class. Everyone reads it. Sometimes the vocabulary is tough and the ideas are new. But that doesn't keep me from having the class read it. In fact, it does the opposite. It encourages me to challenge my students to reach higher, to not fear reading text with new words and ideas, because that's exactly how we *learn* new words and new ideas, by interacting with them in real contexts. Students can also bring in articles. Alissa brought in an article about a legislator who was advocating paying kids to read books, which led to a lively debate.

Once we're finished reading, I'll read the piece aloud to the class. As I read, I may offer definitions of a few words or explain a complex idea. I try to keep my comments to a minimum, because no matter how "neutral" they may appear, the words and ideas that I choose to highlight can end up showing my bias, and what I want is for all of the students to think for themselves. Interrupting reading for explanations can also kill the momentum. After I've read the text to the class, we all react to it in our journals, including me. As we write, I take some time to kid watch, and I can see many of the students working—sometimes *struggling*—to form their thoughts. Forming opinions about complex and controversial subjects isn't always easy. This is an important idea to convey to children, that so many of our questions and concerns don't have easy answers.

Sometimes it helps, particularly at the beginning of the year, to reduce the text down to an open-ended question for the class to respond to. For example, we read a newspaper article about a group of people in a nearby community that was trying to prevent Habitat for Humanity, the organization that builds houses for the poor, from building a house in their neighborhood. The group thought that the rather simple-looking house would make their somewhat historic neighborhood ugly and lower their property values. To make the matter more complicated, Habitat for Humanity had already bought the land for the house from the city. Since the disagreement was going to be settled by the city council voting whether or not to buy the land back from Habitat for Humanity (and prevent them from building), we reduced the article to this question: If you were on the city council, how would you vote and why? Susan and Samantha, who happened to be close friends, had quite different reactions:

> I would have voted that they shouldn't build the house. I think that there are lots of other bare lots where they can put a house. And this town was just about to try and fix up the city, and now an ugly house is going to be built. I think it would look very ugly and awkward to have all those big, beautiful Victorian mansions, and right in the middle would be a small, ugly thing of a house. I think I know how they feel, because in my neighborhood there are a lot of those kinds of houses, and they look quite ugly.
> *Susan*

> I think, who the heck would want to be neighbors with those selfish, unwelcoming, unfriendly people? I think they should have been proud to have a happy home by H for H in their neighborhood, but noooooo! They had to be selfish and creepy, just so they could be a historical sight. THAT GETS ME OFF! If I were on the city council I probably would have voted to give Habitat back their money for it so they could find a neighborhood where families would *appreciate* to have a new family and home on their block. Then those stupid Elgin people could HAVE THEIR STUPID LOT AND HISTORIC SIGHT!
> *Samantha*

The social issue topic that we write about becomes the topic of discussion at that day's class meeting. (Because of this, we read the article and do our journal writing just before our class meeting.) About one class meeting each week comes from social issue journal writing. When we're finished writing our responses, we sit around the rug and those who want to share read what they wrote. As students volunteer to read, I specifically ask for opposing viewpoints. Sometimes students prefer not to read their writing themselves, and ask a classmate to read it for them. After some of the students read from their journals, we have an open discussion about the topic. If many students want to share their writing, we'll read our writing at one meeting and have our discussion the next day. Continuing topics from one class meeting to the next happens often.

The purpose of this discourse is not to determine who is "right" and who is "wrong" on any given issue. First, that reduces an issue down to only two options, when there are a limitless number of options and perspectives on an issue. Second, who is to decide who is right and who is wrong? In the issue concerning Habitat for Humanity, I certainly had my own opinion, but that doesn't make either Susan or Samantha or me more right or more wrong. Each of us listened to the same story about the issue, and then decided for ourselves what it meant to us, and that's the goal here, even if what they think and what they have to say is contrary to what their teacher may want them to think and say. Melinda Fine (1993) has shown that it's not easy for teachers who encourage serious discourse in their classrooms to allow children to truly speak freely and not dictate what is right and what is wrong, or officially validate one point of view. As teachers, we're trained and enculturated to deliver the answers to our students, and as human beings we have our own opinions and beliefs of right and wrong.

Some of the very best social issue writing is situated directly in the lives of the students. For example, last year there was another videotaped beating of suspects by some California sheriff's deputies. The suspects were illegal immigrants from Mexico who had crossed the border in an old, beat-up pickup truck. A long, high-speed chase ensued, and once the truck was pulled over, the officers were videotaped by a news helicopter dragging a woman passenger by her hair and hitting the driver with a nightstick. The officers were suspended pending an investigation. The moment I brought the topic up in class I was met with a chorus of moans. Most of these students were Latino, and many of them were either from Mexico or had relatives living there, and some had relatives who entered the United States illegally. Most of the class had heard about the story, and spoke angrily against the officers.

But then we read a newspaper article on the story, which brought more details to light. For example, during the chase, the truck was traveling at nearly one hundred miles an hour, which everyone agreed could have resulted in someone getting seriously injured or killed. Also during the chase, the newspaper reported that the Mexicans were throwing objects at the pursuing sheriffs, such as empty cans and pieces of the truck. Everyone agreed that this too could have resulted in disaster.

The next day we continued our discussion and Elizabeth told the class that she had heard further reports on the incident that said the Mexicans were *not* throwing things at the pursuing officers. Adam then rang in with the following question to me: "You said that we should be critical, so how do we know if the newspaper is telling the truth?" What a *great* question! I said, "You're right, Adam, we *don't* know if the newspaper's account is true. Or if what Elizabeth heard is true. That's why it's important not to jump to conclusions, but to consider multiple sources and perspectives; to think about what you hear and read and where it's coming from, and to make informed decisions as best you can. That's what it means to be a critically literate person. We need to ask questions and do the best we can."

For some time now, there have been numerous reports coming out about the oppressive working conditions in third world countries that are making products consumed so readily in the United States, such as clothing and sports equipment. One of the companies that's been written about is Nike. According to Bob Herbert (1996) of the *New York Times*, more than one-third of Nike's products are made in Indonesia, where wages are specifically set "below the subsistence level in order to attract foreign investors" (A17). In some countries the wages are as low as $2.20 a day; in others they're $30 a month. At the same time, Herbert points out, Phil Knight, the head of Nike, is worth $4.5 *billion*. After a recent basketball game the press interviewed Michael Jordan (who, according to Herbert, Nike pays $20 million a year), and asked him what he thought about the issue. Jordan told the reporters that it was the concern of Nike.

Since nearly all of my students idolize Michael Jordan, the Bulls, basketball, and hundred-dollar gym shoes, I had them read Herbert's column as well as some Gary Trudeau "Doonesbury" comics on the same issue and write a response to them. We narrowed the issue down to some questions the students could choose from for their response: What is your reaction to what they're paying these workers? Does Michael Jordan have any responsibility for what's going on? Does Phil Knight? What about the people of the United States and its government? What about us? And what, if anything, should be done? The kids' opinions differed greatly:

Does Michael Jordan have any responsibility from this article? In my personal opinion, like everyone in the class, I like Michael Jordan and especially the Bulls. But I think that Jordan and the rest of the Bulls players, or any of them that wear Nike shoes, has to think about the people in Indonesia. They should especially think of the children that are working for some of the factories. . . . Jordan and the other players should give the people in Indonesia just 40% of what they make in a year, or just help them with medical care, food, clothing, and work. In my opinion, I think that's not a lot of money to spend when it's basketball players. If I were in the upper class, I would help the poor people that live in Indonesia or in other countries that have people working like that for just $2.20 a day or $30 a month.
Maria

I think that what Philip Knight is doing to the workers is wrong. I think he should pay them a little more and at least treat them better. I think the government has no responsibility. I think all the responsibility is on Philip Knight. He is the one that owns the company and he should be responsible for all of the problems. I think the people could do something about it. They could stop buying Nike products until Nike realizes that they are against what they are doing to the people of other countries. I personally think I will keep buying Nike products because I think they make good things. I think Michael Jordan has no responsibility. If Philip Knight wants to pay him all that money, why not accept it? It's Philip's problem if he is willing to pay that kind of money for a contract with Jordan. I think what Philip Knight should do is to make smaller contracts with athletes and give the money to the poor people.
Pedro

I think what Nike is doing is definitely wrong (in my personal opinion), because I think that if you want to get a lot of business, look good, and be a famous brand name in the world, you should at least do it the right way. You should get any type of gen-

der to do the job, and pay them the type of money that the job is worth. I also think that Michael Jordan should care for other people and not just himself because of all the money he has. What M. J. said, that that's their business and their problem, is not good. M. J. has a big role in the problem. He has it because he advertises for Nike and makes people want to buy Nike products. He should think about it one day and tell Philip H. Knight that he would not be working for him if he doesn't stop the dirty work. The people in Indonesia deserve to get paid more money for the job they do, and if they get paid a lot, they deserve it, and I think they earned it.
Edgar

Small-Group Talk

John Mayher (1990) is right when he criticizes an overreliance on whole class discussion. This is his point: Let's say you have a thirty-minute class discussion. Let's also say that you have thirty students and every student has an equal turn. Obviously this wouldn't happen, it's unrealistic, but we'll go with this scenario for the sake of argument. Mayher's point is that every child would get to talk for only *one minute*. That's not much time for meaningful talk and expressing our views. So clearly, whole class discussions have their disadvantages. It certainly allows and encourages dialogue, but in the end, each child doesn't get to talk very much. His solution is for teachers to allow their students to talk in small, teacherless groups.

This is something that I haven't done nearly enough of, so I've made a focused effort to concentrate on it within the last year. I think my love for class discussions has kept me from seriously breaking away from them and experimenting with alternatives. I have to admit that there's a degree of control in a whole-class discussion that I like. Having everyone together allows me to maintain control over what occurs and to shift the direction of the dialogue. But control is part of the problem here, not part of the solution. By breaking the class into smaller groups I'll be able to multiply the student talk by six or seven.

Take a Stand

Some years ago I found an old book in a used bookstore called *Teaching Human Beings* (Schrank 1972). The book is chock-full of ideas and activities for promoting thoughtful reflection and social interaction in a classroom. One of my favorite ideas from the book is an activity called "Take a Stand" (42). It's a rather simple idea. On five pieces of cardboard about five inches by ten inches, I write the following: TOTALLY AGREE, SOMEWHAT AGREE, NEUTRAL, SOMEWHAT DIS-AGREE, and TOTALLY DISAGREE. I spread the pieces out on an invisible line in a large open space (desks and tables are pushed out of the way).

With the students sitting on the floor before me, I make a statement. For example, earlier this year I said, "A man goes into a grocery store and shoplifts." At that point everyone stands up and moves to the card that best expresses their feelings.

They sit on the floor in a line behind the card. With this statement, most of the kids moved to the TOTALLY DISAGREE and SOMEWHAT DISAGREE cards. They disagreed with the man's actions. A few of the students paused, thought for a moment, and sat in the NEUTRAL line. They wanted to know what the man stole. They wanted more information. At this point I asked for a few volunteers to stand up ("take a stand") and defend the card that they chose. The rule is that we can't interrupt each other. When the standing person is speaking we need to listen to what they have to say, and when they finish, a student at a different card can rebut the statement, or a student at the same or similar card can support it. (The context of Take A Stand isn't right for restating; it would slow down the process.)

Sometimes the activity will end there. It depends on the topic. If I were to say, "The state of Illinois executes a murderer," that would probably be enough to sustain a debate for some time. What makes Take a Stand so dynamic, however, is that while we're discussing an issue, *students are free to get up and change cards*. So as an issue is being debated, as new ideas and perspectives are being offered, kids might begin to see and think differently, and they might change their minds and move to a new place on the line. It's not uncommon for some students to move multiple times in a single discussion. It's also not uncommon for someone to make a particularly good point, causing a lot of kids to stand up and move at once.

There are times when I'll add to a statement. For example, after a few students spoke about the man who shoplifted, I added, "It was a homeless man." At that point, more than half of the class sitting in the DISAGREE side stood up and moved to the AGREE side. Before, when it was just "a man," they thought it was wrong to steal. But now that the man was homeless, they decided that it was okay for him to steal. Now the students were spread out a lot more. Many of the kids who agreed, who thought it was okay, didn't think it was *totally* okay, so they sat at the SOMEWHAT AGREE card. A few other kids were still at the NEUTRAL card. (There are times when I don't include the NEUTRAL card. For some kids, it's an easy out. Sometimes I may include a PASS card too, for kids who prefer not to comment on a particular topic.) Still, others thought it was wrong for him to steal, homeless or not, and others felt it was wrong, but weren't totally sure. Once again, students stood up and spoke in support of their positions. At times, the debate was charged, with two or three kids standing up, facing each other, and passionately defending their beliefs.

It's possible to keep adding more information to the original statement. Something that continued to come up during the "shoplifter" scenario was the issue of what exactly the man stole from the grocery store. The fact that this point would come up was fuel for further discussion. It means that to some, stealing is not universally a wrong thing to do, that it depends on the circumstances. Others thought that stealing is wrong no matter what. Finally I decided to answer their question. I said that the man stole an orange. Not a single student moved from the AGREE side. In fact, I think it justified their beliefs. "*It was just an orange!*" Some kids moved from the DISAGREE card to the AGREE card, thinking that out of a huge pile of hundreds of oranges, the man stole just one. Near the end of our discussion I decided to backtrack. I said, "Suppose, for the sake of our discussion, the man *didn't* steal an orange, but in fact he stole a thirty dollar steak. What then?" Interestingly, many of the students who had lined up behind the AGREE card stood up and moved to the DIS-AGREE card. Now, they decided, the man went over the line. An orange was okay to steal, but even if he was homeless, he went too far with the steak.

There is an endless list of topics with an endless list of variables that can be brought up in Take a Stand, many of which can explore critical ideas. You can also extend a topic that was written about for social issue journal writing, or a topic from a class meeting. For example, after the class wrote in their journals about the situation with Nike and Michael Jordan, we could have done a Take a Stand on that to make our feelings more public. Afterward, we could have written in our journals again and compared any changes in our thinking. It's also possible to tie a topic into a project that the class is doing. If you're studying nuclear energy, for example, you could explore the class members' thoughts on that. Here are ten Take a Stand ideas:

1. professional sports teams using Native American names and symbols
2. the passing of a handgun control law
3. the lowering or raising of the legal drinking age
4. a boy or a girl dating two people at once
5. kids excluding others from recess and playground activities
6. a parent allowing their child to watch a violent movie or sport
7. a parent buying their child a toy gun
8. a corporation donating money to a political campaign
9. the role of the United States in the Gulf War
10. allowing the police to do random searches of school lockers

It's also possible to tie literature in to Take a Stand. For example, there's a wonderful picture book, *William's Doll*, by Charlotte Zolotow (1972), about a boy who wants a doll. His father won't buy him one and his (male) friends call him a sissy. You could read the book to the class, and then do Take a Stand on gender and social stereotypes.

Voices of Democracy

As I write of developing our voices I cannot help but return to John Dewey's vision of democracy as an "associated living of conjoint communicated experience." This vision requires both thought and expression, both inner and outer voices. School, as it has been traditionally practiced within the dominant paradigm of education for the past two centuries, has been about neither. It is primarily about jumping through one meaningless hoop after another of tests and essays and textbooks and facts. What does it all add up to? Emptiness. Numbness. Superficiality. Vast voids in our hearts and minds and intellects. Maxine Greene (1986) wrote:

> We live, after all, in dark times, times with little historical memory of any kind. There are vast dislocations in industrial towns, erosions of trade unions; there is little sign of class consciousness today. Our great cities are burnished on the surfaces,

building high technologies, displaying astonishing consumer goods. And on the side streets, in the crevices, in the burnt-out neighborhoods, there are the rootless, the dependent, the sick, the permanently unemployed. There is little sense of agency, even among the brightly successful; there is little capacity to look at things as if they could be otherwise. (438)

Why, in a nation that's supposed to have so much freedom, that's supposed to be so smart, that's supposed to be so democratic, is there so "little capacity to look at things as if they could be otherwise"? Why are so many willing to be followers rather than leaders? Why are so many people more excited by a new potato chip or basketball player or movie than prospects for peace and freedom and equality and thoughtfulness? Why are we so complacent in our everyday lives?

We claim to be a democracy, yet where are the voices in our homes, in our streets, in our offices and factories, in our voting booths, in our classrooms? It seems to me that most of the democracy we have is in the hands of a select few, who believe they have the right to make the decisions in our lives. Democracy has been relegated to special interest groups, PR firms, the media, corporations, political spin doctors, Madison Avenue, and Wall Street. Somehow those have become the voices of our nation. Somehow we have become what political journalist William Greider (1992) calls a "mock democracy" (35). He writes:

> American democracy is in much deeper trouble than most people wish to acknowledge. Behind the reassuring facade, the regular election contests and so forth, the substantive meaning of self-government has been hollowed out. What exists behind the formal shell is a systemic breakdown of the shared civic values we call democracy. (11)

Democracy requires *all of us*. It cannot survive—it cannot exist—without *all our voices*. Without this we don't have democracy, we have stagnation. A democratic nation cannot embrace silent classrooms. Democracy thrives on ideas and communication, on asking questions and seeking solutions, on participating in the complexities of life. I cannot help but think, What if schooling was about this? What if from the first day children walked through their school's front doors, they were encouraged to think for themselves, to ask questions, to seek the common good, to act on their original ideas, to be critical readers of society, to share their selves and their cultures and their voices, to explore personally meaningful and relevant interests, to see themselves as creators? What if this were what school was about? I believe we just might be able to create a better world. Not a perfect world, but a better world. A world that's more caring, more thoughtful, more conscious, more democratic. I believe that can happen. And I believe our schools and teachers can help make it happen.

References

AMERICAN ASSOCIATION OF UNIVERSITY WOMEN. 1991. *Shortchanging Girls, Shortchanging America: A Call to Action*. Washington, D.C.: American Association of University Women.

APPLE, M. 1990. *Ideology and Curriculum*. 2nd ed. New York: Routledge.

———. 1993. *Official Knowledge: Democratic Education in a Conservative Age*. New York: Routledge.

APPLE, M. W., and J. A. BEANE. 1995. *Democratic Schools*. Alexandria, VA: Association for Supervision and Curriculum Development.

APPLEBEE, A. N. 1996. *Curriculum as Conversation: Transforming Traditions of Teaching and Learning*. Chicago: University of Chicago Press.

ARNSTINE, D. 1995. *Democracy and the Arts of Schooling*. Albany: SUNY Press.

ASHTON-WARNER, S. 1963. *Teacher*. New York: Simon and Schuster.

ATWELL, N. 1987. *In the Middle: Writing, Reading, and Learning with Adolescents*. Portsmouth, NH: Heinemann.

AYERS, W. 1993. *To Teach: The Journey of a Teacher*. New York: Teachers College Press.

BARASCH, D. S. 1996. "God and Toothpaste." *New York Times Magazine* (22 December).

BARBER, B. 1992. *An Aristocracy of Everyone: The Politics of Education and the Future of America*. New York: Oxford.

BARBOZA, D. 1996. "Mountain Dew's Promotion Angers Children's Advocates." *New York Times*, 27 June, national edition.

BARTH, R. 1990. *Improving Schools from Within*. San Francisco: Jossey-Bass.

BEANE, J. A. 1990. *Affect in the Curriculum: Toward Democracy, Dignity, and Diversity*. New York: Teachers College Press.

———. 1992. "Creating an Integrative Curriculum: Making the Connections." *NASSP Bulletin* 76 (547): 46–54.

———. 1993. "Problems and Possibilities for an Integrative Curriculum." *Middle School Journal* 25 (1): 18–23.

BELLAH, R. N., et al. 1991. *The Good Society*. New York: Vintage.

BERGER, P. L., and T. LUCKMAN. 1966. *The Social Construction of Knowledge: A Treatise in the Sociology of Knowledge*. New York: Anchor Books.

BEYER, L. E. 1996. *Creating Democratic Classrooms: The Struggle to Integrate Theory and Practice*. New York: Teachers College Press.

BIGELOW, B. 1995. "Discovering Columbus: Rereading the Past." In *Rethinking Schools: An Agenda for Change*, eds. D. Levine, R. Lowe, B. Peterson, and R. Tenorio, 61–68. New York: The New Press.

BOOMER, G., et al., eds. 1992. *Negotiating the Curriculum: Educating for the 21st Century*. London: The Falmer Press.

BOWERS, C.A. 1984. *The Promise of Theory: Education and the Politics of Cultural Change*. New York: Longman.

BOWLES, S., and H. GINTIS. 1976. *Schooling in Capitalist America*. New York: Basic Books.

BRUNER, J. 1986. *Actual Minds, Possible Worlds*. Cambridge, MA: Harvard University Press.

BURNS, M. 1992. *About Teaching Mathematics: A K–8 Resource*. Sausalito, CA: Math Solutions.

CAINE, R. N., and G. CAINE. 1991. *Making Connections: Teaching and the Human Brain*. Alexandria, VA: Association for Supervision and Curriculum Development.

CALKINS, L. M. 1986. *The Art of Teaching Writing*. Portsmouth, NH: Heinemann.

———. 1991. *Living Between the Lines*. Portsmouth, NH: Heinemann.

CAPRA, F. 1982. *The Turning Point: Science, Society, and the Rising Culture*. Toronto: Bantam.

CARROLL, L. 1996. *Alice in Wonderland*. New York: Viking Penguin.

CARTER, F. 1976. *The Education of Little Tree*. Albuquerque: University of New Mexico Press.

COCHRAN-SMITH, M. 1991. "Learning to Teach Against the Grain." *Harvard Educational Review* 61 (3): 279–309.

COLES, R. 1996. *The Moral Intelligence of Children*. New York: Plume.

CONNELLY, F. M., and D. J. CLANDININ. 1988. *Teachers as Curriculum Planners: Narratives of Experience*. New York: Teachers College Press.

COOK, J. 1992. "Negotiating the Curriculum: Programming for Learning." In *Negotiating the Curriculum: Educating for the 21st Century*, eds. G. Boomer et al., 15–31. London: The Falmer Press.

COVEY, S. R. 1989. *The Seven Habits of Highly Effective People: Powerful Lessons in Personal Change*. New York: Fireside.

CRONIN, A. 1995. "America's Grade on 20th Century European Wars: F." *New York Times*, 5 December, national edition.

CUBAN, L. 1993. *How Teachers Taught: Constancy and Change in American Classrooms: 1880–1990*. 2nd ed. New York: Teachers College Press.

DAHL, R. 1961. *James and the Giant Peach*. New York: Knopf Books for Young Readers.

DANIELS, H., and B. MINER. 1995. "Whole Language: What's the Fuss? An Interview with Harvey Daniels." In *Rethinking Schools: An Agenda for Change*, eds. D. Levine et al., 115–127. New York: The New Press.

DELPIT, L. 1988. "The Silenced Dialogue: The Power and Pedagogy in Educating Other People's Children." *Harvard Educational Review* 58 (3): 280–298.

DENNIS, J. 1992. *It's Raining Frogs and Fishes*. New York: HarperPerennial.

DENZIN, N. K., and Y. S. LINCOLN. 1994. *Handbook of Qualitative Research*. Thousand Oaks, CA: Sage.

DEWEY, J. [1902/1915] 1990. *The Child and the Curriculum and the School and Society*. Chicago: University of Chicago Press.

———. [1927] 1954. *The Public and Its Problems*. Athens, OH: Swallow Press.

———. [1938] 1963. *Experience and Education*. New York: Collier.

———. [1944] 1966. *Democracy and Education*. New York: The Free Press.

EDELSKY, C. 1992. "A Talk with Carole Edelsky About Politics and Literacy." *Language Arts* 69 (5): 324–329.

———. 1994. "Education for Democracy." *Language Arts* 71 (4): 252–257.

EISNER, E. W. 1985. "Aesthetic Modes of Knowing." In *Learning and Teaching the Ways of Knowing*, ed. E. Eisner, 23–36. Chicago: National Society for the Study of Education.

———. 1992. "Educational Reform and the Ecology of Schooling." *Teachers College Record* 93 (4): 610–627.

———. 1994. *Cognition and Curriculum Reconsidered*. 2nd ed. New York: Teachers College Press.

ELBOW, P. 1973. *Writing Without Teachers*. London: Oxford.

ETZIONI, A. 1993. *The Spirit of Community*. New York: Touchstone.

FANELLI, S. 1995. *My Map Book*. New York: HarperCollins.

FENSTERMACHER, G. D. 1990. "Some Moral Considerations on Teaching as a Profession." In *The Moral Dimensions of Teaching*, eds. J. I. Goodlad, R. Soder, and K. A. Sirotnik, 130–151. San Francisco: Jossey-Bass.

FINE, M. 1987. "Silencing in Public Schools." *Language Arts* 64 (2): 157–174.

FINE, M. 1993. "'You Can't Just Say That the Only Ones Who Can Speak Are Those Who Agree with Your Position': Political Discourse in the Classroom." *Harvard Educational Review* 63 (4): 412–433.

FINKELSTEIN, B. 1984. "Education and the Retreat from Democracy in the United States: 1979–198?." *Teachers College Record* 86 (2): 275–282.

FISKE, E. B. 1991. *Smart Schools, Smart Kids*. New York: Touchstone.

FREIRE, P. [1970] 1990. *Pedagogy of the Oppressed*. New York: Continuum.

GARDNER, H. 1983. *Frames of Mind: The Theory of Multiple Intelligences*. New York: Basic Books.

———. 1991. *The Unschooled Mind: How Children Think and How Schools Should Teach*. New York: Basic Books.

GATES, H. L. 1991. "'Authenticity,' or the Lesson of Little Tree." *New York Times Book Review* (24 November).

GATTO, J. T. 1992. *Dumbing Us Down: The Hidden Curriculum of Compulsory Schooling*. Philadelphia: New Society.

GEERTZ, C. 1973. *The Interpretation of Cultures*. New York: Basic Books.

GIROUX, H. A. 1983. *Theory and Resistance in Education: A Pedagogy for the Opposition*. New York: Bergin and Garvey.

———. 1988. *Teachers as Intellectuals: Toward a Critical Pedagogy of Learning*. Westport, CT: Greenwood.

GIROUX, H. A., and P. MCLAREN. 1986. "Teacher Education and the Politics of Engagement: The Case for Democratic Schooling." *Harvard Educational Review* 56 (3): 213–238.

GLASSER, W. 1969. *Schools Without Failure*. New York: Harper and Row.

GOETZ, J. P., and M. D. LECOMPTE. 1984. *Ethnography and Qualitative Design in Educational Research*. Orlando: Academic Press.

GOLDBERG, N. 1986. *Writing Down the Bones*. Boston: Shambhala.

GOLDING, W. 1953. *Lord of the Flies*. New York: Wideview/Perigee.

GOLEMAN, D. 1995. *Emotional Intelligence*. New York: Bantam.

GOODLAD, J. 1984. *A Place Called School: Prospects for the Future*. New York: McGraw-Hill.

GOODMAN, J. 1992. *Elementary Schooling for Critical Democracy*. Albany: SUNY Press.

GOODMAN, K. 1992. "Why Whole Language Is Today's Agenda in Education." *Language Arts* 69 (5): 354–363.

GOODMAN, Y. 1978. "Kid Watching: An Alternative to Testing." *National Elementary Principal* 57 (4): 41–45.

GRAVES, D. H. 1983. *Writing: Teachers and Children at Work*. Portsmouth, NH: Heinemann.

———. 1991. *Build a Literate Classroom*. Portsmouth, NH: Heinemann.

GREENE, M. 1978. *Landscapes of Learning*. New York: Teachers College Press.

———. 1986. "In Search of a Critical Pedagogy." *Harvard Educational Review* 56 (4): 427–441.

———. 1988. *The Dialectic of Freedom*. New York: Teachers College Press.

GREIDER, W. 1992. *Who Will Tell the People: The Betrayal of American Democracy*. New York: Simon and Schuster.

GRIMMETT, P. P., and J. NEUFELD, eds. 1994. *Teacher Development and the Struggle for Authenticity*. New York: Teachers College Press.

GROFF, P. 1993. "Resolved: Properly Applied, Whole Language Principles Offer Educators an Excellent Means to Develop Active, Literate Citizens" [Con.]. *Curriculum Review* 32 (5): 3–8.

HALBERSTAM, D. 1986. *The Reckoning*. New York: William Morrow.

HANSEN, D. T. 1992. "The Emergence of a Shared Morality in a Classroom." *Curriculum Inquiry* 22 (3): 345–361.

HERBERT, B. 1996. "Nike's Pyramid Scheme." *New York Times*, 10 June, national edition.

HIRSCH, E. D. 1987. *Cultural Literacy: What Every American Needs to Know*. New York: Vintage.

HOLT, J. 1964. *How Children Fail*. New York: Delta.

———. 1989. *Learning All the Time*. Reading, MA: Addison-Wesley.

HOOKS, B. 1994. *Teaching to Transgress: Education as the Practice of Freedom*. New York: Routledge.

HOSIC, J. F. 1921. "Dangers and Difficulties of the Project Method and How to Overcome Them—A Symposium: 2. The Project Method." *Teachers College Record* 22 (4): 305–306.

INGRAM, J., and N. WORRALL. 1993. *Teacher-Child Partnership: The Negotiating Curriculum*. London: David Fulton.

JACKSON, P. W. [1968] 1990. *Life in Classrooms*. New York: Teachers College Press.

JINGSHENG, W. 1997. *Courage to Stand Alone: Letters from Prison and Other Writings*. New York: Viking.

KILPATRICK, W. H. 1918. "The Project Method." *Teachers College Record* 19 (4): 319–335.

———. 1925. *Foundations of Method: Informal Talks on Teaching*. New York: Macmillan.

KLEIBARD, H. M. 1987. *The Struggle for the American Curriculum: 1893–1958*. New York: Routledge.

———. 1992. *Forging the American Curriculum: Essays in Curriculum History and Theory*. New York: Routledge.

KOCH, K. 1973. *Rose, Where Did You Get That Red?* New York: Vintage.

KOHL, H. 1984. *Growing Minds: On Becoming a Teacher*. New York: Harper Torchbooks.

KOHN, A. 1993a. *Punished by Rewards: The Trouble with Gold Stars, Incentive Plans, A's, Praise, and Other Bribes*. Boston: Houghton Mifflin.

———. 1993b. "Choices for Children: Why and How to Let Students Decide." *Phi Delta Kappan* 75 (1): 8–20.

KOZOL, J. 1991. *Savage Inequalities: Children in America's Schools*. New York: Crown.

KUHN, T. S. 1962. *The Structure of Scientific Revolutions*. 2nd ed. Chicago: University of Chicago Press.

LASCH, C. 1995. *The Revolt of the Elites and the Betrayal of Democracy*. New York: W. W. Norton.

LEE, H. 1960. *To Kill a Mockingbird*. New York: Warner.

LEIGH, N. K. 1993. *Learning to Swim in Swaziland*. New York: Scholastic.

LINCOLN, Y. S., and E. G. GUBA. 1986. *Naturalistic Inquiry*. Beverly Hills: Sage.

LITTKY, D. n.d. "Authenticity." *There, Thayer, and Everywhere* 3 (3).

LITTLECHILD, G. 1993. *This Land Is My Land*. Emeryville, CA: Children's Book Press.

LOEWEN, J. W. 1995. *Lies My Teacher Told Me: Everything Your American History Textbook Got Wrong*. New York: The New Press.

MANGUEL, A. 1996. *A History of Reading*. New York: Penguin.

MASUMOTO, D. M. 1995. *Epitaph for a Peach*. New York: HarperCollins.

MAYHER, J. S. 1990. *Uncommon Sense: Theoretical Practice in Language Education*. Portsmouth, NH: Heinemann.

MCGREGOR, D. 1960. *The Human Side of Enterprise*. New York: McGraw-Hill.

MCLAREN, P. 1994. *Life in Schools: An Introduction to Critical Pedagogy in the Foundations of Education*. 2nd ed. New York: Longman.

MCLEOD, A. 1986. "Critical Literacy: Taking Control of Our Own Lives." *Language Arts* 63 (1): 37–50.

MCNEIL, L. M. 1988. *Contradictions of Control: School Structure and School Knowledge*. New York: Routledge.

MEIER, D. 1995. *The Power of Their Ideas: Lessons for America from a Small School in Harlem*. Boston: Beacon.

MEIER, T. 1995. "Standardized Tests: A Clear and Present Danger." In *Rethinking Schools: An Agenda for Change*, eds. D. Levine et al., 175–184. New York: The New Press.

METZ, M. H. 1989. "Real School: A Universal Drama Amid Disparate Experience." *Politics of Education Association Yearbook* 75–91.

MORISON, S. E. 1942. *Admiral of the Ocean Sea: A Life of Christopher Columbus*. Boston: Little, Brown.

MURRAY, D. 1988. "The Listening Eye: Reflections on the Writing Conference." In *The Writing Teachers Sourcebook*, eds. G. Tate and E. P. J. Corbett, 232–237. New York: Oxford University Press.

———. 1990. *Write to Learn*. 3rd ed. Forth Worth, TX: Holt, Rinehart, and Winston.

NATIONAL COMMISSION ON EXCELLENCE IN EDUCATION. 1983. *A Nation at Risk: The Imperative for Educational Reform*. Washington, D.C.: Government Printing Office.

NATIONAL COUNCIL OF TEACHERS OF MATHEMATICS. 1989. *Curriculum and Evaluation Standards for School Mathematics*. Reston, VA: National Council of Teachers of Mathematics.

NAYLOR, P. R. 1991. *Shiloh*. New York: Bantam Doubleday Dell.

NODDINGS, N. 1992. *The Challenge to Care in Schools: An Alternative Approach to Education*. New York: Teachers College Press.

OHANIAN, S. 1994. *Who's in Charge? A Teacher Speaks Her Mind*. Portsmouth, NH: Heinemann.

OSBORNE, R., and P. FREYBERG. 1985. *Learning in Science: The Implications of Children's Science*. Portsmouth, NH: Heinemann.

OWENS, M. 1996. "A Mill Community Comes Back to Life." *New York Times*, 26 December, national edition.

PALEY, V. G. 1992. *You Can't Say You Can't Play*. Cambridge, MA: Harvard University Press.

PARKER, R. E. 1993. *Mathematical Power: Lessons from a Classroom*. Portsmouth, NH: Heinemann.

PARKER, W. C. 1996. "Schools as Laboratories of Democracy." In *Educating the Democratic Mind*, ed. W. C. Parker, 1–22. Albany: SUNY Press.

PAULSEN, G. 1990. *Woodsong*. New York: Penguin.

PERKINS, D. 1992. *Smart Schools: From Training Memories to Educating Minds*. New York: Free Press.

PERRONE, V. 1991. *A Letter to Teachers: Reflections on Schooling and the Art of Teaching.* San Francisco: Jossey-Bass.

PIRSIG, R. M. 1974. *Zen and the Art of Motorcycle Maintenance.* New York: Bantam.

POLACCO, P. 1994. *Pink and Say.* New York: Philomel.

POLYANI, M. 1958. *Personal Knowledge.* Chicago: University of Chicago Press.

POSTMAN, N., and S. POWERS. 1992. *How to Watch TV News.* New York: Penguin.

POWER, B. M., and R. HUBBARD, eds. 1991. *Literacy in Process.* Portsmouth, NH: Heinemann.

PROCTOR, V., and K. KANTOR. 1996. "Social Justice Notebooks." *Voices from the Middle* 3 (2): 31–35.

RAVITCH, D., and C. FINN. 1987. *What Do Our Seventeen-Year-Olds Know?* New York: Harper and Row.

RETHINKING SCHOOLS EDITORS. 1995. "Funding for Justice." *Rethinking Schools* 9 (4).

REYNOLDS, D. S. 1995. *Walt Whitman's America: A Cultural Biography.* New York: Vintage.

RIEF, L. 1992. *Seeking Diversity: Language Arts with Adolescents.* Portsmouth, NH: Heinemann.

RODRIGUEZ, L. J. 1993. *Always Running: La Vida Loca: Gang Days in L. A.* New York: Touchstone.

ROGERS, C. R. 1969. *Freedom to Learn.* Columbus, OH: Charles E. Merrill.

ROGOFF, B. 1990. *Apprenticeship in Thinking: Cognitive Development in Social Context.* New York: Oxford.

ROSENBLATT, L., and B. M. POWER. 1991. "Transactions in Literacy: An Interview with Louise Rosenblatt." In *Literacy in Process*, eds. B. M. Power and R. Hubbard, 128–131. Portsmouth, NH: Heinemann.

ROUTMAN, R. 1996. *Literacy at the Crossroads: Crucial Talk About Reading, Writing, and Other Teaching Dilemmas.* Portsmouth, NH: Heinemann.

RUENZEL, D. 1994. "Classless Society." *Teacher Magazine* January, 20–25.

RUTTER, M., et al. 1979. *Fifteen Thousand Hours: Secondary Schools and Their Effect on Children.* Cambridge, MA: Harvard University Press.

SADKER, M., and D. SADKER. 1994. *Failing at Fairness: How Our Schools Cheat Girls.* New York: Touchstone.

SAPON-SHEVIN, M. 1991. "Cooperative Learning: Liberatory Praxis or Hamburger Helper." *Educational Foundations* 5 (3): 5–17.

SCHON, D. A. 1983. *The Reflective Practitioner: How Professionals Think in Action.* New York: Basic Books.

SCHRANK, J. 1972. *Teaching Human Beings: 101 Subversive Activities for the Classroom.* Boston: Beacon Press.

SCHUBERT, W. H. 1986. *Curriculum: Perspective, Paradigm, and Possibility.* New York: Macmillan.

SENGE, P. 1990. *The Fifth Discipline: The Art and Practice of the Learning Organization.* New York: Currency.

SHANNON, P. 1995. *Text, Lies, and Videotape: Stories About Life, Literacy, and Learning.* Portsmouth, NH: Heinemann.

SHOR, I. 1992. *Empowering Education: Critical Teaching for Social Change.* Chicago: University of Chicago Press.

———. 1996. *When Students Have Power: Negotiating Authority in a Critical Pedagogy.* Chicago: University of Chicago Press.

SHOR, I., and P. FREIRE. 1987. "What Is the 'Dialogical Method' of Teaching?" *Journal of Education* 169 (3): 11–31.

SHORT, K. G., and C. BURKE. 1991. *Creating Curriculum: Teachers and Students as a Community of Learners.* Portsmouth, NH: Heinemann.

SIMON, R. I. 1987. "Empowerment as a Pedagogy of Possibility." *Language Arts* 64 (4): 370–382.

SINGER, I. 1985. "What's the Real Point of 'A Nation at Risk'?" In *The Great School Debate*, eds. B. and R. Gross, 154–157. New York: Touchstone.

SIROTNIK, K. 1983. "What You See Is What You Get—Consistency, Persistency, and Mediocrity in Classrooms." *Harvard Educational Review* 53 (1): 16–31.

SIZER, T. R. 1984. *Horace's Compromise: The Dilemma of the American High School*. Boston: Houghton Mifflin.

SMITH, F. 1986. *Insult to Intelligence: The Bureaucratic Invasion of Our Classrooms*. Portsmouth, NH: Heinemann.

———. 1988. *Joining the Literacy Club: Further Essays into Education*. Portsmouth, NH: Heinemann.

———. 1993. "The Never-Ending Confrontation." *Phi Delta Kappan* 411–412.

SMITH, H. 1995. "It's Education for, Not About, Democracy." *Educational Horizons* 73 (2): 62–69.

SOLOMON, J. 1988. *The Signs of Our Time: The Secret Meanings of Everyday Life*. New York: Harper and Row.

STEINBERG, J. 1998. "Experts Call for Mix of Two Methods to Teach Reading." *New York Times*, 19 March, national edition.

STEVENSON, C. 1993. "You've Gotta See the Game to See the Game." In *Readings in Middle School Curriculum: A Continuing Conversation*, ed. T. Dickinson, 73–82. Columbus, OH: National Middle School Association.

STEVENSON, C., and J. F. CARR, eds. 1993. *Integrated Studies in the Middle Grades: "Dancing Through Walls."* New York: Teachers College Press.

STODDARD, L. 1992. *Redesigning Education: A Guide for Developing Human Greatness*. Tucson, AZ: Zephyr Press.

THOMAS, L. 1974. *The Lives of a Cell*. New York: Viking.

TOLSTOY, L. 1967. *Tolstoy on Education*. Trans. L. Wiener. Chicago: Phoenix Books.

THOMPSON, R. A. 1992. "A Critical Perspective on Whole Language." *Reading Psychology* 13: 131–155.

TUCHMAN, B. W. 1981a. "The Historian as Artist." In *Practicing History*, B. Tuchman, 45–50. New York: Knopf.

———. 1981b. "Mankind's Better Moments." In *Practicing History*, B. Tuchman, 227–243. New York: Knopf.

TYACK, D., and L. CUBAN. 1995. *Tinkering Toward Utopia: A Century of Public School Reform*. Cambridge, MA: Harvard University Press.

TYLER, A. 1995. *Ladder of Years*. New York: Fawcett Columbine.

ULTRA GAMEPLAYERS EDITORS. 1998. "Review of 'Grand Theft Auto.'" *Ultra Gameplayers* (April): 70.

VYGOTSKY, L. S. 1978. *Mind in Society: The Development of Higher Psychological Processes*. Cambridge, MA: Harvard University Press.

WELLS, G., and G. L. Chang-Wells. 1992. *Constructing Knowledge Together: Classrooms as Centers of Inquiry and Literacy*. Portsmouth, NH: Heinemann.

WELTY, E. 1984. *One Writer's Beginnings*. New York: Warner.

WHITMAN, W. [1855] 1959. *Leaves of Grass*. New York: Viking.

WIGGINTON, E. 1985. *Sometimes a Shining Moment: The Foxfire Experience*. Garden City, NY: Anchor.

WILSON, E. O. 1992. *The Diversity of Life*. New York: W. W. Norton.

———. 1996. *In Search of Nature*. Washington, D.C.: Island Press.

WOLK, S. 1994a. "Project-Based Learning: Pursuits with a Purpose." *Educational Leadership* 52 (3): 42–45.

———. 1994b. "Adolescents, Poetry, and Trust." *Language Arts* 71 (2): 108–114.

WOOD, G. H. 1984. "Schooling in a Democracy: Transformation or Reproduction?" *Educational Theory* 34 (3): 219–239.

———. 1988. "Democracy and the Curriculum." In *The Curriculum: Problems, Politics, and Possibilities*, eds. L. E. Beyer and M. W. Apple, 166–187. New York: SUNY Press.

———. 1992. *Schools That Work*. New York: Dutton.

X, MALCOLM. 1964. *The Autobiography of Malcolm X*. New York: Ballantine.

YOLEN, J. 1992. *Encounter*. San Diego: Harcourt Brace Jovanovich.

ZEMELMAN, S., H. DANIELS, and A. HYDE. 1993. *Best Practice: New Standards for Teaching and Learning in America's Schools*. Portsmouth, NH: Heinemann.

ZINN, H. 1995. *A People's History of the United States: 1492–Present*. Revised and updated ed. New York: HarperPerrenial.

ZOLOTOW, C. 1972. *William's Doll*. New York: HarperTrophy.

Index